MW00784981

THE SHOOTING SCRIPT®

# DREAMCATCHER

# THE SHOOTING SCRIPT®

# DREAMCATCHER

SCREENPLAY BY **WILLIAM GOLDMAN** AND **LAWRENCE KASDAN**

BASED ON THE BOOK BY **STEPHEN KING**

INTRODUCTIONS BY **STEPHEN KING, WILLIAM GOLDMAN,**
AND **LAWRENCE KASDAN**

A Newmarket Shooting Script® Series Book
NEWMARKET PRESS • NEW YORK

The Newmarket Shooting Script® Series is a registered trademark of
Newmarket Publishing & Communications Company.

This book is published simultaneously in the United States of America and in Canada.

All rights reserved. This book may not be reproduced, in whole or in part,
in any form, without written permission. Inquiries should be addressed to:
Permissions Department, Newmarket Press, 18 East 48th Street, New York, NY 10017.

FIRST EDITION

02  03  04  10  9  8  7  6  5  4  3  2  1

ISBN: 1-55704-566-6 (paperback)

ISBN: 1-55704-567-4 (hardcover).

Library of Congress Catalog-in-Publication Data is available upon request.

QUANTITY PURCHASES

Companies, professional groups, clubs, and other organizations may qualify for special terms when ordering quantities of this title. For information, write to Special Sales, Newmarket Press, 18 East 48th Street, New York, NY 10017; call (212) 832-3575 or 1-800-669-3903; FAX (212) 832-3629; or e-mail mailbox@newmarketpress.com.

Website: www.newmarketpress.com

Manufactured in the United States of America.

OTHER BOOKS IN THE NEWMARKET SHOOTING SCRIPT® SERIES INCLUDE:

| | |
|---|---|
| *About a Boy: The Shooting Script* | *Igby Goes Down: The Shooting Script* |
| *Adaptation: The Shooting Script* | *Knight's Tale: The Shooting Script* |
| *The Age of Innocence: The Shooting Script* | *Man on the Moon: The Shooting Script* |
| *American Beauty: The Shooting Script* | *The Matrix: The Shooting Script* |
| *Ararat: The Shooting Script* | *Nurse Betty: The Shooting Script* |
| *A Beautiful Mind: The Shooting Script* | *The People vs. Larry Flynt: The Shooting Script* |
| *The Birdcage: The Shooting Script* | *Punch-Drunk Love: The Shooting Script* |
| *Blackhawk Down: The Shooting Script* | *Red Dragon: The Shooting Script* |
| *Cast Away: The Shooting Script* | *The Shawshank Redemption: The Shooting Script* |
| *Dead Man Walking: The Shooting Script* | *Snatch: The Shooting Script* |
| *Erin Brockovich: The Shooting Script* | *Snow Falling on Cedars: The Shooting Script* |
| *Gods and Monsters: The Shooting Script* | *State and Main: The Shooting Script* |
| *Gosford Park: The Shooting Script* | *Traffic: The Shooting Script* |
| *Human Nature: The Shooting Script* | *The Truman Show: The Shooting Script* |
| *The Ice Storm: The Shooting Script* | *U-Turn: The Shooting Script* |

OTHER NEWMARKET PICTORIAL MOVIEBOOKS AND NEWMARKET INSIDER FILM BOOKS INCLUDE:

| | |
|---|---|
| *The Age of Innocence: A Portrait of the Film*★ | *Frida: Bringing Frida Kahlo's Life and Art to Film*★ |
| *ALI: The Movie and The Man*★ | *Gladiator: The Making of the Ridley Scott Epic Film* |
| *Amistad: A Celebration of the Film by Steven Spielberg* | *Gods and Generals: The Illustrated Story of the Epic Civil War Film*★ |
| *The Art of The Matrix*★ | *The Jaws Log* |
| *Bram Stoker's Dracula: The Film and the Legend*★ | *Men in Black: The Script and the Story Behind the Film*★ |
| *Catch Me If You Can: The Illustrated Screenplay*★ | *Planet of the Apes: Re-imagined by Tim Burton*★ |
| *Chicago: The Movie and Lyrics*★ | *Saving Private Ryan: The Men, The Mission, The Movie* |
| *Cradle Will Rock: The Movie and the Moment*★ | *The Sense and Sensibility Screenplay & Diaries*★ |
| *Crouching Tiger, Hidden Dragon: A Portrait of the Ang Lee Film*★ | *Stuart Little: The Art, the Artists and the Story Behind the Amazing Movie*★ |
| *Dances with Wolves: The Illustrated Story of the Epic Film*★ | *Windtalkers: The Making of the Film About the Navajo Code Talkers of World War II* |
| *E. T. The Extra Terrestrial From Concept to Classic—The Illustrated Story of the Film and the Filmmakers*★ | |

*★Includes Screenplay*

# CONTENTS

# ALL STORY, NO BACON

## BY STEPHEN KING

"I can't wait for the bacon sandwiches. They didn't take out the bacon sandwiches, did they?" —My wife, Tabitha

"Just tell me they didn't leave out the raw bacon." —My publisher, Susan

"The part *I'm* waiting for are those fucking bacon sandwiches!"
—My editor, Chuck

What they were all talking about and hoping for, just in case you're one of those good-for-nothing lazybones who goes to see the movie but never reads the book, is a sequence in the novel version of *Dreamcatcher* where the alien invader, Mr. Gray (who has grown quite fond of using his host's sensory equipment), chows down on a few pounds of raw bacon and then whoops it all back up. It's not in the movie. The good news is that a lot of other stuff *is* in it, including a small but vital something that usually gets left out: namely, the spirit of the story.

I'm qualified to talk about this because I may just be the most adapted novelist in modern times . . . and I don't say that with pride so much as with a kind of stunned bemusement. Several honorable adaptations have come from this thirty-year spew of celluloid. The best of them have been done by Castle Rock, the company that co-produced *Dreamcatcher*, and the best of those have had few of the elements I'm best known for: science fiction, fantasy, the supernatural, and pure gross-out moments like those raw bacon sandwiches. The books that *do* have those elements have, by and large, become films that are either forgettable or outright embarrassing. Others—I'm thinking chiefly of *Christine* and Stanley Kubrick's take on *The Shining*—should have been good but just . . . well, they just aren't. They're actually sort of boring. Speaking just for myself, I'd rather have bad than boring.

What seems to happen is that some filmmakers get blinded by the visual possibilities of sequences they want to adapt, and then get their heads in a box: They believe they are making genre films. In my case the genre is horror—after all, haven't I been dubbed "the master of the modern horror story" by the media? Yow, get the special effects! Get the blood-bags and the squibs! The complexity of the story tends to get lost. So do the characterization and the tonal changes. And speaking of tonal changes . . . sure, I like to make people scream, but I also like to make 'em laugh. Best of all, I like to get the readers of a story to a place where they want to do both at the same time. So far as I can tell, only the version of *Dreamcatcher* scripted by Bill Goldman (who also wrote the screenplays for *Misery* and *Hearts in Atlantis*) and Lawrence Kasdan has succeeded in transferring this emotional paradox to the screen. It comes most notably in the scene where Jonesy and Beaver discover Rick, the hapless lost hunter who they've taken in, sitting on the toilet in their isolated camp and giving birth to a monster. At this writing, only one preview audience has seen *Dreamcatcher*, and I wasn't there. But I have no doubt that as the scene played out, half the audience was screaming and half of it was laughing its collective ass off. And it's at that moment that a movie (or a story) transcends itself and becomes pure magic. It's no longer about what's happening on the page or the screen; it's about what's going on in the viewer's heart and mind. And we sense the truth of this mixed reaction. Real life isn't neatly divided up into genres, like items in a TV dinner, each part of the meal in its own little compartment: Real life is a glorious stew, with everything mixed together, and the best movies are able to give this back. *Dreamcatcher* is that kind of movie.

It's also the most difficult sort of novel to adapt, the kind that, more and more often, filmmakers have a tendency to shun. Instead of one protagonist, there are five: Henry, Jonesy, Beaver, Pete, and Douglas Cavell (known as Duddits). Added to this is a *sixth* protagonist, Owen Underhill, and a larger-than-life villain, Colonel Curtis (Kurtz, in the novel). In most adaptations, the director and the writer or writers would have opted to combine two of these characters and (probably) drop a third one entirely. Lazy, but easier.

Adding to the problem of too many characters is the fact that Henry, Jonesy, Beaver, Pete, and Duddits are doubled: We see them not only as adults, but as children. Most adaptations would deal with *this* problem by dropping the childhood stuff entirely or simply settling for one or two quick flashbacks, one at the beginning of the film and one about three quarters of the way through, where Everything Is Explained. In adaptations of this sort, the whole question of character is given little more than a quick wink and a promise. After all (the reasoning goes), it's a horror movie, isn't it? What does the audience care about character or how adults may be formed out of certain pivotal childhood experiences? Yow, let's hurry up and get to the special effects and the blood-bags! Let's hurry up and get to the monster!

Well, the truth of the matter is that most audiences care very much about character because without character there is no horror, no laughter, no empathy, no *nothing*. A blood-bag with no people to put it in context is just a splat. Without character in a so-called horror movie, you're left with nothing but the unappetizing slaughter that characterizes so many films of the Jason-Freddy-Michael Myers type, and those movies ceased being box-office bonanzas long ago. Producers are loath to let these franchises go because all too many of those guys have been afflicted by greed-induced stupidity. Originality is the very last thing in which they are interested, and even now they seem unaware that most of these films go direct to home video after a token week or two at the local multiplex.

I think *Dreamcatcher* is a brilliant exception to the rule, a classic suspense film that will eventually go on the same shelf with movies like *Jaws* and *Alien*. If it does, and if it's a box-office success in the bargain, the entertainment and business writers will be a lot more interested in the numbers than they are in the story elements that created the numbers. Where they *do* touch on those elements, they'll mostly get it wrong . . . which goes a long way toward explaining why very few entertainment and/or business writers have ever made a successful movie or written a successful novel. That sounds insufferably snotty, I know. The truth often does.

It's not my job to tell you why this particular adaptation works so well. You have the screenplay in front of you, and if you haven't read the novel, you can buy an inexpensive paperback copy at your local bookstore (or take it out of the library, if you're a tightwad). I'll just say that a close and thoughtful comparison of the two will teach you a great deal about the delicate and difficult art of turning a complex 600-page novel into a film that runs two hours and ten minutes. William Goldman has written several essays on adapting novels for film (one is in this book), and I recommend them to you enthusiastically. Few writers know what they are doing, even when they are doing it well. Bill is a wonderful exception to the rule.

One thing that startled and delighted me was how *much* of the novel made it into the finished movie. I had to look at it three times to see most of these things, and I have no doubt that additional viewings will show me more (I cannot imagine watching *Graveyard Shift* three times without a gun to my head, and maybe not even then). The Bridgton Pharmacy at the beginning of the movie, for instance, looks like the real Bridgton Pharmacy (yes, there is such a place). The exterior of the Bridgton Main Street also looks like the real one. There really is a Quabbin Reservoir, and the shaft house in the movie looks almost exactly like the one standing at Quabbin's east end. Someone cared enough to make the fictional version look like the real one, and the cumulative effect of all this painstaking work is powerful, indeed. The devil's in the details, they say, and there's plenty of hell raised in *Dreamcatcher*.

At the risk of repeating myself, this is one of the very, very good adaptations of my work, and the book that follows is a valuable artifact showing how successful adaptation is accomplished. Maybe the most notable thing is what you *won't* find here: the easy shortcuts, the stereotyping, the reliance on shock effects to replace the work of building characters the audience is willing to care about. Believe it or not, I have never been particularly interested in horror; what I care about is how people react to the unexpected, the painful, and the terrible—Jonesy's accident, for instance, which isn't a bit supernatural. The business of good fiction, whether on film or the printed page, is saying something true about how we live, how we get along, and how we die. I talked about some of those things in *Dreamcatcher*, and I was delighted to see Larry Kasdan's film talking about them as well . . . and in much the same language.

Of course, the book *also* talked about raw bacon sandwiches, but I guess you can't have everything.

Bangor, Maine<br>
December 19, 2002

# ADAPTING KING

## BY WILLIAM GOLDMAN

Mostly what we do are adaptations.

Bergman, the greatest screenwriter, was famous for originals, and Wilder, our master, did a bunch of them too. But adaptations carry the day out there.

When I am offered one, I am very careful before I say yes or no. Because from experience I expect the task to take six months of my remaining life on earth. It does not take that long for writing reasons. It's more the building up confidence that this time, yes lord, my work will not suck.

I do a lot of research if I possibly can. It makes me feel smarter I guess. And sometimes you find stuff that helps in the search for the spine of the story.

Which is only everything.

The other thing I do those first four months—the writing takes the last two—is reread the source material, over and over again, each time with a different colored pen. And I make a mark in the margin every time I come across a line of dialog or a scene I think might be in the movie.

I read the material half a dozen times and by the end of that, I hope to have the story. And pages that have no marks, or maybe one, will not be in the screenplay. Those with five or six will make the cut.

That's how I do it anyway. So it's pretty obvious I hope that I only do movies I want to do. If I didn't, I would be insane by the time I read something I disliked half a dozen times.

The advice I give young writers is always this: *You had better give a shit.* About anything you write. Now and forever.

I have done three King adaptations and the rest of this is about why I said yes.

### Misery

The story of a best-selling commercial writer, Paul Sheldon, who is finishing a novel in Colorado. When he is done, he starts to drive back to New York, hits a blizzard, suffers a terrible car crash, almost dies.

But the Gods are smiling, ho ho ho, and he is rescued by a nurse, Annie Wilkes by name, who brings him back to life in her desolate home.

By which time he knows she is his number one fan. And also crazed. Not to mention very violent.

Okay, I am reading happily along, not sure if I want to make a movie out of it or not. Then this moment happens: Paul Sheldon—Jimmy Caan—has managed to wheelchair his way around the house but Annie— Kathy Bates—returns before expected, and there is a mad race to see if he can get back to bed before she finds out.

He is successful.

Or thinks he is.

But she knows and I know, sitting there reading, that she has a terrible temper and is going to exact revenge on the one man on earth she loves. But I did not think she was going to cut his feet off.

Most horrific fucking thing I ever read and when I was finished, I knew I had to try the adaptation. Because of that single scene where Annie, who loves Paul so much and is so afraid of losing him, hobbles him forever.

The script is finished, a second draft, then the search for a director. First choice: the great George Roy Hill—who says *yes*.

Hallelujah.

You will never know how rare that is. To get the director you want. And right out of the chute. Amazing.

We meet, and Hill who never changes his mind has changed his mind. He cannot bring himself to direct what he calls "the lopping scene." We shout, I beg, no good.

Now Rob Reiner, who eventually directed but at this point was just going to produce, begins to conduct an informal poll at Castle Rock, the company he cofounded, about "the lopping scene." Was it too much?

Eventually, when he had decided to direct, he and Andy Scheinman, his producer, did a pass on the screenplay—and changed "the lopping scene" to what you saw if you saw the flick: She breaks his ankles instead of making him a permanent cripple.

I fought the good fight, called them a couple of gutless assholes (we were and are friends), explained the lopping scene was the main reason I took the fucking job, and that they were not just breaking my heart, they were ruining the movie.

I was only wrong.

When we had our first sneak, the ankle-breaking scene caused all the screams you would ever want. If we had done what King wrote and I loved, the audience would have hated us, hated Kathy Bates, and the movie, I believe, would have failed.

It's hard to be smart.

### *Hearts in Atlantis*

A more than 500-page novel made up of five interconnected stories. They take place over forty years. And they vary tremendously in length, complexity, you name it. The book is about the Vietnam experience.

Story 1) *Low Men in Yellow Coats*, 1960, 254 pages
Tells of ten-year-old Bobby Garfield. And his cheap mother. And his friend Sully. And the girl of his dreams, who he loves hopelessly, Carol Gerber, who lives across the street. And what happens when a strange gifted man, Ted Brautigan, comes to live upstairs in Bobby's boarding house. One of many crucial incidents is when Carol is brutally savaged by some older boys, and Bobby somehow finds the superhuman strength to carry her up a steep hill to Ted who will save her.

Story 2) *Hearts in Atlantis*, 1966, 150 pages
About a crazed hearts game at college. And a lot of other stuff. Carol Gerber goes to the college.

Story 3) *Blind Willie*, 1983, 46 pages
About one of the men who savaged Carol, now married and living in the suburbs, who makes a living as a blind beggar in New York City.

Story 4) *Why We're in Vietnam*, 1999, 44 pages
About the death of Sully, who was the third of the Bobby-Carol trio and dated Carol after Bobby moved away. A war hero in Vietnam.

Story 5) *Heavenly Shades of Night Are Falling*, 1999, 13 pages
About Sully's funeral. Bobby comes back to his hometown of Harwich, Connecticut, where the long opening story happened, for the first time in almost forty years.

There is so much King stuff in the first four stories. *Blind Willie* could be a movie by itself. A guilt-wracked war vet who lives with his wife in the country and commutes to the city, where he disguises himself as a blind beggar. And who is hassled by a cop. And maybe his life is going to be exposed so what does he do?

I don't know about you, but I'm pretty interested in that guy and how did he get that way and what happens next?

But my problem was this, doctor: I felt that this novel was the story of Bobby and Carol. Their time together takes up half the book. And one or the other of them is involved in the other stories.

So as I started the last of the five, I had zero idea if I could figure something that would enable me to say yes, I want to do this!

I start the final very short story. Page 509. And thank God, it's about Bobby. And he's back where the first story took place, where he and Carol met, fell in love, had their magical first kiss on the Ferris wheel.

Look—I wrote *The Princess Bride*. I believe in true love and high adventure. And I knew somehow, as I rushed to finish, that some damn way, Stephen King was going to bring Bobby and Carol back together.

I zip through 509, all well and good, same with 510, 511's fine.

It's on 512 that King lets me know that Carol Gerber is dead.

You did that, I thought to King. You fucking had to go and do that. Ten pages left and I put the book down, went to the kitchen, heated a cup of coffee, sat with the sports section to see if I could find anything optimistic about the Knicks.

I'm alone in my place. Dead silent like it usually is. And then, and this does not happen often, thank God, but it did that day, I burst into hysterical tears.

And I knew somehow I had to try and make a movie out of this strange and wonderful piece of narrative. (And guess what: On page 514, it turns out Carol is alive, and they meet again after forty years, and the novel ends with Bobby and Carol on a park bench, listening to the Platters as the sun goes down. . . .)

Lots of problems for me as screenwriter, sure, but as Billy Jean King said, "If it was easy, everyone could do it."

Of the five stories, I kept the first and fifth, pitched the other three. I told the story in flashback, Bobby coming to the funeral, being told Carol was dead, devastated, going back to the street where he lived, remembering the summer.

Then, at the very end, flashback over, he returns to the part of the park where so much of the story happens, and there Carol finds him, forty years after they last saw each other.

We got lucky with the cast. Anthony Hopkins as Ted, Anton Yelchin and Mika Boorem as Bobby and Carol. And Scott Hicks, the director, is one of the real gents in the field. Shooting went wonderfully. Or as "wonderfully" as that awful period can ever go.

Understand something: I have been connected, one way and another, with maybe fifty films and of those, there are only three I love: *Butch Cassidy and the Sundance Kid* back in 1969, *The Princess Bride* in 1987, and *Hearts in Atlantis* in 2001.

*Butch* was one of the most popular movies of the decade, a prizewinner here and abroad. *The Princess Bride*, not a huge commercial success upon release, has become, and thank you, God, a huge cult favorite everywhere.

*Hearts in Atlantis* tanked. Critically and commercially. Have no more idea why than I can tell you why audiences took to *Butch*. Nobody knows anything, as somebody must have said. I do know we came out two weeks after 9/11 and the country had other things on its mind in those terrible days.

You already know the reason I took *Misery* never made the final cut. Well, to my amazement, the reason I took *Hearts in Atlantis* never made that movie either.

Here's what happened. Scott Hicks went to see *Billy Elliot*, with a special kid, Jamie Bell, in the title role. An English film and a nice one, about a working-class kid in a mining town around 1980 who wants to be a ballet dancer. All kinds of family strife, all kinds of difficulties to be somehow overcome.

And you know the fates are never going to allow the boy to get his silly dream. But guess what? As the last scene unfolds and we see Adam Cooper dancing so beautifully as Billy, we realize the kid made it after all and . . .

. . . and hold the phone. You should be asking yourself about the typo you just read where I said Adam Cooper was dancing when just a paragraph earlier, I was raving on about Jamie Bell.

Here's the deal: Adam Cooper, a British ballet dancer, played Billy as a grown-up. Jamie Bell played the child.

*The final dance scene took place fifteen years later.*

Scott Hicks was troubled. He liked the movie, liked it a lot, but not so much the ending because it dealt with someone we had never seen before, the adult Billy. The fifteen years older Billy.

Well holy shit, here we were in *Hearts* with a couple smooching on a park bench who have not seen each other in *forty years.*

Forty very long years.

David Morse, who is always splendid, played the adult Bobby Garfield. But we had spent time with him already in the opening of the movie, seen him as a successful photographer, then going off to the funeral. Driving around town. Maybe ten minutes with Morse. We were okay there.

But to end with a romance. To bring in, maybe five, maybe seven minutes before the very end an adult Carol who we had never met?

Scott, a bright fellow, had terrible problems seeing how to make that work. How do you move an audience with a brand new lady? Can you move them? Can you make them care?

We talked a great deal about the problem which was never a problem for me because I had already spent months with the book and Bobby and Carol. I had the memory and knowledge that King had done it, made it work, brilliantly and movingly.

But that was the book—in the book, you're the writer, you're the director, you supply the pictures, you can flip back and forth, reacquaint yourself with the couple, and also have the memory of Carol in the other stories.

We changed it. Made the decision that in the movie Carol was indeed dead, and it was her teenage daughter who lived across the street, who grown-up Bobby had a sweet scene with. And Mika Borrem was more than skillful enough to play both Carol and Carol's daughter.

What if we had done it the way King wrote it, the way that moved me so to tears?

The truth? Two, actually. The first: I don't think it would have made any difference at all. The second: We will never know.

### Dreamcatcher

The number 906 resonates. My memory is that I was sent a typed version of *Dreamcatcher*. I think 906 was the number of pages. Not sure, doesn't matter, but I will never forget the poundage when I was lying in bed, reading it.

The story is about four Maine friends, friends for twenty-five years and more, all failures now, at least to themselves, who one week a year go off to a hunting cabin in the woods where they can drink and tell stories and sing old songs.

And where, this year, a rocket ship lands. Filled with not the friendliest of folk.

The novel is crammed with adventure. And fright. And sadness. And the bathroom scene is going to be talked and screamed about for a very long time.

The reason I did the adaptation? The character called Duddits. Douglas Cavell is his real name and he is one of King's major creations, a Down's syndrome child the four boys save and befriend.

And on his sick frail shoulders rests this task: to save the world.

I see the movie next week and as far as I know, Duddits is still in the flick.

Hope he stays . . . I saw it, and he does.

# CONTROLLING THE FEAR

## BY LAWRENCE KASDAN

I became aware of Stephen King's new novel *Dreamcatcher* sometime after the release of my last film, *Mumford*. That movie, a comedy set in a small West Coast town, was concerned with issues of identity, secret lives, and human connection. It completed what I considered a loose trilogy about certain American lives that started with *The Big Chill* in 1983 and continued with *Grand Canyon* in 1991. By the time I'd finished *Mumford*, I was in the mood to tell a different kind of story. I'd had my fill of gentle, humanistic ensemble comedies. I wanted to deal with more robust material, a story that allowed a more exuberant and outrageous use of the things movies do best.

When I read *Dreamcatcher*, I was delighted and bemused. There were many connections to the kind of story I'd been telling all along. The novel begins, in fact, with a story of friendship among five men who are struggling with difficult issues of life in America. I had been working that material in various ways for years and remained fascinated by it. But the bonus for me was that the story of the friends' connection was just the jumping-off point for a story of great horror and exhilarating action. If this had been one of my stories, the friends would have gone off on their annual hunting trip, talked about their troubled lives, then headed back home. With Stephen King, they head off for a comforting week of camaraderie and wind up facing an alien invasion. It was the kind of riveting tale I was primed to tell.

When I talked to the people at Castle Rock, the production company that owned the rights and had made several of King's best movie adaptations, I discovered that an old friend of mine, William Goldman, had already begun work on the script. Bill had been a hero of mine when I was struggling to enter the movie business, a role model for many aspiring screenwriters. He and I had gotten friendly during a Writers Guild-sponsored trip to the Soviet Union a decade before. Happily, when I entered the process, he agreed that we would work together on another draft of the script. Then I would go away and use that screenplay as the basis for a shooting script that I could commit to produce and direct.

Although I've been writing screenplays for a long time, I have never tried my hand at a horror film. I like them, but have trouble seeing them in a movie theater. I hate jumping in surprise in a packed auditorium with a crowd of strangers, the very aspect of these movies that aficionados enjoy the most. For me, all that proximate humanity makes my own fears and anticipation almost unbearable. When I went to see Ridley Scott's film *Alien*, I had to prepare by reading the comic book first. I needed to know where the shocks were, when they were coming. The experience is so intense otherwise, I get no enjoyment from the movie.

Once over that hurdle, I tend to love a well-done scary movie. I was attracted to the idea of making one partially because of my own uneasiness. I thought I knew exactly what made me squirm, and I wanted to see if I could make an audience equally nervous.

When I finally got up the nerve to see *Alien*, it turned out to be an important film for me, one of my favorites. I've seen it many times by now and always find something new to admire about it. *Alien* sits in my pantheon of scary movies with *The Exorcist, The Shining, Silence of the Lambs*, and *Carrie*—all of which have influenced the kind of movie I wanted to make of *Dreamcatcher*. It's no coincidence that two of that small list are based on Stephen King novels. Around eighty of Stephen's stories have made their way to some kind of filmed version, often more than once. He writes filmable stories—up to a point. More about that later.

I had read the novel of *The Shining* and was totally engrossed by it. Though I am a huge fan of Stanley Kubrick's work, I felt a certain alienation from the movie upon first viewing. But I found, as time went on, that it was a movie that kept drawing me back time after time. The first hour particularly, before all hell breaks loose, is full of scenes made ominous simply by the banality of the writing, staging, and playing. There's an almost documentary quality to the scenes of Jack Nicholson interviewing for the job, as with the intercut scenes back in Denver where his wife and son are visited by a child psychologist. Kubrick takes a long time with these scenes, and the ones that follow where the family is introduced to the hotel. I love the way the sense of menace grows in these leisurely scenes. And the hyper-realistic tone pays dividends in the second half when things become stranger and stranger.

When *Carrie* came out in 1976, I had been writing screenplays and trying to sell them for seven years, with no success. *Carrie* electrified me. It had been made by a filmmaker not much older than myself, Brian DePalma, who was already operating with enormous skill and confidence. Full of wonderful actors, most even younger than me, the movie simply stoked the burning, frustrated ambition in me to make my own films. Moreover, it wasn't just a scary movie. It was a character study and a dead-on portrait of the casual cruelty we all remember well from high school. Stephen King, it seemed to me, had found a perfect metaphor— telekinetic powers—to express the rage of the girl at the center of the story, the lonely outcast in the crowded high school.

The movie was surprising, scary, witty, and very sexy. From the sensual opening in the girls' locker room that turns to horror for the heroine, the movie never goes off point. It's a relentless workout with insistent resonance for everyone who's ever felt the sharp edge of rejection.

Though I had wanted to be a movie director since I was thirteen years old, I had studied English literature in college. The thing I found most thrilling in the good books I was exposed to was the satisfying ways metaphor could be used to express ideas and emotions. It became a life-long pursuit for me, finding the right metaphor to carry my work. When you find it, it lifts up the whole enterprise. And when you fail to find it, everything just lies there, obvious, literal, and embarrassing. I know, because I've experienced both sides.

Stephen King is a master of metaphor. I don't know at what point he decided that horror would be his métier, but he must have understood perfectly how much access he had to the earthly embodiments of our deepest fears. In story after story, he takes some familiar object, situation, or moment, and pushes it to extravagant lengths to scare the hell out of us. *Dreamcatcher* is a perfect example.

My personal worldview is that people spend their lives trying to control their fear of a dangerous, chaotic universe. We have found an endless variety of strategies in this struggle. Some people try to impose order by obsessive work, some by obsessive play. Some abuse drink and drugs, some maintain an antiseptic living space. Some find comfort in religion, others in libertine decadence. But in all cases, the human mind seeks a way to hold off the encroaching darkness. That darkness, in which all the scary, uncontrollable demons live, exists mainly in two different realms. There is the darkness *out there*, in the night, in the shadows, in the forest, in space. And there is the darkness *in here*, in our minds and in our bodies, where destructive evil can grow and flourish, out of our view, taking over our beings before we even know there's a problem.

*Dreamcatcher* takes those fears, and the two fronts from which they attack, and makes them tangible. The story involves not only the threat from space, from the black void above our heads each night, but also the threat in our bodies, the fear that some cancerous entity can eat away our insides, actually gaining nourishment as we are consumed. And, of course, both threats work on our minds, poisoning our thoughts, destroying our confidence, weakening our resistance. In the face of such terror, our mind may be our only defense—but our mind is peculiarly vulnerable to decay.

On the face of it, the story was simple and apparently easy to adapt to the screen. Four friends have bonded in childhood around a heroic act that brings a fifth child—strange, damaged, "challenged"—into their lives. Twenty years later, they are all struggling with their adult roles. At the annual gathering, a week's hunting trip, they all expect some temporary succor from the tumult of their lives. Instead, they find themselves facing an alien incursion. Heroism is once again demanded of them. And the place that the fifth child, the "challenged" one, holds in their destinies is finally clarified.

One of the scariest pieces Stephen King has ever written is his account of his accident and recovery. Hit by a speeding van on the shoulder of a country highway, he endured multiple surgeries, long rehabilitation, and excruciating pain. *Dreamcatcher* was the book he wrote during this period.

I don't know a writer who isn't in awe of Stephen's output. It seems impossible to all mortals. I was saying long before I'd had any contact with him that clearly he was himself an alien, prolific beyond human capacity. But even with that extraordinary history, the writing of *Dreamcatcher* represents some new level of accomplishment. Unable to sit comfortably at his computer, he wrote the entire more than 600-page novel *longhand*. Personally, I could not even copy out this book longhand in six months, much less compose it while in pain.

And how beautifully composed it is. Not neat, not cohesive, not structurally efficient. But dazzling in its style, its sentences, its ideas, its invention. Dazzling in the risks it takes so casually and in the rate at which those risks pay off. Dazzling in the way it processes the physical and psychological pain of its author into art for the story, muscle for the narrative.

Some of its invention created problems for the adaptation to movies. There are wonderful conceits that neither William Goldman nor I—after long discussion—could figure how to visualize. There are long tangential explorations that simply couldn't fit in the rigorous economy of a movie. But there were some delicious ideas that I simply refused to give up on. On those, I struggled long and hard, and muscled them into the script despite their resistance. Whether I was right to do so, only the individual viewer of the movie will be able to judge.

Before I give two examples, I'll say something in the interest of full disclosure. Whenever I've released a movie, I've had people ask me—"Whose idea was that scene? Who thought of that camera move? Who came up with that bit of behavior?" The truth is that when a satisfying movie experience is happening, the large group collaboration that filmmaking actually is, no one can remember where the ideas—good or bad—originated. I find this to be acutely true in the creation of *Dreamcatcher*, the movie. I had never before had so much fertile source material to draw on. My brother Mark, an associate producer of the film, helped me organize and integrate it all as I wrote the shooting script. I had instant access not only to Stephen King's novel, but also to two William Goldman script drafts and all the notes of our joint script discussions. At this point, I honestly can't remember where any particular detail in the script came from.

(In the five or six telephone conversations I've had with Stephen King during this process, I've been delighted not only by his down-to-earth, self-deprecating charm, but also by what I take to be his confusion—identical to mine—about what was in the novel and what entered during the script stage.)

Having said that, I'll give a couple of examples of ideas I took from the novel and struggled to make work in the script and film. They're closely related conceits. Jonesy, the college professor friend who is hit by a car at the beginning of the story, thinks of his mind as a Memory Warehouse, overflowing with remnants of his life up to the present. I related strongly to that idea, since I have often described my memory that way to friends, with the added fillip that the place has become so overcrowded with useless trivia that I have to throw something out to make room every time I learn something new.

This Memory Warehouse takes on added importance later in the story, because of a second fascinating but difficult-to-visualize idea. For reasons that are not apparent until late in the narrative, Jonesy has become the perfect host for the alien presence—Mr. Gray, as he is known—who invades the Maine woods. Using Jonesy's body as both disguise and vehicle, Mr. Gray moves out of the quarantined area and heads off to take over the world. But the original Jonesy is not consumed or even completely subsumed by Mr. Gray; his persona remains alive, sharing his body with the alien. This presents the rich—and challenging—opportunity in the film to have one actor embodying both our human protagonist and his alien adversary. (The actor Damian Lewis took on this daunting task with vigor and invention.)

And the place that Jonesy uses as a haven from the intrusion of Mr. Gray, the last remaining place, it seems, that the alien cannot penetrate, is that part of his mind we've identified as the Memory Warehouse. Not only does Jonesy use it as a refuge, but he is also able to view the action of the story out the window of the place. At times this means that Jonesy (Damian Lewis) stands at the window of the warehouse and watches as Mr. Gray

(Damian Lewis) makes his way through a blizzard on his nefarious mission.

In shooting and cutting scenes like this, a director in modern America finds himself on a teeter-totter of confidence. One knows, on the one hand, that audiences are sophisticated about visual ideas and are capable of instantly comprehending complicated conceits. On the other hand, a filmmaker knows that if an idea is not presented just right, it's easy to lose the audience, throwing them out of the story for long stretches when you need them to be deep inside it.

Unfortunately, it's impossible to know how you've met that test until much later in the life of the movie. And even then, you may never get a definitive answer. Movies are mysterious and no one really knows why one idea, scene, or entire movie "works," while another does not. A story like *Dreamcatcher*, rich in ideas and potential fun, lets a filmmaker explore those mysteries to the fullest extent.

# DREAMCATCHER

by
William Goldman
and
Lawrence Kasdan

Based on the book
by
Stephen King

10/1/01

Because something is happening here
But you don't know what it is
Do you, Mister Jones?

                    Bob Dylan
                    "Ballad of a Thin Man"

TITLES BEGIN over PANNING abstract shots of SOMETHING THAT WE
CANNOT QUITE MAKE OUT. EXTREME CLOSE-UPS on, well, on <u>something</u>.
It hangs in darkness, moving gently -- like some kind of spider's
web. An organic feeling, almost alive. Otherworldly, too, and
dangerous. We DON'T SEE it whole here, but get some sense of its
shape. It is **The Dreamcatcher.**

TITLES END.

1    INT. HENRY'S OFFICE (BOSTON) - DAY                            1

PENCIL MARKINGS. We're so close we can see the grit of the lead.
We HEAR the SCRATCHING. BEGIN PULL BACK. We make out some of the
words: "compulsive overindulgence... suicidal guilt... SLOW
SUICIDE by cholesterol... Barry, Barry N., B. Neiman..."

                    BARRY (V.O.)
          ... Carl's Jr. has this $6 Burger, which
          really only costs $3.95, you know, so you
          think you're getting some deal, but the
          truth is it may be the best franchise
          burger out there...

The pencil jumps down and begins an elaborate DOODLE: circles
full of spidery intersecting lines, like we saw under the TITLES.

                    BARRY (V.O.)
          ...I went there yesterday and ordered
          three and, by golly, those suckers almost
          filled me up. When I got home I still had
          to have a box of Eggos...

The doodling stops and the pencil prints this last bit large,
lots of pressure on the paper, four letters:    **SSDD**

CUT TO floor level, the wooden feet of a psychiatrist's couch.
They're CREAKING under the weight of BARRY NEIMAN. We BOOM UP to
see the man himself -- Barry weighs almost 400 pounds.

                    BARRY
          ... But that doesn't take away from Carl's
          achievement. I mean, here's a guy who's
          got to go through life as Carl <u>Junior</u>,
          right --

                    HENRY (V.O.)
          Barry --

                    BARRY
          -- like he can never get out of the shadow
          of his dad, right, the original Carl, I
          guess --

                         HENRY (V.O.)
          <u>Barry</u>!

Barry stops, surprised; he cranes to see the doctor behind him --

DR. HENRY DEVLIN. [This story is about FOUR FRIENDS, and **HENRY** is
the first we meet.]

Henry went to Harvard on scholarship and is one of the top young
shrinks in Boston. One problem -- he's been seriously suicidal
for some time now.

                         HENRY
          Barry, do you think your eating problem
          stems from thinking you killed your
          mother?...

Barry is shocked. Henry's never said anything like this before.

                         HENRY
          ... That you're trying to eat yourself to
          death as punishment? You <u>do</u> think you
          killed her.

                         BARRY
          I -- I never said that --

                         HENRY
          She called out for you, said she was
          having chest pains, begged you to dial
          911.

                         BARRY
          I never told you <u>any of that</u>. How could
          you know this? You shut up now --

                         HENRY
          But she was <u>always</u> calling out for you,
          wasn't she? She'd been crying wolf her
          whole life. Why should you take her
          seriously this time?

                         BARRY
          You weren't there! <u>How could you know what
          happened</u>? <u>How</u> --?

                         HENRY
          That doesn't matter... What matters is, it
          was an understandable mistake. You've got
          to stop blaming yourself...

Barry is trying to get up -- it's a titanic struggle, but he
keeps at it, sofa GROANING beneath him.

> BARRY
> STOP IT, YOU MONSTER! STOP IT. You're the
> devil...

> HENRY
> ... if you don't, you'll eat yourself into
> an early grave. And there's no reason for
> that, Barry. It wasn't your fault --

Barry manages to roll/fall off the couch, his final lurch
BREAKING ALL FOUR LEGS of the sofa. He gets up, throws a
horrified look at Henry, and charges out of the office. The door
SLAMS behind him. Ashamed, to himself --

> HENRY
> Congrats, Mr. Hippocratic Oath, you're now
> doing more harm than good.
>> (gazes at wrecked couch)
> That's gotta be some kind of sign.

He goes to sit at his desk. He pulls open a bottom drawer and
takes out a .38 revolver. He checks the cylinder, then swivels in
his desk chair so he can look out at the gray spring day.

We're BEHIND HIM as he puts the revolver to his temple and draws
the hammer back with his thumb. All he has to do now is squeeze.
Silence. Then, very loud -- RING!! RING!!

His phone. Astonishingly, he hasn't killed himself in surprise.

> HENRY
> Jonesy.

He lowers the gun and gingerly releases the hammer. IT GOES OFF
with an ear-splitting BANG! The bullet smashes into his framed
medical diploma on the wall.

Henry is shocked and somewhat deafened. He looks over at the
damage, then puts the gun down on the desk, carefully. He works
his pinkie in his ear before picking up the phone.

> HENRY
>> (into phone)
> Hey.

> JONESY (PHONE)
> Hey, yourself. How ya doin', Henry?

> HENRY
> What? What'd you say? I missed that.

                    JONESY
          Are you going deaf now? I said, how ya
          doin'?

                    HENRY
          Oh. You know... SSDD.

                    JONESY
          What else?

WE BEGIN TO INTERCUT WITH --

2    INT. JONESY'S OFFICE (BOSTON) - DAY                        2

GARY JONES -- **JONESY** -- sitting at his desk in his small office.
He's the second of the four friends, an Associate Professor of
History at a decent but not great college in Boston. People have
always taken to him, and he has no idea why.

                    JONESY
          I was thinking if you were free this
          weekend, we might go see Duddits.

                    HENRY
          Yes, absolutely. He's been on my mind a
          lot too.

Someone KNOCKS on Jonesy's office door.

                    JONESY
              (calling out)
          It's open.
              (into phone again)
          I've got a thing here, gotta go. H., I'll
          see you Saturday.

                    HENRY
          Right...

Henry hangs up, puts the revolver back in the drawer.

                    HENRY
          ... see you Saturday.

3    INT. JONESY'S OFFICE - DAY                                 3

DAVID DEFUNIAK comes through the door. Just a worried kid. Skinny
and underfed, one earring. Jonesy gestures. Defuniak sits in the
chair across. Nervous. The old-fashioned, black and white
Converse sneakers he's wearing are in tatters. Jonesy notes them.

                    JONESY
       So, Mr. Defuniak. Do you know we're both
       escapees from Maine?
            (Defuniak tries to smile)
       You're from Pittsfield.

Defuniak nods, and you can see his panic. Jonesy reaches into a
folder on his desk, takes out an exam.

                    JONESY
       David? Do you know what happens to
       scholarship students who are caught
       cheating on exams?

Defuniak is in a nightmare now. Suddenly, tears. Jonesy tosses
him a box of Kleenex. Jonesy's hiding it, but right now he feels
as bad as Defuniak looks. Then something wonderful happens -- a
life-changing moment for the kid -- Jonesy <u>begins to rip up the
exam</u>.

                    JONESY
       You had the flu that day, didn't you,
       David? Isn't that why you didn't take the
       exam?

For a moment, the kid doesn't get it.

                    JONESY
       You missed the test, David. And since <u>you
       were ill</u>, David, why not write me an essay
       instead -- three thousand words on the
       short-term results of the Norman Conquest.

                  DEFUNIAK
           (knows he's being saved now)
       I was <u>just so sick</u> that morning, Professor
       Jones -- 105 fever --

                    JONESY
       -- came on suddenly, did it? --

                  DEFUNIAK
       -- oh, yessir, out of the blue --

                    JONESY
       Go get started. I'd like it by Monday.
           (Defuniak stands)
       Pittsfield's a better place to be from
       than to go back to.

                  DEFUNIAK
       Yessir, thank you sir.

                    JONESY
          And, David, the next time you think of
          buying beer, buy some boots instead. I
          wouldn't want you to catch the flu again.

                    DEFUNIAK
          Okay. I will. Buy some boots, I mean. I
          really will.

Defuniak nods, hurries to the door, opens it, looks back. He
wishes he could resist asking, but he can't --

                    DEFUNIAK
          How did you know? You weren't even there
          that day.

Jonesy's not sure how he wants to answer. Finally --

                    JONESY
          Sometimes I just know.

Defuniak leaves. Jonesy sighs, goes back to a huge pile of exams.

4    INT. MACDONALD MOTORS (BRIDGTON, MAINE) - DAY                4

**PETE** MOORE, car salesman, stares out at the drizzling afternoon.
Gloomy. Pete's the best-looking of the friends. He thought he was
going to be an astronaut. Now he's tiptoeing toward alcoholism,
which worries him a lot. When he isn't drinking.

PETE'S POV: A WOMAN is crossing the wet street, headed this way.
Pushing thirty, attractive. She comes in and hurries toward Pete.

                    TRISH
          This probably isn't going to work.

                    PETE
          Never start that way with a car salesman --
          we love challenges. I'm Pete Moore.

                    TRISH
               (really upset)
          In one hour I'm showing a house up in
          Fryeburg -- it's a big commission -- and
          I've lost my damn car keys.  Could you
          possibly make me duplicates?

                    PETE
          That takes at least a day.

                    TRISH
               (fighting tears)
          Oh boy, I just <u>knew</u> it.

                    PETE
          Whoa. Easy, Trish, maybe I can help. I've
          always been good at finding things.

He gives her his killer smile --

                    TRISH
          Did I tell you my name? I don't remem--

                    PETE
          I guessed.

TRISH gives him a wary smile.

5    EXT. STREET - DAY                                    5

Pete and Trish hurry across the street toward a drugstore.  Under
the awning, they stop for a moment.

                    PETE
          You had a headache... stressed-out about
          showing the house, right?
               (Trish nods)
          You stopped for coffee, came to the
          drugstore for aspirin...

6    INT. DRUGSTORE - DAY                                 6

Pete and Trish enter. To RACHEL, the girl at the counter --

                    PETE
          Rachel.

                    RACHEL
          Hey, Pete... Miss, I looked again -- I
          don't see 'em.

                    PETE
               (to Trish)
          Okay, I need your help. You had the coffee
          in your hand, you bought aspirin, paid for
          it, went to your car outside, realized the
          keys were gone. That everything?

                    TRISH
          Yes...

Pete looks at her a moment, not sure how to introduce this --

                    PETE
          Look, this is gonna seem weird, but it's
          just a thing I do to help me think.

He closes his eyes, makes a fist with his right hand, pops up his
index finger, waggles it back and forth. Whatever he's doing, it
makes Trish uneasy. Rachel giggles -- she's seen this before.
Pete opens his eyes, drops his hand, looks around.

WHAT PETE SEES: <u>A path in the middle of his view</u> that's more
vivid than everything around it, clearer, more intense. (The four
friends refer to it as "THE LINE.") And right now it goes to one
side of the candy display.

Pete walks over there.

                    PETE
          You bought a candy bar before the
          aspirin... a Mars Bar.

Trish is stunned. She nods.

7    EXT. STREET - DAY                                          7

Pete sees The Line heading toward a Taurus. Trish follows him.

                    PETE
          Yours, right?

She nods, keeping her distance now. At the car, he turns to her.

                    PETE
          One more question: if I find your keys,
          would you let me buy you dinner? The West
          Wharf? Six-thirty? Best fried clams in
          Maine. It's right on your way back --

                    TRISH
          I know The West Wharf.
              (hesitates)
          Sure. Okay. That would be nice.

                    PETE
          All right... so you got here, opened your
          purse -- aspirin, coffee, candy, juggling
          it all around... and that's when --

He bends suddenly, his hand dipping into the flowing gutter, then
out again, makes a magician's flourish, a big smile --

                    PETE
          -- you dropped your keys.

Trish gapes at the car keys in his hand. But she doesn't reach
out for them. Pete's smile fades. He's scared her.

                              PETE
                    Just luck is all.

Trish takes her keys, careful not to touch his hand.

                              TRISH
                    Thank...you.

She unlocks her car, gets in quickly.

                              PETE
                    The West Wharf, right? Half past six? Best
                    fried clams in this part of the state.

She's not going to be there and they both know it.

                              TRISH
                    You got it.

She pulls away. Pete waves, stands there in the rain as the last
of his smile falls away. Sad --

                              PETE
                    Another fuckarow.

8    INT. BAR (PORTLAND, MAINE) - NIGHT                          8

CLOSE ON a TOOTHPICK in a man's mouth. He's working it from tooth
to tooth, expertly, with no hands. Now, more surprising, he lifts
a glass of Canadian Club to his lips and drains it, <u>without
removing the toothpick</u>. As he puts down the glass, we meet --

-- JOE CLARENDON -- **BEAVER** to his friends. He's wiry, with
glasses; looks like either a math genius or a serial killer. In
fact, he is a carpenter. Always wears Doc Martens. He has the
most generous heart of our four friends. Sure, maybe the smallest
brain, but since childhood his first instinct in any new
situation is to smile.

But he's not smiling now, alone in this bar. He goes out.

9    EXT. STREET - NIGHT                                         9

Beaver takes a deep breath, moves on. We can see this in his
face: the man is miserable. And lonely.

10   INT./EXT. PHONE BOOTH - NIGHT                              10

Beaver dials, puts in change.

11     INT. JONESY'S OFFICE - NIGHT                                    11

Jonesy is about to leave his office as the PHONE RINGS. He has to
come back from the door to pick up the phone --

                    JONESY
          Jones.

12     INTERCUT OFFICE/PHONE BOOTH                                     12

Beaver, in the booth, is writing letters with his fingertip in
the fogged glass.

                    BEAVER
          How you doing?

Jonesy's glad to hear Beaver's voice.

                    JONESY
          You know, Beaver. Same shit, different
          day.

Beaver's mood instantly lifts. We can now SEE the letters he
printed on the fogged glass:  **SSDD.**

                    JONESY
          You okay?

                    BEAVER
          Like always.

                    JONESY
          You want to talk?

                    BEAVER
          No, you're trying to get home.

                    JONESY
          Screw that.

                    BEAVER
          No, really, I got nothing. Go home.
               (hesitates, then --)
          ... Jonesy?

                    JONESY
          Yuh, Beav?

                    BEAVER
          You be careful.

Jonesy reacts. Not big, but it's not nothing either.

                    JONESY
          Be careful of what?

                    BEAVER
          Wish I knew.

13    EXT. BOSTON STREET - NIGHT                              13

Jonesy, hurrying along a busy Boston sidewalk. He comes to a
major street and stops at the crosswalk. Lots of traffic. Jonesy
flinches, then turns to the STRANGER next to him.

                    JONESY
          What'd you say?

                    STRANGER
          I didn't say anything.

                    JONESY
          Right. Sorry.

PUSH IN as he tries to shake a weird feeling. Then, stunned, he
stares at something across the street which we don't see --

-- and suddenly he plunges into the street.

This big old clunker of a car, an ANCIENT MAN at the wheel,
driving way too fast, SMASHES INTO JONESY. He spins crazily in
the air, then crashes down onto the pavement. As his SCREAMING
gets louder and louder --

JONESY'S POV: A CROWD OF PEOPLE around him, but he's having
trouble looking up, so what he's seeing mainly is their shoes.

Someone is saying, "Get a cell phone, call an ambulance!", and an
OLD WOMAN replies, "It won't do any good." And now the ANCIENT
MAN who hit him pushes his way through the crowd. Jonesy can see
his antique brown wingtips --

                    ANCIENT MAN (O.S.)
               (early Alzheimer's)
          I looked away for one second and then I
          heard a thump... What happened?

Jonesy sees something he recognizes: a pair of tattered, black
and white Converse sneakers have worked their way forward.

                    DEFUNIAK (O.S.)
               (distraught)
          Omigod, that's Prof. Jones! He can't die.

On that, Jonesy's eyes close. WE GO TO BLACK and in the darkness
WE HEAR the WAIL OF A SIREN.

14  INT. AMBULANCE - NIGHT (TRAVELING)   14

FADE UP ON JONESY'S POV: he's on a stretcher as TWO EMT'S cut away his trousers. He tries to see what's revealed, but he can't quite lift his head enough.

       EMT #1
   Jesus.

EMT #1 suddenly has two large paddles in his hands and he's slapping them (out of Jonesy's view) on his chest --

       EMT #2 (O.S.)
   Clear!

-- the juice flows and Jonesy's body jerks like a fish on a hook.

       EMT #2 (O.S.)
   No good -- <u>flatline</u> -- <u>hit it again</u>!

Jerking again, Jonesy closes his eyes. SCREEN GOES BLACK BRIEFLY.

       EMT #2 (V.O.)
   Whaddya think?

       EMT #1 (V.O.)
   I think it's no good... I think he's gone.

Jonesy opens his eyes again, or at least it seems that way, but there's something strange: <u>the face of the EMT #1 has changed</u> --

-- now it's the face of someone we haven't met yet, but will. A mentally-challenged child of thirteen by the name of DOUGLAS CAVELL -- **DUDDITS** to those who love him.

       DUDDITS
   Awch out fo Ister Gay.
   *[Watch out for Mr. Gray.]*

Jonesy's eyes close; the SCREEN GOES BLACK AGAIN.

       EMT #2 (V.O.)
    (defeated, quiet)
   That's it... this one's dead.

Blackness. The SIREN FADES AWAY. Quiet. A TITLE appears:

15      **SIX MONTHS LATER.**     15

16      INT. HOLE IN THE WALL CABIN (MAINE WOODS) - NIGHT      16

THAT SOMETHING WE COULD NOT MAKE OUT under the OPENING TITLES. It hangs in the darkness, but the EXTREME CLOSE-UPS give way to LOOSER SHOTS, more recognizable textures: twigs, twine, beads, feathers.

And then -- <u>lights hit it</u>. It is a weaving that hangs from the center rafter of this cabin. <u>Four spidery circles held in place by sticks around a larger circle</u>. The design Henry was doodling -- **The Dreamcatcher.**

SOUND OF AN ENGINE; a vehicle is approaching. The lights are coming from its bouncing headlights. As it gets closer, we begin to HEAR MEN'S VOICES -- <u>loud with excitement</u> --

TILT DOWN from The Dreamcatcher to a window, through which WE SEE an old INTERNATIONAL HARVESTER SCOUT pull up. Our four friends pile out -- Henry, Jonesy, Pete and Beaver.

17      EXT. HOLE IN THE WALL - NIGHT      17

They're all grabbing stuff as they exit the Scout -- duffels, suitcases, grocery bags, gun cases. <u>Jonesy moves with a bad limp</u>, and some pain.

They bustle to the cabin, which, over forty years, has become part of these woods. Beaver unlocks the door. We SEE our guys as they go in... and they look very happy.

18      INT. HOLE IN THE WALL - NIGHT      18

LATER. The cabin: open downstairs area -- living room, kitchen. Funky mix of furniture accumulated over years. Navajo rug. Two bedrooms in the rear. Bathroom in the corner. Steps upstairs. One wall has a big picture window.

Beaver and Pete are cooking, banging around the kitchen, drinking beer (Pete goes through them fast). Beaver's adding hot sauce without conscience to some hamburger/onion/potato mishmash.

                  BEAVER
          (shouting toward the window)
     Ten minutes.

                  HENRY (O.S.)
          (from outside)
     We hear you.

                  BEAVER
          (gestures toward the window)
     Henry's pretty gloomy even for Henry, wouldn't you say?

Pete agrees, takes another beer. He frowns at the beer supply --
not deep enough for his tastes.

                    BEAVER
          Got blown last night.

                    PETE
          Good for you. First time?

                    BEAVER
          Bite my bag. Met this lady at bingo, went
          back to her place and it turned into a
          pretty nice fuckaree --

                    PETE
          As opposed to a fuckarow...

                    BEAVER
          Obviously... though I'll admit I've had
          perfectly good fuckarees turn into
          fuckarows in an flash.

                    PETE
          Try Viagra.

                    BEAVER
          Viagra! I'm practically at full salute all
          day long. I'm, whaddya call it --
          privatic, prismatic? Henry'll know.

                    PETE
          I think you're remembering yourself in the
          fourth grade.

                    BEAVER
          What, you having wood problems?

                    PETE
               (unfazed)
          You haven't tried it, have you?

                    BEAVER
          Hell, no.

                    PETE
          You won't believe it. Drop that little
          blue bomb and you're hard as a Louisville
          Slugger for twelve hours.

Beaver stops working the frying pan, incredulous.

                    BEAVER
          Twelve hours?

                              PETE
            I'm talking Yastremski. You don't have to
            need it to love it.
                    (catching up)
            Bingo? Did you say bingo? Like the game in
            church basements?

                              BEAVER
                    (defensive)
            There's trim there...

                              PETE
            Ooh, Beaver... I thought my deal was
            pathetic.

19      EXT. HOLE IN THE WALL - NIGHT                        19

Same time. Cold. Henry and Jonesy are loading wood into a
wheelbarrow from stacked cords. Jonesy, stiff, bends with some
difficulty, picks up a log -- a quiet GASP.

                              HENRY
            You just watch, that's your job.

                              JONESY
            I'm fine. 100%.

                              HENRY
                    (unconvinced, helps him)
            Really?

                              JONESY
            Well... 83% anyway.
                    (watches Henry)
            H., you been thinking of Duddits more than
            usual?

Henry nods, gathers more wood.

                              JONESY
            Remember, we were going to go see him that
            weekend? Then I got hit --

                              HENRY
            I remember.

                              JONESY
            You been to see him since?

Henry, guilty, "no." Jonesy indicates that he hasn't either. He
glances toward the kitchen window, then lowers his voice --

                    JONESY
          I've got to tell you something weird...

Henry nods, pays attention while he works.

                    JONESY
          The night I got hit, I was standing on
          that sidewalk and there, across the
          street... I saw Duddits --
               (this stops Henry, for a moment)
          -- just like he was that day we first saw
          him, back in Derry. He was calling out for
          help and everyone was ignoring him,
          passing him by. And then he looked over at
          me -- directly at me -- and he motioned
          for me to come to him.
               (pause)
          For six months I've had no memories of the
          accident. None. Then this morning, when I
          started packing to come up here, it all
          came back.
               (Henry says nothing)
          You believe I saw him, don't you?

                    HENRY
               (nods -- soft)
          I do, yessir.

                    JONESY
          It just rocked me... Duddits loves me, I
          know that. He loves us all. He would die
          before he'd ever hurt us.
               (beat)
          So why was he calling me into the street
          to get hit?

Henry takes a long time before he answers, not satisfied with
what he's come up with.

                    HENRY
          Maybe there's more to the story we don't
          get yet...

20   INT. HOLE IN THE WALL - NIGHT                            20

The four friends are sitting at the big table, well into dinner.

                    PETE
          Name it!

                    BEAVER
I'll name it... <u>after</u> we make a small
wager. Say fifty bucks?

                    HENRY
What's the subject?

                    PETE
In the movies, when people wake up
together in the morning, they immediately
start kissing, nuzzling and goin' at it.
But what they <u>never do</u>, is get up first,
take a leak and brush their goddamn
teeth... which, I don't think I'm alone in
feeling, is pretty much <u>necessary</u> when you
wake up.

                    BEAVER
        (remembering, to Henry)
What's it called when you got a constant
woody and it won't go down?

                    HENRY
You mean, priapism?

                    BEAVER
        (to Pete)
I'm practically priasmic!

                    HENRY
Priapismic.

                    BEAVER
Whatever, it's hard.

                    JONESY
That's what you're betting on?

                    BEAVER
No. I'm sayin' I can name the one movie
where they acknowledge the scuzzy facts of
life. But not without some cash on the
line.

                    JONESY
<u>I'm</u> so curious, I'll give ya a quarter.

                    BEAVER
Okay... *PROMISED LAND*.

                    PETE
*PROMISED LAND*? Never heard of it.

                    BEAVER
               (instant gloat)
          Meg Ryan and, what's-his-name, Reefer
          Sutherland --

                    JONESY
          Keifer...

                    BEAVER
          -- from, I dunno, 1988 or something. Meg
          Ryan wakes up and she says, 'Where's the
          cat?' And the guy says, 'What cat?' And
          she says, 'The cat that shit in my mouth.'
               (to Pete)
          That'll be 50 small.

                    PETE
          Bullshit, you made that up.

                    HENRY
          Could Beaver make that up?

                    BEAVER
          You other bozos can have that priceless
          piece of cinematic trivia absolutely free.

                    JONESY
          You mind if I file that in the 'Who-gives-
          a-shit?' section of my Memory Warehouse?

                    BEAVER
          What's the Memory Warehouse?

                    PETE
          You don't remember about the Memory
          Warehouse? You're shitting me...

                    BEAVER
               (sheepish)
          I musta forgot.

The other three laugh.

                    JONESY
          That's a joke, right? You <u>forgot</u> about the
          <u>Memory</u> Warehouse.

                    BEAVER
               (it's not)
          Just remind me, don't give me a lot of
          shit.

19.

                         PETE
                    (takes pity on Beaver)
          It's in his head, B. We've all got one.

                         HENRY
          Hasn't that place been condemned?

                         JONESY
          Not yet, it's just that it's so crowded
          now I have to throw something out every
          time I learn something new. When I got my
          new laptop, I had to throw out all my
          files of rock 'n roll lyrics...

Surprisingly, we begin to SEE Jonesy's MEMORY WAREHOUSE --

21   INT. MEMORY WAREHOUSE (IN JONESY'S HEAD)                    21

This vast storage facility has a funky, burnished quality, like
some aging, Victorian library. The overall design is circular --
level upon level of overloaded stacks spiraling up into the
gloom. It's so impossibly big and crowded and baroque, it could
only exist in a dream, or in someone's imagination.

TIGHT SHOT, somewhere in the stacks, of several aging file boxes
labeled *"ROCK 'N ROLL LYRICS -- Real and Mis-remembered."*

Jonesy, as he is today, minus the limp, is barely glimpsed as he
loads the files on a dolly. In their place, he stacks a new box
labeled *"APPLE G3 Laptop -- how the damn thing works."*

BACK TO SCENE. The friends are laughing.

                         PETE
          My warehouse was washed away in a flood
          about ten years ago. It's gone now.

                         BEAVER
          I didn't know there was enough beer in
          Maine for a flood.

                         PETE
                    (reacts, points)
          Hey, hey, hey!

                         HENRY
          Jonesy...
                    (an old group joke)
          ... *if that really is your name...*
                    (the others laugh)
          ... what do you do with the discarded
          files?

                         JONESY
              I burn 'em.

22      INT. MEMORY WAREHOUSE (IN JONESY'S HEAD)                    22

The dolly loaded with old files is SQUEAKING over the warped
wooden floors. We pass endless shelves with printed CATEGORY
HEADINGS: *"OLD PHONE NUMBERS... SPORTS HUMILIATIONS... JERK-OFF
FANTASIES (AGES 12-16)... GIRLFRIENDS' PARENTS' NAMES... etc."*

CUT TO a huge, Deco-style INCINERATOR DOOR. Jonesy pulls it open,
revealing a RAGING INFERNO. He starts throwing in the old files.

BACK TO SCENE at the dinner table.

                         BEAVER
              Don't tell me you threw away the words to
              *'Blue Bayou'*?

The other three react. This has special meaning to them.

                         JONESY
              No... if I really can't let go of
              something, I sneak it back to an office
              I've got there...

23      INT. JONESY'S OFFICE, MEMORY WAREHOUSE (IN JONESY'S HEAD)   23

Jonesy comes in the door of a decrepit old office. We can SEE the
stacks of the Memory Warehouse out the door. He takes the small
clutch of files he's got in hand and places them carefully in an
old filing cabinet in the corner.

                         JONESY (V.O.)
              ... where I keep all my secret stuff.

BACK TO SCENE at dinner table. The others are quiet for a moment.
Beaver gets up and goes to a shelf in the living room area.

                         BEAVER
              Where do you keep the stuff on Duddits?

                         JONESY
              Oh, he's got a special section all his own
              on the third level.

Beaver takes down a huge HUNTING KNIFE in a decorated leather
scabbard. He walks over to the front door, pulls out the gleaming
blade and proceeds to <u>add a notch on the jam</u>, above older ones.

                         PETE
              I can't stop thinking about the Duds
              lately. How 'bout you guys?

                    BEAVER
              (as they all agree)
         It's this place. He's all around here even
         though he's never been here.

He finishes his knife-work and takes up the beer he's set aside.

                    BEAVER
         This is our twentieth year comin' here to
         Hole in the Wall. And, fuck me Freddy,
         here's to twenty more.

                    JONESY
         ... twenty more...

The others raise their drinks. Beaver moves to the center of the
room and lifts his beer toward The Dreamcatcher hanging from the
center rafter. Slowly, the other three get up and join him.

                    BEAVER
         And here's to Duddits... our Dreamcatcher.
         Wish he was here...

                    PETE
         ... to the Duds...

                    HENRY
         ... to Douglas Cavell...

                    JONESY
         ... to Duddits.

CUT TO ANGLE from above, The Dreamcatcher hanging in the
foreground, the four friends toasting from below. SLOW FADE OUT.

FADE UP.

24    EXT. SIDE STREET, DERRY, MAINE (FLASHBACK -- 1982) - DAY    24

We're back 20 years, in Derry, Maine. A perfect October
afternoon. Our FOUR FRIENDS, 13 years old, on their way to play
ball. They toss a basketball around, never stop their chatter.

They pass a small school -- people in Derry refer to it as "The
Retard Academy" -- for what we today would call "challenged"
children. Several of those children wait now to be picked up.

One of them, a girl, stands off alone. JOSIE RINKENHAUER is her
name and she's twelve, has frizzy blonde hair. She waves. The
boys smile, wave back. They take off into a vacant lot --

25      EXT. TRACKER BROTHERS WAREHOUSE (1982) - DAY            25

-- at the end of which is a square building with a rotting sign
that reads **TRACKER BROTHERS.**

>                    JONESY
>          Why would Tina Jean Schlossinger's pussy
>          be on the wall of Tracker Brothers?

>                    BEAVER
>          Because I said so. It's a picture.

>                    PETE
>               (excited)
>          Have you seen it?

>                    BEAVER
>          No... but the kid sits behind me in shop,
>          he <u>saw</u> it.

>                    HENRY
>          But the building's been deserted for
>          years.

CLOSER NOW, clearly deserted. Broken windows, weeds all around.

>                    BEAVER
>          Hey, you don't want to see the homecoming
>          queen's pussy, don't come!

>                    JONESY
>               (quoting)
>          *"I've got a bad feeling about this."*
>               (blank looks)
>          Han Solo.

Suddenly Beaver stoops and picks up a piece of colorful cloth.

>                    BEAVER
>          Fuck me Freddy, some kid's shirt.

>                    PETE
>          So?

>                    BEAVER
>          It's new.

He holds the shirt up now -- it may indeed be new -- but it's
been badly ripped at the back collar. Beaver drops it, moves on.

SOMETHING ELSE up ahead in the field. Jonesy hurries to it, picks
it up. A yellow, kid's lunch box: Scooby-Doo and his friends.

                    PETE
          I hate that show -- they never change
          their clothes --

JONESY turns the lunch box over, reads a sticker on the side --

                    JONESY
          'I BELONG TO DOUGLAS CAVELL. IF THE BOY I
          BELONG TO IS LOST, PLEASE BRING HIM TO 19
          MAPLE LANE, DERRY, MAINE. THANKS.'

                    BEAVER
          Must belong to one of those kids from the
          Retard Academy, you think?

They stand there for a moment in silence. And then, THIS SCREAM
and it's full of pain. And <u>surprise</u> -- the awful surprise of
someone who has never been hurt this way before.

The boys take off around the corner of the building. And we HEAR
the VOICE of an 18-year-old.

                    RICHIE GRENADEAU (O.S.)
          Go on and eat it. Eat it and you can go.

AROUND THE CORNER come the boys, reacting before we see what they
see. Beaver shouts --

                    BEAVER
          Hey you guys, quit it -- <u>just fucking quit</u>
          <u>it</u> --

WHAT THEY SEE: FOUR PEOPLE in all. Two are huge Derry High School
football linemen, DUNCAN and SCOTTIE.

RICHIE GRENADEAU is between them. Six-two, one-ninety, he's
everybody's high school dream -- perfect face, perfect body. He
wears a golf glove and holds <u>a large dog turd</u>. Which he is trying
to force a half-naked child to eat.

The child, clearly the afternoon's entertainment, kneels on the
gravel wearing only his underpants and a single sneaker. His face
is smeared with blood and dirt and snot and tears.

THIS IS **DUDDITS.** Same age as the friends, but hard to tell that.
Whatever has gone wrong in his biological history, whatever has
made him "challenged," has had an effect on his appearance.

                    RICHIE GRENADEAU
               (whirling on the friends)
          Who're you?

                    JONESY
          What are you <u>doing</u>? You trying to make him
          <u>eat</u> that? What's <u>wrong</u> with you?

                    RICHIE GRENADEAU
          You got it, snotface -- I'm gonna make him
          eat this dog turd. Then he can go.  You go
          right now, unless you want half.

                    DUNCAN
          Take a hike, girls -- while you have the
          chance.

                    SCOTTIE
          Yeah, piss off --
               (one step toward them)
          -- that was your final warning.

The friends don't budge.

                    HENRY
          You better watch it.

                    RICHIE GRENADEAU
          Why's that?

CU on Henry, finger pointing dead at Grenadeau --

                    HENRY
          <u>I -- know -- who -- you -- are</u>!

                    RICHIE GRENADEAU
          I'm trembling with fear.

                    HENRY
          You're Richie Grenadeau -- you're the
          quarterback.

                    RICHIE GRENADEAU
          So?

                    JONESY
          So what do you think people will say when
          we tell them what we caught you doing?

                    SCOTTIE
               (coming toward them)
          You're not telling anybody anything cause
          you'll be <u>dead</u>.

                    HENRY
          Get ready, Pete.

Pete moves away from his friends now.

                  PETE
Give the word, Henry.

                  HENRY
Pete can fly... and when you come for us,
all we have to do is get in your way.

                  SCOTTIE
    (scoffs)
I can't catch that little dick?

                  JONESY
You know who that is? That's Pete Moore.

Scottie's smile drops, he looks over at Richie. He's heard of
this kid, even though Pete's only a freshman.

                  HENRY
That's right, fat ass, Pete Moore. No one
can catch him.
    (instructing Pete, too)
And he's going straight to his house, to
tell his mother what you did and she'll
call the cops and... <u>then we'll see</u>.

For a moment, it's up for grabs. Grenadeau indicates Duddits --

              RICHIE GRENADEAU
You know him, is that it?

                  BEAVER
Never saw him.

              RICHIE GRENADEAU
Then why are you asking for trouble? This
is not somethin' to get the crap beaten
out of you for. Just look at the moron, he
<u>likes</u> this! He's getting attention --

                  JONESY
How do you know what he likes?

The high school boys exchange looks. Beaver picks up some rocks,
clanks them together. Pete dances. Jonesy and Henry close ranks.

                  BEAVER
<u>Come on you dickweeds</u>.

              RICHIE GRENADEAU
You <u>want</u> to fight us?

                    BEAVER
          Yes! Yes!

                    PETE
          I'm gone, Henry, just say the word.

                    RICHIE GRENADEAU
          Why? You'll lose -- <u>why</u>?

Jonesy, screaming, indicates Duddits.

                    JONESY
          <u>Because you can't do that</u>! It's wrong.
               (losing it)
          And I want to tell the world -- tell
          everybody!

The older boys suddenly realize this: it's over, they've lost.

                    RICHIE GRENADEAU
          You want us to leave, is that it?

Jonesy nods. Beaver is boiling over.

                    BEAVER
          No, let's kick their asses!

Everyone present thinks Beaver's nuts. They ignore him.

                    RICHIE GRENADEAU
          How do we know you won't tell?

                    HENRY
          If no one gets hurt, there's no story to
          tell.

Grenadeau considers this, then nods. To his pals --

                    RICHIE GRENADEAU
          Let's go.

He starts off, trying to strut. The others give dirty looks to
the boys, and follow him away. Richie turns back once --

                    RICHIE GRENADEAU
          We'll get him later, you know that. We'll
          get you all later.

And they are gone. The boys turn their attention to Duddits, half-
naked, crying, making an awful WAILING SOUND. They go to him.

                    HENRY
          I hate that sound.
               (to Duddits)
          It's okay, you can stop now.
               (Duddits cries louder)
          Do something somebody.

For a moment, no one moves. Then, Beaver, embarrassed --

                    BEAVER
          If I do, and if you tell anybody, I'll
          never hang with you again.

Mystified, they all agree. Beaver kneels down next to Duddits,
who, eyes squeezed shut, chest heaving, doesn't see him. Beaver
takes Duddits in his arms. And begins to sing, beautifully --

                    BEAVER
          'I feel so bad I've got a worried mind
          I'm so lonesome all the time...'

Duddits opens an eye, looks at Beaver.

                    BEAVER
          'Since I left my baby behind on
           Blue Bayou.'

The crying begins to subside. The boys are stunned.

                    HENRY
          I never knew Beav could sing --

                    BEAVER
          'Savin' nickels, savin' dimes
          Workin' til the sun don't shine
          Lookin' forward to happier times on Blue
          Bayou.'

Duddits stops crying. Beaver stops singing.

                    PETE
          Beaver, that's beautiful.

                    BEAVER
          I mean it, not one word.

He starts to get up, but Duddits holds on.

                    DUDDITS
          Eever. [Beaver.]

                    JONESY
        You've got a fan.
            (offers the lunch box)
        This yours?

Duddits takes it, kisses Scooby. Pete appears with Duddits' pants
and torn shirt, then struggles to get the distracted kid in them.

                    DUDDITS
            (singing as best he can)
        Ooby-Ooby-Doo, where are oo?
        We ot-sum urk oo-do-now.
        *[We got some work to do now.]*

                    JONESY
            (helping him up)
        Douglas Cavell, that's your name, right?

CU Duddits. And now for the first time we find out something: he
has the most wonderful smile. He raises his arms high --

                    DUDDITS
      I Duddits.

                    JONESY
        Duddits?

                    BEAVER
        Duddits.

                    HENRY
        C'mon, Duddits, we got to get you home.

The group starts walking back to the street. Suddenly Beaver
remembers something and breaks away. He runs over to the window
at the back of the building and peers inside.

                    BEAVER
        Hey, guys! Come here. Leave the kid there.

Henry turns to Duddits as the others run to join Beaver.

                    HENRY
        Stand right here, Duddits. Right there
        with Scooby, okay?

Duddits smiles at him, hugs his lunch box. Henry runs to the
window. **[Painted in fading letters on the wall beneath the window
is an old admonition: NO BOUNCE, NO PLAY]**

AT THE WINDOW the boys jostle to get a look. They have to cup
their hands to cut the glare and see through the grime.

WHAT THEY SEE: Tracker Brothers office. Desk on end, overturned chairs. Some used rubbers on the floor. **[What we notice: this is the same office that sits in Jonesy's Memory Warehouse.]**

On a bulletin board across from the window: a map of New England trucking routes, and a Polaroid of a woman holding her skirt up to reveal white panties. She's no beauty and no high school girl.

> BEAVER
> Jesus-Christ-bananas.

The boys, rich with disappointment, turn on Beaver.

> JONESY
> No way is that Tina Jean Schlossinger.

> HENRY
> Maybe her grandmother. Good going, Beav.

> PETE
> Holy god, we came all the way down here
> for that?

Jonesy thinks, then jerks his thumb behind them, toward Duddits.

> JONESY
> No, we came for him.

They turn to look at Duddits -- their new responsibility, their new friend, <u>their new link to each other</u>. He stands across the grass, lunch box hugged to tiny chest, smiling beatifically at them. THE SCREEN GOES SLOWLY TO WHITE.

FADE UP on a WHITE SNOWSCAPE. We're looking at --

26    EXT. WOODS NEAR HOLE IN THE WALL (PRESENT DAY) - DAY        26

Morning. A thick layer of snow on the ground. The woods are beautiful under glaring gray skies. More snow coming.

27    EXT. HUNTING STAND - DAY                                    27

The stand is in a tree near the cabin. Jonesy is set up here as comfortably as his body will allow; that is, only middling. He's got his lower body (and damaged hip) in a sleeping bag.

His deer rifle is propped nearby, but he's got mixed feelings about using it since his accident. He's focussed on a paperback and a thermos of hot coffee. Suddenly, he's <u>startled by</u> -- the SCREAM of a bird in pain. Nearby, branches rustle and a bird SHRIEKS as it takes off. One wing isn't working right.

28      EXT. GOSSELIN'S MARKET - DAY                          28

Start on an old sign on a tall post:
**GOSSELIN'S MARKET -- BEER BAIT OUT-OF-STATE LICS. LOTTERY TIX**

PAN OFF to a standard beer and deer place in the Jefferson Tract.
A store, a barn, a corral. No business -- just Henry's Scout in
the parking lot. Pete is loading supplies -- and a <u>lot</u> of beer.
Henry, carrying the last box, comes out with OLD MAN GOSSELIN.

                    OLD MAN GOSSELIN
          Weather moving in.
               (worried)
          Double storm. Alberta Clipper first --
          maybe eight inches. With a nor'easter on
          its tail. Get on back to the cabin, Henry.

                    HENRY
          Heading straight there, Mr. G.

                    OLD MAN GOSSELIN
               (as though Henry were a kid)
          Don't mess around.

                    HENRY
          Yessir.

29      EXT. WOODS - DAY                                      29

Beaver sits silently on a fallen tree, rifle at the ready. Could
be a statue except for the way he's working his toothpick. He
looks up at the sky. <u>A single snowflake lands on his glasses</u>.

30      EXT. HUNTING STAND - DAY                              30

Jonesy looks up from his book as <u>snowflakes start to fall all
around</u>. He considers the quiet scene, smiles, and then HEARS
something: the WHISPER of moving brush, the SNAP of a twig.

Instantly, he is alert. Instinct takes over and he reaches for
his rifle. Another twig SNAP. Jonesy twists his body around and
raises his rifle to his eye.

WHAT HE SEES in his sight: <u>the head of a deer</u>, a buck, through a
tunnel of interlocking branches. Brown fur, black eyes.

Jonesy. Balanced, ready. He begins his pre-shot ritual: he takes
a deep breath, tightens his finger on the trigger, blinks once to
clear his eye and sights one final time -- and reacts in shock.

WHAT HE SEES: <u>the head of a man</u>. The brown color was his coat,
the black eye a button, the antlers branches.

Jonesy is rocked, as the realization of what he almost did hits him. He swings the barrel up, falls backwards on his butt, pain shooting from his hip. Wincing, he looks down over the edge at --

THE MAN he almost killed. A big guy, maybe 60, dressed in upscale gear (incredibly, he's wearing a bright orange hunter's cap and vest, unnoticed by Jonesy until now). He's unsteady on his feet.

The Man looks around, stops. He has spotted Hole in the Wall. A CRY of relief escapes him. He staggers toward the cabin.

Jonesy puts his rifle on safety and begins his painful descent.

31      EXT. HOLE IN THE WALL - DAY                          31

A granite slab serves as a front stoop. The Man, wiped out, falls down as he reaches it. Jonesy comes hurrying up behind him.

                    JONESY
          Easy, fella, easy, you're all right now,
          you're okay.

Still down, The Man swivels, sees Jonesy, totally loses it.

                    THE MAN
          Thank God!  Oh gee, thank God, I'm lost,
          I've been lost in the woods since
          yesterday...

                    JONESY
          Let's just get you inside and get you
          warm, how would that be?

                    THE MAN
          S-S-Sure. I thought I was going to die out
          here. I...I...

As Jonesy helps him up, their faces are close together. His breath is bad, but Jonesy hides his reaction. The Man is dead pale in the face -- except for a red mark on his cheek.

32      INT. HOLE IN THE WALL - DAY                          32

Jonesy puts his rifle behind the door. The Man starts to take off his coat, but his zipper gets stuck. He looks at it, like a helpless child. The Man, RICK MCCARTHY, drops his hands to his sides like a first-grader and lets Jonesy take his coat off.

                    THE MAN
                 (holds out his hand)
          Rick McCarthy.

                    JONESY
          Gary Jones, but it's Jonesy to everybody.
          Our damn cell phones are on the blink now
          so I can't call for help -- but our car'll
          be back soon.

                    MCCARTHY
          I didn't think I'd make it. I lost the
          folks I was with.  You saved me, that's
          for sure.

McCarthy looks at The Dreamcatcher.

                    MCCARTHY
          What's that?

                    JONESY
          Dreamcatcher.
             (McCarthy looks confused)
          Indian charm. Catches nightmares, keeps
          them away, keeps you safe down here.

                    MCCARTHY
          I've had enough nightmares.

Suddenly this incredible BELCH comes out of him. Louder than any
belch you ever heard. He's mortified.

                    MCCARTHY
          Been doing that all night. Ate some
          berries in the dark. I think they must
          have upset me.

Jonesy studies him. Is he imagining it, or has the red mark on
his cheek grown? Another thing, McCarthy's chest is huge.

33    EXT. HENRY'S SCOUT, DEEP CUT ROAD (MAINE WOODS) - DAY        33

MOVING SHOTS: deep woods in heavy snowfall, beautiful but
ominous. Henry and Pete are driving on this rutted logging road.

34    INT. HENRY'S SCOUT (TRAVELING) - DAY                        34

Henry at the wheel. Pete's got a beer in one hand, cell phone in
the other. He dials, listens, then holds the phone up to Henry.

                    PETE
          You ever hear a signal like that before?

We HEAR it now too -- it's strange. Henry shakes his head. Pete
flicks on the radio -- STATIC. He switches stations -- STATIC.

                    PETE
          What is this? Must be the storm.
               (nervous)
          You think it's the storm?

                    HENRY
          I will if you will.

Pete reaches back, brings up a new beer; catches Henry's glance.

                    PETE
          I know what you're thinking.
               (Henry shrugs, 'what?')
          You're thinking that anyone who starts
          drinking at 11 A.M. probably needs to take
          the cure. But I only do it up here. In the
          real world, this shit never passes my lips
          until after five. And if it ever does,
          buddy, I'm on the wagon for life.

                    HENRY
          I'm glad to hear it.

They ride in silence for a while.

                    PETE
          What's the matter with you?

                    HENRY
               (laughs)
          What are you talking about?

                    PETE
          Spare me, H. You know we can't hide this
          shit from each other.

                    HENRY
               (considers, finally)
          Six months ago, the day Jonesy got hit, I
          did something terrible with a patient.
          Humiliated him, drove him away. Two days
          ago I saw his picture in the paper. He ate
          himself to death.

                    PETE
          You mind if I don't use that story next
          time I'm trying to sell a Mustang?
               (Henry smiles)
          Henry, you were a lead balloon long before
          this porker munched his way to eternity.

                         HENRY
               You're a great comfort, Pete. Delicate
               touch -- <u>Whoa</u>!

The car has gone into a slide, but Henry rights it quickly.

                         HENRY
               Sorry.

                         PETE
               Can I ask you something?
                   (Henry: 'of course')
               Does Jonesy know he died twice in the
               ambulance that day?

                         HENRY
               <u>Once</u> in the ambulance, <u>once</u> at the
               hospital.

                         PETE
               Does he know?

                         HENRY
                   (not sure)
               If he knows, he hasn't let on.

                         PETE
               Don't you think that's creepy?

Henry glances over, then shrugs, peers out ahead.

                         PETE
               I wish we were back at the cabin.

                         HENRY
               Hold tight -- I'm goosing it.

Pete nods. Henry starts driving faster. A lot faster.

35    INT. HOLE IN THE WALL - DAY                              35

On the couch, McCarthy gratefully accepts a bowl of soup from
Jonesy. The door bursts open and here's Beaver, glasses fogged
up, half blind, covered in snow. In addition to his own gear,
he's got the stuff Jonesy left behind. Stamping his feet --

                         BEAVER
               Jesus-Christ-bananas, some fuckarow this
               is turning into!

Only when he's wiped his glasses clean and replaced them does he
notice McCarthy. And the sweetest smile comes to his face.

                BEAVER
I'm Joe Clarendon. Call me Beaver.

                JONESY
Rick McCarthy here had a bad night in the
woods.

                BEAVER
Welcome.
    (shakes hands, points)
That frostbite?

                MCCARTHY
    (touches the red spot)
I get the same thing from peanuts --
allergy.

Beaver heads back to take off his coat, sharing a look with
Jonesy at the stove. They don't think it's an allergy.

                JONESY
Grilled cheese anyone?

                MCCARTHY
This soup is fine for me, thanks.

                BEAVER
I'll bite. Sail it over here.

                MCCARTHY
My mother always used to feed me pea soup
when I was feeling --

Another BELCH, even bigger and louder. Beaver whirls.

                BEAVER
Bitch-in-a-buzzsaw! I've heard some mighty
burps in my time but that's the blue
ribbon baby.

                MCCARTHY
I am _so_ embarrassed --

                JONESY
-- Rick ate some berries in the woods.

                MCCARTHY
Oh _no_ --

And now, ladies and gentlemen, this FART. It starts as a LOW
RASPING NOISE -- and goes on and on. Beaver and Jonesy can't
believe it. They can barely keep from laughing out loud.

                    MCCARTHY
          Omigod, that's awful. I'm so sorry --

                    BEAVER
          Rick, buddy, don't worry about it --
          there's more room out than in, anyway...
               (opens a window)
          What've you been eating, woodchuck turds?

Jonesy stares at McCarthy. The older man's swollen chest is
normal now, but <u>his stomach is huge -- he looks pregnant</u>.

                    JONESY
          You know what I think? I think you need to
          lie down and take you a little nap.

McCarthy, in a heavy sweat now, manages to make it to his feet.

                    MCCARTHY
          You know, I bet you're right. I'm tired,
          that's all it is...

36   INT. BEDROOM, HOLE IN THE WALL - DAY                    36

Jonesy settles McCarthy in a bed. The mark is larger and redder.

                    MCCARTHY
          Thank you for taking me in. Thank you
          both.

                    BEAVER
          Ah, shit, anybody woulda.

                    MCCARTHY
          Maybe. Maybe not.

Beaver puts a wastebasket next to the bed.

                    BEAVER
          This is in case you have to, you know...
          <u>urk</u>, if you can't make it to the bathroom.
               (points)
          Which, by the way, is the <u>third</u> door to
          your left. If you go in the first, you'll
          be taking a shit in the linen closet.

                    JONESY
          Something we frown on.
               (McCarthy is past jokes)
          You need anything, we're outside.

McCarthy's eyes are closing, his breath deepening. Beaver and
Jonesy tiptoe out, closing the door behind them.

37    INT. KITCHEN, HOLE IN THE WALL - DAY                    37

They quietly enter, but immediately break up, desperately trying
to suppress their laughter. Beaver opens the outside door --

                    BEAVER
          Fuck me Freddy, gimme some air!

                    JONESY
               (laughing)
          We got any gas masks handy? We need a
          biohazard team in here.

                    BEAVER
               (gestures, 'stop')
          Shut up, will ya?  What're we into here? I
          hate this kind of thing.

                    JONESY
               (breaking up again)
          Oh, like this happens a lot? You want to
          hear something that'll freak you out more?

                    BEAVER
          Not really.

                    JONESY
          You know his huge stomach? Well, when he
          got here, his stomach was normal but his
          chest was out to here. Looked like Anna
          Nicole Smith.

                    BEAVER
          I wish Henry was here.

                    JONESY
          He's a shrink, not an internist.

                    BEAVER
          He went to med school... Did you?

38    INT./EXT. HENRY'S SCOUT, DEEP CUT ROAD (TRAVELING)- DAY    38

Henry, driving through the storm, Pete alongside, with beer.

                    PETE
          You want a beer?

                    HENRY
          Later.

Pete chugs his beer, then points up ahead -- a steep hill.

                    PETE
          Better get a run at it.

Henry guns the gas, squints to see. The Scout takes the hill with
no problem. As they fly over the crest, Pete's eyes go wide --

                    PETE
     Watch it!

                    HENRY
          I see him!

A man is sitting in the center of the road, a hundred feet down
the slope of the hill. Just sitting there, like a serene Buddha.
The headlights flood him. The guy does not move an inch.

Henry twists the wheel to the right. The Scout's tires fight to
get out of the deep ruts. Still no movement from the man in the
road as the car rushes closer and starts to SKID broadside.

Pete braces his hands on the dashboard. Henry fights the car,
turning the wheel the other way now.

FROM BEHIND the man in the road: the Scout skidding toward us,
about to obliterate this guy.

Henry gets a close-up view out his side window and reacts in
surprise -- it's a woman. Her hooded face flashes by Henry's
window as the Scout misses her by inches.

FROM OVERHEAD we SEE the Scout slide by her, practically taking
off her kneecaps. But that's the end of good fortune. The Scout
hits a buried log and the car starts to roll over.

INSIDE THE CAR Henry's seat belt breaks and he falls to the roof
of the car. Everything's spinning now. His leg hits the turn
signal stalk, which breaks and jams into his thigh -- he CRIES
OUT in pain.

The Scout -- over and over it goes. Slowing.

Then it stops. Upside down in the blizzard. Wheels spinning.
Wipers going. The headlights shining into falling flakes and dark
woods. We begin to HEAR Pete SCREAMING --

                    PETE
          I broke my leg! Oh man, my damn leg!

INSIDE THE CAR. The WHICK-THUMP of the wipers is louder.

                    HENRY
          Shut up for a second and let me get outta
          here.

                         PETE
            Henry, help me! I'm caught! I can't --

Henry finds the door handle, fights it open, manages to unhook
his legs, and pops out of the car like a cork from a bottle.

                         HENRY
            Just a minute.

Henry lies there for a moment, breathing deeply. When he starts
to get up, he realizes his leg is soaked with blood.

                         HENRY
            My leg, oh man, my bloody leg --

                         PETE
                 (stops his moaning)
            Yours broken too?

                         HENRY
            No, it's just bloody, but I had to make
            you shut up somehow.

Henry limps around the car to Pete's side, goes to his knees,
yanks the door open with both hands.

                         HENRY
            Unbuckle your belt, Pete.

Henry pulls Pete out of the car. They both fall backwards into
the snow. Now they can't help it, both start to laugh. Like kids.

                         PETE
            The fuck are you laughing about?

                         HENRY
                 (doesn't know)
            How's the leg?

                         PETE
            It ain't broken. Just locked up is all.
                 (at Henry's leg)
            You're gushing pretty good.

                         HENRY
                 (looks, dispassionate)
            Yeah. I think it's stopping.

Remembering simultaneously, they look off at the figure of the
woman in the road. She has not even turned in their direction.

39          INT. KITCHEN, HOLE IN THE WALL - DAY                    39

Jonesy sits at the kitchen table marking on a grocery bag with a
felt marker. The page is full of doodles and written notations:
down in one corner is roughly the same sketch of The Dreamcatcher
Henry had made in his office. There's a primitive series of
drawings of a figure (McCarthy) with first a huge chest, then a
huge stomach, a mark on his face. And some lists: **"Farts... Lost
at sea in the woods... H.& P., phone home!... DUDDITS calling..."**

Beaver pulls a brand-new jar of peanut butter out of the cupboard
and comes over to sit opposite Jonesy. Quietly --

                    BEAVER
          ... You don't suppose he got exposed to
          radiation, do you? I saw that in a movie
          once. Guy ended up bald as Telly what's-
          his-fuck.

He glances at Jonesy's doodling and gives him a wary look. Then
he unseals the jar, breaking the vacuum seals -- POP-POP!

                    JONESY
          This guy's got plenty of hair. But I'll be
          damned if that red mark didn't get bigger
          while I was watching it --
               (looks at Beaver)
          What are you doing?

Beaver is repeatedly dipping his index finger into the virgin
peanut butter and sticking big dollops in his mouth.

                    BEAVER
          What? Peanut butter calms me down.

                    JONESY
          Somebody else might want to use that jar.

                    BEAVER
          I'll leave some.

Jonesy's eyes shift past Beaver toward the living room and he
reacts, mesmerized. Beaver extracts a new toothpick, lovingly,
from his pocket; he doesn't notice Jonesy's stare.

WHAT JONESY SEES: Out the living room picture window (beyond
Beaver, FOREGROUND) an extraordinary thing is happening: dozens
of animals are all moving through the yard in the same direction.

                    JONESY
          Beav?

                    BEAVER
          Radiation would explain those nu-cular
          farts he's got...

                    JONESY
               (stands up)
          Beaver...

Beaver looks up at him, then turns to look. Whispering --

                    BEAVER
          Criminettlies...

40   EXT. PICTURE WINDOW, HOLE IN THE WALL - DAY            40

We're LOOKING IN at the two friends as they come to stand at the
window. But WHAT WE NOTICE is the reflection in the window of the
ANIMAL EXODUS that's happening outside in the snowstorm.

41   INT. PICTURE WINDOW, HOLE IN THE WALL - DAY            41

FROM INSIDE, over the friends, we SEE the biggest animal parade
since the Ark. Deer, raccoons, woodchucks, squirrels... and,
right along with them, bears and wildcats. Animals that usually
attack each other. None of the animals pays any attention to the
others. They just keep moving quickly in the same direction. A
lot have red-gold moss on their fur -- like on McCarthy's cheek.

42   EXT. SCOUT WRECK, DEEP CUT ROAD - DAY                  42

Henry and Pete are finally up to making a move. Henry helps Pete
up and they hobble toward the woman in the road.

                    PETE
          I ought to warn you -- when we get up
          there, I'm gonna strangle this broad.

                    HENRY
          If I had to guess, I'd say she's dead.

                    PETE
          I don't care... I'll strangle her anyway.
          She almost got us both killed.

MOVING POV of the woman as they approach her from the back, heavy
snow obscuring their view. It's pretty creepy.

REVERSE MOVING SHOT: The two limping friends bring us to the
figure so we SEE her from the front before they do.

                    HENRY
          Hello! Here we come, ma'am, so don't be
          startled.

                        PETE
          I thought you said she was dead.

Henry shrugs. They come around her. She seems to be a frozen
corpse. Just sitting there in her hooded coat and an orange vest.
Her face white with frost. Eyes wide open. Blank. Staring.

                        HENRY
          Hello.

Nothing.

                        PETE
          Forget it, H., she's gone.

Pete pulls his gloves off and leans down close to her face, where
he CLAPS his hands loudly in front of her nose.

                        PETE
          Hello!

Suddenly the woman's hand shoots up and grabs Pete's leg! Henry
jumps, but Pete SCREAMS, pulling away in terror and falling on
his ass in the snow. Henry drops down in front of the woman.

                        HENRY
          Ma'am, can you hear me? Are you okay?
          Hello!

In reply, she FARTS deafeningly. Henry has to back off.

                        HENRY
          I wonder if that's how they say 'hello' in
          these parts?

                        PETE
          Phew! Listen, Miss Roadkill, you almost
          got us dead... say something.

The woman, BECKY, turns, registers them as if for the first time.

                        BECKY
          I have to find Rick.

As she stares wildly around in the blizzard we SEE, in the shadow
of her hood, an ugly red growth running down her neck.

43   EXT. HOLE IN THE WALL - DAY                              43

Jonesy and Beaver have come outside. They stare in wonder at the
animals, then at each other, then back to the animals again.

                    BEAVER
          What's that red stuff on their fur?


                    JONESY
          Like McCarthy's cheek, right?


                    BEAVER
          I never saw anything like this before.


                    JONESY
          Even the bears look scared.


                    BEAVER
          Of what, man? And where're they all going?


                    JONESY
          It's not where they're going that worries
          me. It's what are they running away from?

And at that moment, the animals react to something and begin to
move even faster. Now, we HEAR it too -- WHUP-WHUP-WHUP.

                    BEAVER
          What-the-hell?

WHUP-WHUP-WHUP. The animals start running. From right over the
roof of the cabin -- a large HELICOPTER appears.

                    BEAVER
          This could be perfect -- they can get
          Stinky to a hospital.

Up beyond the first helicopter is a SECOND SMALLER HELICOPTER, a
two-man KIOWA, hovering above its mate like a pilot fish near a
whale. The big copter drops to thirty feet, whipping the snow.

                    BEAVER
          Hey you guys -- we need help!
               (points toward cabin)
          Got a sick guy inside!

The copter door opens, REVEALING a HELICOPTER GUY with a
bullhorn. He's wearing a biohazard suit.

                    HELICOPTER GUY
               (amplified)
          HOW MANY ARE YOU? SHOW ME ON YOUR FINGERS.
          THIS AREA IS UNDER TEMPORARY QUARANTINE.
          YOU MUST STAY WHERE YOU ARE!


                    BEAVER
          What do you mean, quarantine? We got a
          sick guy down here!

                         BEAVER AND JONESY
                         (overlapping)
               -- We need help here! --
               -- Real sick guy here! --

                         JONESY
               Take him with you now!

                         HELICOPTER GUY
                         (booming on)
               GREAT. YOU MUST NOT LEAVE. THIS AREA IS
               UNDER QUARANTINE.

                         BEAVER
                         (screaming)
               What's so damn great? We got a guy here
               could be dying! We need some help!

                         GUY IN HELICOPTER
                         (makes an A-OK sign)
               GLAD YOU'RE OKAY. THIS SITUATION WILL BE
               RESOLVED IN 24 TO 48 HOURS.

Stunned, Beaver and Jonesy watch the big copter fly away.

                         BEAVER
               Kiss my bender.

They stare in frustration, their attention now shifting to the
smaller copter, which continues to hover. CUT TO:

44    INT. SMALLER HELICOPTER - DAY                          44

The solitary man in here is going to figure prominently in
everything that happens from now on -- **COLONEL ABRAHAM CURTIS.**

CURTIS' POV: Beaver and Jonesy. Beaver flips him the finger.

Curtis considers them with interest, then pulls up and away.

45    EXT. LOGGERS' SHELTER, DEEP CUT ROAD - DAY             45

A LOGGERS' SHELTER by the road. Primitive: four posts, a tin roof
collapsed in back to form an accidental lean-to. Henry and Pete
appear out of the snow, supporting Becky between them.

                         PETE
               Let me ask you, old buddy, 'cause I'm
               confused -- is this SSDD or not?

                         HENRY
              Definitely not. <u>Different</u> shit today,
              Pete. And a pretty weird day so far, if
              you want to know.

As they lay Becky down in the shelter, she BELCHES.

                         PETE
              I guess that's an improvement.

Now they see her stomach is gigantic. They share a look of
dismay, but say nothing. They start picking up firewood and
knocking off the snow.

                         HENRY
              It's nine miles to Hole in the Wall. I
              think I can manage that. Then I'll bring
              the snowmobile back and get you both.

MINUTES LATER. A FIRE is going. A pile of wood nearby. Becky
MOANS, looks glassy-eyed and terrified. Another FART. Pete moves
a few feet away from her. Henry, about to go --

                         HENRY
              Now Pete, you listen to me -- don't go
              back to the car for beer.  Stay with her.
              Keep her warm.

                         PETE
              My right hand to God, Doctor D. --

He looks after Henry, who's heading off through the storm. Yells:

                         PETE
              <u>Henry, this is important</u> --
                   (Henry stops, turns)
              -- if we die before you get back? Promise
              you'll tell everybody she wasn't my date.

They both laugh, salute. Henry's smile fades a second before he
turns away. He gives his friend one last concerned look, leaves.

46   INT. HOLE IN THE WALL - DAY                              46

Jonesy and Beaver are inside. Jonesy heads over toward the
bedrooms, then stops suddenly. Beaver comes up next to him.

WHAT THEY SEE: <u>a trail of blood</u> from the bedroom door to the
closed bathroom door.

They exchange a look and then turn to the open bedroom door. They
can't see inside from where they stand. They step carefully over
the blood and approach the door. [We're WITH THEM as they go.]

The room comes into view: there is blood on the floor. On the bed itself, halfway down the sheet, is a large <u>bloody blotch</u>. They exchange a look of dread and turn to the closed bathroom door. Avoiding the blood, Jonesy and Beaver approach the door.

> JONESY
> Rick? You okay?

> MCCARTHY (O.S.)
> (from inside)
> I'm a little sick, fellows. I just need to make a little room.

> BEAVER
> McCarthy! Rick! Open up, man!

> MCCARTHY (O.S.)
> Go away.

Jonesy tries to turn the knob. Locked. Beaver pounds on the door.

> BEAVER
> Open the door, or we have to break it down.

> MCCARTHY (O.S.)
> (shouting now)
> <u>Can't a man have some privacy</u>?

> JONESY
> Rick! Where you bleedin' from, buddy?

> MCCARTHY (O.S.)
> Bleeding? I'm not bleeding.

Jonesy and Beaver exchange a look, then eye the door.

> JONESY
> Let's do it.

> BEAVER
> I'm not all that absolutely positive I want to go in there.

> JONESY
> What if he's dying?... 'Scooby-Dooby-Doo, we got some work to do now.' On three. Ready? One...two...
> (suddenly embarrassed)
> <u>Hold it</u> -- What if we just bounce off?

> BEAVER
> No bounce, no play.

> JONESY
> Right. No bounce, no play.

They take a step back, turn their shoulders to the door.

> BEAVER
> One and a two and <u>three</u> --

They hurl their bodies at the door, <u>which bursts open</u> --

47    INT. BATHROOM, HOLE IN THE WALL - DAY                    47

Jonesy and Beaver stumble into the bathroom, skidding on bloody floor tiles. Spastically, they grab the doorjamb and each other to keep from going down. When they've steadied themselves, they look at the scene before them, <u>thunderstruck</u>.

> BEAVER
> Ah, fuck... Ah, man -- <u>fuck</u>.

WHAT THEY SEE: <u>and it's nothing you've ever seen before</u>. The blue tile floor has blood on it, sure, but what it has a lot more of is <u>reddish-gold mold</u>. It's everywhere now. And IT'S GROWING.

McCarthy is sitting on the toilet, wearing only his thermal top and hunting cap. He stares ahead at the blue shower curtain. The red mold now covers half his face.

> BEAVER
> I don't want to see this, Jonesy -- man, I can't see this. I dunno, man...

> JONESY
> Shut up a minute. Mr. McCarthy? Rick?

> BEAVER
> Is he still alive?

> JONESY
> I don't know. Rick? Rick, are you --

Suddenly, a SPLASH in the toilet below McCarthy.

> BEAVER
> Oh... man. Jonesy, if he can still do that, he must be alive. I mean, c'mon...

> JONESY
> Rick? Can you hear me? I think he's dead.

> BEAVER
> Bullshit he is. He just dropped a clinker, I heard it.

                    JONESY
          I don't think that was --

Beaver, flipping out, reaches to grab McCarthy's shoulder --

                    BEAVER
          That's enough, fella! Snap out of it!

McCarthy falls into the tub, pushing the shower curtain ahead of
him -- Jonesy and Beaver SEE something and simultaneously SCREAM.
We SEE it for only a split second (12 frames):

McCarthy's ass has a giant, bloody crater in its center, <u>as
though a shotgun had fired from inside</u>. McCarthy's body flops
into the tub and, thank god, the shower curtain hides the horror.

Suddenly there is ANOTHER SPLASHING SOUND in the water of the
toilet. Beaver leans forward to look inside the bowl, but Jonesy
reaches in front of him and SLAMS the lid down.

                    JONESY
          No!

                    BEAVER
          No?

                    JONESY
          No.

ANOTHER SPLASH and the lid bumps up. Beaver quickly sits on it.

                    JONESY
          Good move, Beav.
               (thinking out loud)
          Whatever it is, it's trapped... Got
          nowhere to go but the septic tank...

Beaver's face lights up and instantly he FLUSHES the toilet. They
listen to the water as it clears the bowl. They wait, tensely.
It takes forever. FLUSHING ends. SILENCE. Beaver reaches into his
pocket -- nervous compulsion -- and pulls out some toothpicks.
He's about to select one when there is a huge THUMP from inside
the bowl. The toothpicks go flying.

                    BEAVER
          <u>Shit</u>!

                    JONESY
          Listen, Beaver, we're going to change
          places.

                    BEAVER
          What?

                    JONESY
     One of us has got to go out to the shed.

                    BEAVER
     One of us? No way --

                    JONESY
     Shut up and listen! There's friction tape
     out there, isn't there? You're going to
     get it, come back here and we'll tape the
     lid down. Then we'll get the hell outta
     here.

Another THUMP! Beaver winces. He thinks, looks down.

                    BEAVER
     You get the tape, Jonesy.

Jonesy gives him a long look. He loves this guy.

                    JONESY
     Beav -- don't be brave. You're faster than
     me.  You get the tape, I'll sit on
     Thumper.

                    BEAVER
     No -- because if it does somehow get out,
     you can't fight it -- not with your hip.

Jonesy wavers; he understands what Beaver's doing.

                    BEAVER
     Goddamit, go!

Jonesy takes off. Beaver is alone now. In this horrible place.
Creepy quiet. Then, Jonesy is suddenly back in the doorway.

                    JONESY
     And Beaver...?

                    BEAVER
     Yeah?

                    JONESY
     Sit tight, buddy.

-- and on that he breaks out laughing. So does Beaver. They just
roar. Then Jonesy is gone.

Beaver checks his pocket -- no more toothpicks. He looks at two
that have landed clear of the fungus, on clean tiles. He
scrunches up his face -- even in desperation, is that too gross?

No. He needs a toothpick, now more than ever. Without lifting off the lid, Beaver strains to reach the closer toothpick. No good, he's a couple inches short. He gives up, frustrated. His glance falls on the mess in the bathtub, the late Mr. McCarthy.

>                    BEAVER
>          Blow it out your ass.

That kind of cheers him, but only for a moment. He looks around, closes his eyes. And then he starts to SING, glorious and pure --

>                    BEAVER
>          'I feel so bad I've got a worried mind
>          I'm so lonesome all the time
>          Since I left my baby behind on
>          Blue Bayou.'

He trails off and slumps into silence. Then, calling out --

>                    BEAVER
>          Earth to Jonesy, come in, Jonesy!

48    INT. SHED, HOLE IN THE WALL - DAY                        48

Jonesy is in the shed outside; it's crammed with stuff. He looks around for the friction tape -- and can't find it.

>                    BEAVER (O.S.)
>               (distant)
>          Jonesy... I miss you!

Jonesy grabs a bicycle horn, squeezes -- OOHGAH!--OOHGAH! Loud.

49    INT. BATHROOM, HOLE IN THE WALL - DAY                    49

Faintly, Beaver HEARS the horn and it comforts him. He looks for more comfort, and there it is -- waiting on the clean tile, a toothpick. He looks at it longingly. Suddenly Beaver shouts --

>                    BEAVER
>          Find the damn tape!

50    INT. SHED, HOLE IN THE WALL - DAY                        50

Jonesy, wild with frustration, because he can't find it.

>                    JONESY
>          Where is it? --

And he SLAMS his fist down on a table full of stuff. A stack of nail boxes topples over and there it is: the fat roll of tape. Jonesy grabs it and starts limping out of the shed --

51      INT. BATHROOM, HOLE IN THE WALL - DAY                    51

A toothpick. TILT UP to Beaver. He can't take it anymore, he
needs the solace of that wooden sliver. And he's convinced he can
get away with the four-inch move that will bring it to his grasp.

Quickly now, he bends forward enough to grab the toothpick -- off
the lid for just a moment -- a moment too long.

Something hits the lid of the toilet with terrifying force -- the
lid catches Beaver in the balls and sends him pitching forward.
He tries for balance by grabbing the shower curtain but --

-- the curtain pulls free: CU ANGLE of the bar with a metallic
CLITTER-CLACK of rings popping free.

The toilet seat flies up so hard that it CRACKS the porcelain
tank. Water pours out.

Beaver's face is on the bloody floor; his glasses have fallen
off. He's in pain from his groin, but then something much worse
happens: SOMETHING lands on his back (we catch only a glimpse
from this angle, he can't see it at all) and he SCREAMS. Whatever
it is, it's on his back, attached there somehow. Beaver pushes up
from the floor and looks down his body in time to see:

The Thing's muscular tail come right between his legs, open its
hideous tail pincers, and grab hold of Beaver's groin.

Beaver's face lifts up as he CRIES OUT in agony, but not defeat.
With a mighty effort, Beaver rolls over and slams his body down,
trying to crush the Thing on the floor. It cries out, with an
awful high-pitched CHITTERING SOUND.

ABOVE BEAVER now, we SEE the pincers release. In a BLUR, the
Thing wriggles out from under Beaver and EXITS THE FRAME. As
Beaver sits up, we SEE that his neck has a horrible wound and is
gushing blood. He gropes for his glasses, finds them and stands
up, bringing his glasses to his face.

BEAVER'S POV: First blurry, without his specs, then, as he brings
them up to his eyes, clarity. And, oh man, it's bad --

-- WE SEE IT FOR THE FIRST TIME, clinging to the doorway about
halfway up, this Thing, this muscular tentacle, several feet
long, with two feverish black eyes. There's no way around it, all
things considered, you've got to call it a **SHIT WEASEL**.

Now, the lower part of the head splits down along its body,
revealing a nest of razor-sharp teeth.

It strikes at Beaver like a snake, then withdraws too fast to see. Beaver has raised his hands to his face to ward it off. For a moment he's confused about what's happened, but then --

-- he CRIES OUT again -- because four of his fingers are gone --

> JONESY (O.S.)
> (distant, entering cabin)
> I'm comin', Beav --

The Shit Weasel coils on the doorjamb and then launches itself across the room and onto Beaver's chest.

Beaver is knocked backwards, the back of his knees catching the top of the toilet bowl. He sits down violently into the bowl, this horror WRIGGLING on his chest -- tail wrapping around his torso, pincers stabbing to grip.

The Weasel draws back to strike at Beaver's face, and does, but at the very moment when we expect to see the worst, Beaver's good hand comes up gripping a toilet brush with a stout wooden handle and gets it between them.

The Weasel catches it square in the mouth and is stopped an inch from Beaver's eyes. For this one second, one time, Beaver has triumphed. The Weasel is confused. It draws back and CHOMPS through the 3/4" handle with no trouble, SPRAYING splinters and WET SLIME, then arches to strike again.

Jonesy, at last, arrives in the doorway.

> JONESY
> Beaver! Beav, what—

The Shit Weasel turns to look at Jonesy. For a moment it seems it might release Beaver and attack Jonesy instead. Beaver senses this and does the most extraordinary thing: he wraps his arms around the Weasel to keep it from launching at Jonesy.

> BEAVER
> Jonesy, get outta here! Get out! Shut the door!

Jonesy registers Beaver's last, incredible sacrifice.

> BEAVER
> (weak)
> ...run Jonesy...

CU BEAVER, blood-splattered face turned for his last look at Jonesy. He turns back to his enemy, in time to see --

BEAVER'S POV: the Weasel has returned its attention to him and is at this moment ready to strike -- DIRECTLY AT CAMERA, teeth and maw coming right at Beaver's eyes. BEAVER'S WORLD GOES BLACK.

Jonesy watches in horror as Beaver is driven backwards over the toilet (where, mercifully, we can't fully see the damage). In a split second, pop goes the Weasel, reappearing at the base of the bowl and <u>slithering fast</u> right at Jonesy.

Halfway across the room, it lifts its head and launches at Jonesy -- who manages to SLAM the door just as the Shit Weasel hits. The door quakes and the wood distorts at the impact point, but holds.

52    INT. OUTSIDE BATHROOM, HOLE IN THE WALL - DAY              52

Jonesy grips the door knob with both hands. From inside, angry CHITTERING. The door begins to SHAKE.

CU the doorknob, as Jonesy holds it. <u>Now it starts to turn</u>.

Jonesy strains to maintain his grip. The doorknob <u>keeps on turning</u>, until... the pressure on the doorknob subsides.

Jonesy takes a breath. He leans in close to adjust his grip. Suddenly, <u>right next to Jonesy's head</u>, the Weasel is attacking the door with its teeth, punching at the wood, again and again.

Jonesy, terrified, knows there's not a thing he can do to stop it biting through the door. But his terror is replaced by a realization and hot tears begin to pour down his face --

> JONESY
> You killed him. You killed Beaver!
> (screaming)
> <u>You killed him, you fuck</u>!

The doorknob begins to turn again, with such force that Jonesy cannot hold it. The rod connecting the knobs SNAPS, the doorknob comes loose. The door starts to open.

Now something happens that makes Jonesy shudder: <u>a shadow passes over him. He's not alone</u>. Jonesy turns.

**MR. GRAY** is standing behind him. He's an extraterrestrial. You can tell because he's got that look we've seen a thousand times, in a hundred subtle variations, in movies and tabloids:

Huge black eyes, gray skin, spindly legs. Something almost <u>benevolent</u> about his appearance. He's seven feet tall and while it's pretty horrifying actually having him there in the room...

... it could be worse. We're so familiar with this look, it's almost as comforting as Mickey Mouse.

Jonesy is frozen. Mr. Gray comes closer. And closer still.

AT FLOOR LEVEL, the Shit Weasel slithers out of the bathroom, between Jonesy's feet, and over to Mr. Gray's legs, where it heads upwards, spiralling gracefully up the ET's body.

TILT UP with the Weasel as it zips around Mr. Gray's skinny chest and settles on his shoulder. The Shit Weasel coils, as if to strike at Jonesy, but abruptly turns to look in the direction of the bedroom, then launches itself off that way, landing with a wet SMACK on the floor and undulating away.

Mr. Gray takes no notice. He leans down so that his head and Jonesy's are just inches apart.

                    JONESY
          What do you want?

Suddenly, violently, LOUDLY, Mr. Gray's head EXPLODES in a cloud of wet, red-gold particles.

**WHAT WE SEE:** (and Jonesy probably doesn't as he flinches in surprise) is that **under the benevolent husk -- the good Grayboy disguise -- is the TRUE MR. GRAY.** And that is a truly horrible sight. Imagine the Shit Weasel grown to seven feet, completely covered in the red-gold slime, and fully equipped with hideous articulation. We see it for only 8 frames.

The red-gold slime-cloud of particles completely engulfs Jonesy's upper body.

Jonesy inhales them. He breathes them all in...

53      EXT. GOSSELIN'S MARKET - DAY                      53

We're LOOKING UP at the old sign we saw before: **GOSSELIN'S MARKET.** The small helicopter we saw at Hole in the Wall comes WHUP-WHUP-WHUPPING by, then the big helicopter, then another, and another. We become aware of a HUGE DIN.

CRANING UP past the sign and REVEALING that Gosselin's has been transformed: the world of the military has arrived. Buses and Humvees, trucks and trailers, Quonset huts and helicopters have arrived en masse -- and keep right on arriving.

All the MILITARY PERSONNEL wear unmarked green coveralls. They move about quickly, the air sharp with tension and efficiency.

Light towers are going up. A powerful electric fence is almost finished, enclosing the entire property -- store, barn and corral. In the distance, the SOUND of AUTOMATIC WEAPONS FIRE.

ANGLE ON the small helicopter as it lands, closest to camp. The bigger birds land beyond, guided by a bevy of waving GROUND CREW. Out of the small copter comes the fellow we saw before --

-- COL. ABRAHAM CURTIS. He's more impressive than anybody you're likely to meet. In his sixties, tall, fit, with white eyebrows -- a great soldier. There's something savage (and funny) about his ferocious mien. He heads toward a big Winnebago parked among trailers. Curtis looks with interest at the corral.

TWO DOZEN HUNTERS, from crusty old-timers to stylish L. L. Beaners, are milling about the corral and barn. More HUNTERS and LOCALS are being brought in now in trucks, or herded in on foot. (Some show the red-gold fungus on exposed skin.) Everyone goes into the holding area. The place looks like a prison camp.

Curtis steps up to enter his Winnebago when HE SEES, through the swarming activity --

A large GRAY SCHOOL BUS rolling into camp, loaded with SOLDIERS. What interests Curtis is the man at the open front door: he's munching from an open Burger King bag, looking around with cool, noncommittal interest at the activity. His name is --

**OWEN UNDERHILL,** fortyish, and he's the other great soldier we're going to meet. The guy you want alongside you when things go bad. Feeling Curtis' gaze even at this distance, he looks up at him.

Curtis smiles.

54      INT. CURTIS' WINNEBAGO, GOSSELIN'S - DAY                        54

CLOSE ON a shiny silver .45 Colt automatic with ivory grips. Curtis has been polishing it at his desk, lovingly, and now slides in a full clip and chambers a round.

A KNOCK at the door and Owen comes in without waiting for a response. Curtis' face lights up as he goes to Owen. The men embrace. Curtis holds Owen just a second too long and too tight.

                    CURTIS
          Owen.

                    OWEN
          Boss.

                    CURTIS
          How's Rita and the little angel?

                    OWEN
          Good.

                    CURTIS
          I'll get you back to them quick as I can.

Curtis lives in the Winnebago; it's loaded with electronics and
secret stuff. On the walls, photos: woods, cabins, people and
animals <u>with and without the fungus</u>. Owen looks --

                    CURTIS
          The men call the red stuff 'Ripley,' after
          the broad in the *ALIEN* movies. We're
          eradicating the animals as they flee the
          Blue Zone.

                    OWEN
          And the populace?

                    CURTIS
          The civilians are being brought here to
          Gosselin's. We'll detain 'em till we
          figure this out. And Owen, this time the
          ET's belong to you...
               (an honor)
          ... You'll be Blue Boy Leader.

                    OWEN
          Finally... How many left?

                    CURTIS
          About a hundred.

Owen reacts: "that's odd." Curtis picks up on it.

                    CURTIS
          Yeah, not nearly enough for a serious
          incursion. My guess is it's a crash
          landing. They've never picked terrain like
          this before or even cold weather.

                    OWEN
          What's your call?

                    CURTIS
          I'd say the real threat is them getting
          out of our net. Crash landing or not, I
          guarantee they're gonna send out scouts...
          see if they get lucky. I always say,
          they've never visited a world they
          wouldn't rather own.

Owen watches him intently.

                    CURTIS
They're up to their old tricks... using
the standard Grayboy look, with the
innocent doggy eyes and baby-butt skin.
They project what they think we want to
see. But I've had a look at the real thing
and, believe me, you wouldn't want it
marrying your sister.


                    OWEN
There's a difference of opinion about the
Ripley.

                    CURTIS
        (reacts)
Really. Who's got an opinion?

                    OWEN
Who do you think?

                    CURTIS
General Matheson.

                    OWEN
Three-star General Matheson.

                    CURTIS
        (winces, that stings)
Three? When did you see him?

                    OWEN
They called me in yesterday.

                    CURTIS
And what is the vaunted opinion of those
enlightened cocksuckers... who've never
been within three states of an ET?

                    OWEN
They say the fungus doesn't take hold in
all the victims. That some people will
just get over it.

                    CURTIS
And the Shit Weasels, the ones blasting
out the basement door? Matheson think
folks 'get over' one of those puppies?

                    OWEN
The theory they're working on is... the
creatures will only grow in a small
percentage of the exposed population.

> CURTIS
> You like that theory, bucko?

There is a long pregnant pause. They look into each other's eyes.

> OWEN
> I think it's crap.

> CURTIS
> So, if you thought someone had been
> exposed...

He goes to the window and pulls up the blinds, giving them a snowy view of the holding area and its growing population.

> CURTIS
> ... and you had 'em in your grasp?

> OWEN
> (hard, cold)
> I wouldn't want them walking out of here
> to wander as they wish.

Curtis likes that response. He puts his arm around Owen.

> CURTIS
> Bucko, I believe we are on the same
> page... pissing in the same latrine. If
> the Ripley gets out of this pine-tree
> paradise... well, it cannot be allowed to
> do that. I've quarantined the entire
> area. Nothing leaves alive.

> OWEN
> Roger that, Boss.

Again, a SHARP KNOCK on the door, but this time no one enters.

> CURTIS
> Come!

Two soldiers climb aboard: CONKLIN, a tough sergeant-type, and the man he's escorting, MAPLES. Curtis moves behind his desk.

> CONKLIN
> I've got Maples here, boss.

Maples is nervous; he's never been in here before. He begins to salute, catches himself halfway and then speaks uncertainly --

> MAPLES
> Corp. Maples, sir! I mean, boss --

                    CURTIS
          I know who you are, Maples. I've
          handpicked every man in Blue Boy Group.
          And sometimes I wonder about my judgement.

                    MAPLES
          Yes, sir. I'm sorry -- boss...

                    CURTIS
          Maples, do you know the Blue Unit
          Catechism?

                    MAPLES
          Yes, boss. The B.U.C. for all buckos.

                    CURTIS
               (the next exchanges are very fast)
          Is Blue Unit part of regular Army?

                    MAPLES
          No, boss! Better, boss.

                    CURTIS
          How does Blue Unit operate?

                    MAPLES
          Under the radar. We do not salute. We do
          not display rank. We do not say, "sir"! We
          are a force unto ourselves.

                    CURTIS
          And regular Army compared to Blue Unit?

                    MAPLES
          Pussies, boss!

                    CURTIS
          Under what rules does Blue Unit operate?

                    MAPLES
          Rules of combat.

                    CURTIS
          That's right, bucko. When a soldier
          disobeys his superior's orders he puts
          everyone at risk. And he is to be punished
          immediately by appropriate command
          personnel -- that's me. *Capishe*?

Maples begins to sweat, nods.

                    CURTIS
          Good. Then answer me one simple question
          and you can boogie out of here. But you
          have to answer me honestly.

Maples's throat is constricting with fear, but he nods.

                    CURTIS
          You were on containment detail at 0600
          this morning in Sector 14 of the Blue
          Zone. Did you or did you not allow a young
          woman and her four-year-old daughter to
          exit the Zone in their own vehicle on
          Hickam Valley Road?

                    MAPLES
          Col. Curtis --
               (realizes his mistake, but goes on,
                desperately)
          -- she hadn't been in the Zone. She'd made
          a wrong turn a few miles back. She
          couldn't have been contaminated.

                    CURTIS
          You know this for a fact or because she
          told you so?

                    MAPLES
          For a fact, boss.

                    CURTIS
          Scout's honor?

Maples is confused.

                    CURTIS
          Can you raise your hand and tell me
          honestly that you knew this for a fact?
               (Maples blinks)
          Then do it, Maples. Swear on it... Scout's
          honor.

Maples can't believe this, but he raises his hand.

                    MAPLES
          ... Scout's honor, boss...

In a flash, Curtis has raised the Colt and fired off one
deafening round through Maples's palm. The bullet hits the
ceiling. Shock all around. Maples screams, clutching his ruined
hand, but Curtis is instantly in his face, gun at his temple.

CURTIS
Stop that blatting, laddie-buck!

Maples starts to drop in a faint, but Conklin catches him. Owen
watches from across the room, ready to stop a potential murder.

CURTIS
Laddie, you've just avoided a court-
martial. Ever lie to me again, you'll be
facing a firing squad.
(to Conklin)
Now get him out of here before I change my
mind.

Conklin supports Maples across the room, where Owen opens the
door and says something to a Sentry, who rushes to help Conklin
remove the wounded man. Owen turns to find Curtis wiping up the
blood with a towel, as though nothing had happened.

OWEN
Jesus, Abe...

CURTIS
I warned him. He could have got off with a
slap on the wrist --

OWEN
-- instead of taking his whole hand?

CURTIS
He crossed the Curtis Line. Came into my
house and told me lies. You think I'm
crazy, Owen?

OWEN
A little.

CURTIS
I lost my temper there, maybe. But that
little worm did something a lot worse. The
pretty mom he let pass this morning is
down in the barn right now, crawling with
the Ripley.

He stands up wearily and drops the towel in a wastebasket. He
picks up the Colt and inserts a new shell in the clip.

CURTIS
It's twenty-five years I've been going out
to fight these alien bastards -- show them
they came to the wrong neighborhood and
knocked on the wrong fucking door -- and,
frankly, laddie, the tank is running a

                    CURTIS (cont'd)
          little low.
               (looks up at Owen)
          Luckily for me, there's one piece of good
          news in this blizzard of bullshit.
               (dramatically)
          I have you to lead the assault today...
          and to take over for me tomorrow.

                    OWEN
          What are you talking about, Abe?

                    CURTIS
          Owen, this is my last dance. From now on,
          you'll be leading the band.

He hands Owen the gun.

                    CURTIS
          You know where I got that, don't you?

                    OWEN
          John Wayne.

                    CURTIS
          That's right, laddie. He gave it to me and
          I'm giving it to you.

                    OWEN
          Abe, I don't know how to --

                    CURTIS
          Let's not get all girly with each other,
          Owen. This is hard enough. Just tell me
          how we do it...

                    OWEN
               (an old mantra)
          'We go in fast and hard...'

                    CURTIS
          And how do we come out, bucko?

                    OWEN
          '... we come out clean and ...'

                    CURTIS AND OWEN
          '... smilin'!'

55    EXT. DEEP CUT ROAD - DAY                              55

MOVING SHOT along the ragged trail that Pete is making as he
drags his bad leg through the deepening snow.

CATCHING UP to him as he makes his way back to the Loggers'
Shelter from the wreck of the Scout. He's done exactly what Henry
admonished him not to do, and he's struggling with an overload of
beer bottles in grocery sacks that seem ready to burst.

56          EXT. LOGGERS' SHELTER - DAY                          56

Pete reaches the lean-to. The fire is still going and Becky seems
to have made herself comfortable before falling asleep. She's
lying on her side, eyes closed, face toward the fire.

                    PETE
          Honey, I'm home... just hadda see a man
          about a horse...

Pete drops down on the other side of the fire, his back to a
snowbank. He opens a beer, looks her over --

                    PETE
          Good idea, catch a little shut-eye. Save
          your energy for those horrendous farts...

CUT TO REVERSE over Becky's reclining figure, Pete beyond the
comforting flames. BOOM DOWN to ground level: in the shadow cast
by the bright fire in front, we SEE that Becky's ass is a bloody
mess, having been blown out exactly like McCarthy's. A bloody
trail leads into the deep snow, then disappears.

57          EXT. SHED, HOLE IN THE WALL - DAY                    57

ANGLE ON THE DOOR TO THE SHED, open now to the swirling blizzard.
Quiet, peaceful -- until, from inside the shed, the ear-splitting
ROAR of a snowmobile engine starting up.

An ARCTIC CAT SNOWMOBILE explodes out of the shed, travels twenty
feet and skids to a stop AT CAMERA. The driver appears to be --
surprise -- none other than Jonesy. But there's something wrong --

CU **JONESY/MR. GRAY.** They're using one body now -- the one
formerly operated exclusively by Gary Jones, Ph.D. -- but now
controlled by Mr. Gray. His eyes lack Jonesy's warmth. Even so --

Jonesy is still in there. And Mr. Gray knows it, knows there's
some part of Jonesy he can't get at. For now, Jonesy's body is
good enough for his purposes -- to move through this world and
complete his mission.

WHAT BOTH JONESY AND MR. GRAY KNOW: a battle has begun.

Jonesy/Mr. Gray REVS the engine of the Arctic Cat and heads off.

WIDE SHOT, snow falling on the lovely woods. In the distance,
Pete sits by the fire, apparently in conversation with someone.

AT THE FIRE. Pete is pretty sloshed. Lots of empties around. He
throws some more wood on the fire.

PETE'S POV: the leaping flames, and through them, Becky,
apparently in blissful sleep.

>           PETE
> ... well, it's very nice of you to say so.
> I find you very attractive, also. I have
> the feeling you're one of those rare women
> who could handle the full-size Ford
> Expedition, 'the truck that handles like a
> luxury car'... a <u>really big</u> luxury car...
>           (laughs, losing it)
> ... but seriously, folks, there is one
> issue I'd like to bring up, just in case I
> should, you know, kick the bucket out
> here... turn into a goddamn Petesicle...
> not that I think that's inevitable...

IN THE SNOWBANK behind Pete, we SEE that <u>something is moving
under the snow</u>, creating a raised, moving map of its progress
toward Pete's back. Pete takes a final swig and flips the empty
over his shoulder into the snowbank -- <u>the moving bulge stops</u>.

>           PETE
> ... I'm sure Henry or Jonesy or Beaver
> will be coming to get us soon. They're my
> friends, see, we're all best friends, and
> friends don't let each other down...

The bulge in the snow starts moving toward Pete again.

>           PETE
> ... which relates to what I wanted to
> mention here... Now, ma'am, don't get
> freaked out or think I'm some kind of
> weirdo who you shouldn't meet for the best
> fried clams in Maine -- just some <u>innocent
> fried clams at The West Wharf</u>!--
>           (catches himself)
> ... Sorry about that... see, the four of
> us, these best friends, we all have this
> <u>other</u> friend, by the name of Duddits. And
> our friend Duddits... well, he's not your
> average ole buddy. No ma'am, he is not
> your average anything. One day, a long
> time ago, he gave us all this gift. It's

                        PETE (cont'd)
this kinda... how should I put it?... this
<u>ability</u>. This ability to <u>know things</u>, to
talk to each other without talking at all,
just -- <u>mind to mind</u>... Do you see what
I'm getting at?

Pete looks through the flames at the unresponsive Becky.

                        PETE
I knew you would. Well, here's the dicey
part. Lately, I've been having this
dream... and <u>in the dream</u> I understand how
our friend Duddits could give us a gift
like that. And do you know what it is I
understand? Do you, darlin'? It's this --
    (looks around, confidential)
-- I think maybe our friend Duds is not
from this planet. I think that Duddits is
from somewhere else and he came here to
<u>prepare us for something</u>...

Pete suddenly falls silent. Glumly, he opens a new bottle. The
moving bulge in the snowbank is right behind him now.

                        PETE
Crazy, huh? I'm talkin' shit about the
only perfect person I ever knew. He's so
goddam good, I can't believe he's a
human... Man, I should be singing his
praises, not questioning what galaxy -- I
gotta pee... that's what I should be
doing...

Pete stands up, painfully, and turns to face the snowbank. He
unzips his pants, with some difficulty, then writes in the snow
with his piss:  **"D-u-d-d-"**

                        PETE
Here's to you, Duds, the highest civilian
decoration--

He pisses the vertical stroke of the **"i"** and then dots it:

The snow melts away under the warm stream, REVEALING the noded,
red-gold head of Becky's SHIT WEASEL!

Pete squints, not sure what he's seeing --

                        PETE
Lord, I will never drink again...

The Weasel launches itself out of the snow directly at Pete's
crotch. We CAN'T SEE where the impact happens, but it's bad.

Pete doubles over in agony and grabs the slimy, wriggling Weasel, trying to pull it off. The Weasel's CHITTERING merges with PETE'S SCREAMS. They begin a whirling battle --

CUT TO: Becky's peaceful, dead countenance -- a mute witness.

The Weasel's tail is around Pete's thigh, trying to imbed its pincers in his lower back. Pete staggers, seems about to fall. But even drunk and hurt, he's still an athlete. Still gripping the Weasel, he looks down and <u>hurls himself into the fire</u>.

IN THE FIRE, Pete isn't feeling the heat yet through his heavy clothes, but the Weasel reacts with a deafening SCREECH. It releases its hold on Pete and shoots out of the fire, CHITTERING wildly. Pete rolls out of the fire, tears of pain rolling down his cheeks. He grabs a burning piece of wood as he goes.

OUT OF THE FIRE now, Pete looks around desperately to locate the Weasel, which has disappeared from view.

PETE'S POV: desperately scanning the area -- the snowbank, the roof of the shelter, the litter of bottles and bags -- finally settling on Becky's lifeless body.

Pete squints at Becky through flooded eyes. He holds the torch in front of him defensively, hesitant to look down at his damaged groin. Now he looks down, winces in horror, then HEARS the grotesque CHITTERING. He looks up to see --

-- the Weasel rise from behind Becky's head and launch itself. Pete dodges, but the Weasel has got hold of him near his left ear. The creature swings out to full length from Pete's head as he spins around, then wraps its tail under his arm and <u>prepares to bury its tail pincers in his neck</u>.

At that moment, in the second before the mortal strike, Pete brings the flaming torch up and SLAMS it into the head of the Weasel, even though it means burning his own face. The Weasel SCREECHES in shock and flies off into the snow.

Pete, crazed, bloody, burnt -- a fearsome sight -- locates his adversary and goes after it, torch in hand -- RIGHT PAST CAMERA.

59    EXT. DEEP CUT ROAD - DAY    59

Henry trudges through the blizzard. The only sound the steady FLUMPH-FLUMPH of each footfall, until --

-- he HEARS something ahead: the APPROACHING WHINE of the Arctic Cat's engine. Henry stops, his expression brightens.

                   HENRY
Jonesy! <u>Way to go</u>, motherfucker...
here you come to save the day --
     (singing)
'<u>Mighty Mouse is on the way</u>!'

The Arctic Cat is ROARING, just over that next rise. Henry's
smile disappears; it looks like he just got a migraine --

                   HENRY
... What in the hell -- Who's Mr. Gray?
What are you trying to tell me, Jonesy?

Henry struggles to understand the message he's getting.

                   HENRY
-- <u>You're not Jonesy</u>!

CUT TO the rise ahead, as the Arctic Cat sails over, Jonesy/Mr.
Gray at the controls. TRACKING WITH IT as it bears down on the
spot where Henry was just standing. It comes, and comes... and
<u>goes right by</u>.

No Henry in sight. The snowmobile speeds through the next turn
and disappears. The engine's WHINE recedes in the distance.

A DITCH: a deep drift of snow stirs to life. Henry appears, looks
after the departing Arctic Cat, his expression grim.

60    EXT. ARCTIC CAT, DEEP CUT ROAD - DAY          60

TRAVELING SHOT with Jonesy/Mr. Gray as they speed along. A beat.
And then <u>a really strange thing begins to happen</u>:

Jonesy and Mr. Gray (both in Jonesy's body) <u>begin what will</u>
<u>become a long debate</u>. This dialogue takes several forms, but we
can identify who's speaking at any moment for a simple reason:
<u>Mr. Gray has chosen a distinctive accent</u> for his work in this
world. **When he speaks, either OUT LOUD (when we see Jonesy's lips
moving) or *VOICE OVER* (when they communicate by thought), Mr.
Gray sounds as though he is BRITISH.** Jonesy, of course, sounds
like Jonesy.

                 MR. GRAY
What was that, Mr. Jones? What did we just
pass on the road there?

                 JONESY
Are you speaking to me?

                 MR. GRAY
Yes, I am, Mr. Jones. Or is it... Jonesy?
That's what your friends call you, isn't

MR. GRAY (cont'd)
it? Let's be friends -- What was that,
<u>Jonesy</u>?

JONESY
(to himself)
*Why does <u>it</u> sound like a Brit?*

MR. GRAY
I admire this accent... much prefer the
sound of the King's English as spoken by
that refined and spirited people... before
it was appropriated and butchered by you
chaps.
(again)
What <u>was</u> that?

JONESY
What was <u>what</u>?

MR. GRAY (V.O.)
*We just passed something and you're trying
to keep it from me.*

JONESY (V.O.)
*I don't know what you're talking about.
But I've got a question...*

MR. GRAY (V.O.)
*At your service.*

JONESY
Why are you letting me live?

MR. GRAY
I'm borrowing you. We're going to take a
little journey.

JONESY
Beaver never did anything to anyone, and
you killed him.

MR. GRAY
Your friend had nothing in his head. I've
already found something useful in yours.

JONESY (V.O.)
*Fuck you.*

MR. GRAY (V.O.)
(pleased)
*I know what that expression means! I've
studied the Foul Language section of your
Memory Warehouse. Rather distasteful, I
must say.*

                        JONESY
            How 'bout this, <u>Mr. Gray</u>? Eat shit and
            die.

Mr. Gray reacts, flinching.

                        MR. GRAY
            Why do you call me 'Mr. Gray'? Has someone
            told you about me?

                                        SMASH CUT TO:

A61    INT. AMBULANCE (FLASHBACK -- SIX MONTHS EARLIER) - NIGHT    A61

JONESY'S POV: Duddits hovers over him in the swaying ambulance.

                        DUDDITS
            Awch out fo Ister Gay.
            *[Watch out for Mr. Gray.]*

B61    EXT. ARCTIC CAT, DEEP CUT ROAD (BACK TO SCENE) - DAY        B61

Jonesy snaps out of his memory --

                        MR. GRAY
                    (insistent)
            <u>Who</u> told you about me?

                        JONESY
            If you want to know, why don't you just
            read my mind?

                        MR. GRAY
            Surprisingly, you're able to keep a few
            things from me. I don't understand it, but
            I'm sure I'll figure it out soon.

Jonesy reacts to that idea, but Mr. Gray has already moved on --

                        MR. GRAY
            Your friend Pete has a gift for finding
            things, does he not?

                        JONESY
            I don't know any Pete.

                        MR. GRAY
                    (dismisses that: 'spare me')
            I need to find my way out of these woods.
            But I'm afraid he won't help me if he
            hears this voice.
                    (a fair imitation of Jonesy's voice)

MR. GRAY (cont'd)
And I haven't got the hang of yours just
yet.

Jonesy is stunned that Mr. Gray has got that far. What next?

MR. GRAY
If you care about Pete, you'll help me out
here.

61    EXT. LOGGERS' SHELTER - DAY                          61

Snow has obscured much, but we SEE: the Shit Weasel, dead and
burnt crisp, in the dying fire. Becky, lying dead.

Jonesy/Mr. Gray stops the Arctic Cat and looks around. For a
moment, nothing. Then, a low MOAN. From a mound of snow, Pete
rolls into view. Jonesy/Mr. Gray goes to him.

It's really the remains of Pete. Ripley is all over his face and
throat; his burned face has been partially eaten away. There's a
huge dark blood stain at his crotch.

JONESY
Aw, Pete, Jesus --

PETE
(weak)
...motherfucker tried to bite my dick off,
Jonesy. I always thought it'd be my ex-
wife did that...

JONESY
(lifts Pete up)
Let's get you to some help.

Jonesy supports him as they start toward the snowmobile.

JONESY
Can you still see The Line, buddy?

PETE
I don't need the damn Line to get to
Gosselin's.

JONESY
I know that, but --
(hesitates, torn)
-- if we didn't want to go to Gosselin's
...how would you get us out to 95?

PETE
95? Who gives a shit? I'm hurtin' here,
Jonesy --

Pete pulls away, falling over in the snow. He peers at Jonesy.

>           PETE
> What's wrong with you?... Wait a minute,
> you're not --

>           JONESY
> Shut up, Pete! You're too messed up to
> know what you're saying --

Suddenly, Mr. Gray cuts him off in British accent.

>           MR. GRAY
> -- Too late for that. Pete, I need you to
> get on the snowmobile right now.

>           PETE
> Who the fuck are you? You sound like one
> of those James Bonds... this has somethin'
> to do with that fuckin' eel, doesn't it?
> You're not --

The Ripley at Pete's neck jerks to life, tightening like a
python. Pete GASPS, grabs at the fungus. Mr. Gray's dead eyes
look down at Pete, who is slowly choking to death. We begin to
PULL BACK from this excruciating sight --

-- through a window frame, and past a figure watching from inside
the window -- Jonesy! We are --

62    INT. JONESY'S OFFICE, MEMORY WAREHOUSE (IN JONESY'S HEAD)    62

Jonesy's in his office in the Memory Warehouse.

>           JONESY
>         (shouting)
> Stop it, stop it! I'll get him to help.
>         (at Pete)
> Pete, tell him what he wants to know!

63    EXT. LOGGERS' SHELTER - DAY                              63

Mr. Gray blinks and the Ripley relaxes. Pete, breathing again,
looks in terror at Jonesy/Mr. Gray.

>           MR. GRAY
> Now, Pete, which way to I-95? I need to go
> to Massachusetts.

Pete raises his index finger and begins to wag it, looks.

WHAT PETE SEES: As in the drugstore, <u>a path in the middle of his view</u>, The Line going off into the woods... RIGHT PAST THE WATCHING MR. GRAY.

<u>Mr. Gray jolts and sidesteps</u>, as though The Line were a physical thing which has almost hit him. He recovers quickly.

>                    MR. GRAY
>           My, my... That <u>is</u> a gift.
>                (to Pete)
>           Who taught you that?

>                    JONESY (V.O.)
>                (quickly)
>           *I did.*

>                    MR. GRAY (V.O.)
>                (reacts, smiling)
>           *I don't think so, Professor. But I'll know*
>           *soon enough.*

He heads for the snowmobile, flipping up the hood of his parka.

>                    MR. GRAY
>           You're going to be a big help, Pete. Climb
>           aboard.

64      INT. JONESY'S OFFICE, MEMORY WAREHOUSE (IN JONESY'S HEAD)    64

At the window Jonesy breathes a sigh of relief, his friend saved. Suddenly, POUNDING on the door of the office. Jonesy goes to the quaking door and peeks out through the peephole.

WHAT HE SEES (FISH-EYE DISTORTION): His view of the stacks is instantly blocked by the True Mr. Gray, who is outside, looking back at him. (So close Jonesy can't see what he looks like.)

Jonesy is confused. He spins to look out the window, but <u>there's nothing out there</u> except the now-deserted Loggers' Shelter. More POUNDING. From outside the door:

>                    MR. GRAY (O.S.)
>           Show's over out there, buddy. Let me in.

CU Jonesy, his mind racing. Mr. Gray has total access out there.

>                    MR. GRAY (O.S.)
>           What have you got in that part of your
>           mind, Professor?  Your memories are out
>           here in the warehouse, aren't they?
>                (beat)
>           I want to know who warned you about me.
>           And who taught Pete that nifty trick...

MR. GRAY (O.S.) (cont'd)
I'm sure the answers are in these files.
It'll just take me a while to find them.
(moving away)
... Back in a bit. Think about letting me
in. It's the polite thing to do...

65   EXT. HOLE IN THE WALL - DAY                          65

WIDE SHOT. Everything looks okay from here. Beautiful, in fact:
weathered cabin, heavy snowfall, embracing forest. Here comes
Henry slogging to the end of his long walk.

CLOSER SHOT: with Henry now, seeing <u>what</u> he sees, <u>when</u> he sees
it. He stops on the granite slab and looks inside.

66   INT. HOLE IN THE WALL - DAY                          66

The interior, overrun with red-gold fungus, COMES INTO VIEW as
Henry edges inside. SERIES OF SHOTS: We can actually <u>see the fuzz
growing</u>, like slow-moving lava. Henry looks up, stunned.

REVERSE, BOOMING UP so what he's looking at is REVEALED at the
top of the move -- The Dreamcatcher, all but obliterated by the
growth, like a red-gold wasps' nest, only a bit not yet engulfed.

HENRY
You caught a hell of a nightmare this
time.

Suddenly, Henry gets a chilling feeling that <u>something is behind
the door</u> he's standing next to. He quickly pulls the door closed,
terrified. There <u>is</u> something -- Jonesy's deer rifle. Henry picks
up the rifle, checks the chamber, then takes it with him as he
moves carefully into the room, watching where he steps. There is
a pile of something (hidden in mold) by the bathroom door.

HENRY
What <u>is</u> this?
(calling out)
Beav?

Shining in the pile is the doorknob; next to it lies the roll of
friction tape, where Jonesy dropped it. (We have the feeling that
something could spring from the pile at any moment.)

Henry looks into what this morning was a blue bathroom and is now
a <u>red cave of fungus</u>. Henry sees a Doc Marten boot sticking out
from the space beyond the toilet. His worst fears are confirmed.

HENRY
Ah, Beaver, shit... fuck me Freddy.

Huge tears roll down his cheeks. Suddenly, he FLINCHES. He's
standing in the <u>exact spot</u> where Mr. Gray's head exploded.

WE SEE IT HAPPEN AGAIN, as does Henry, in a <u>futzed, distorted image</u>. Mr. Gray's outer husk explodes and Jonesy is engulfed in the cloud of red-gold particles, which Jonesy inhales.

Henry is <u>devastated</u>. He backs away from that spot, as though he's just seen the actual event happen.

He HEARS something, stops, tries to identify what it is -- a CHITTERING SOUND. Henry lifts the rifle as he inches toward a view of the bedroom. The NOISE gets LOUDER. Henry reaches the door, looks inside and reacts in horror.

CHITTERING angrily on the blood-soaked bed sits the Shit Weasel that killed Beaver. Mouth open, fangs ready, huge eyes staring at Henry. Its muscular body is wrapped protectively around --

-- <u>one hundred eggs</u> the size of big marbles, orange-brown, covered with a murky wet substance. Inside each one, a <u>hairlike shadow moves</u>. The Weasel lifts up, but the speed we saw before is gone -- the laying of the eggs has sapped that.

Henry unshoulders his rifle. The Weasel CHITTERS like crazy. Henry fires; a deafening GUNSHOT and -- <u>he missed</u>.

                    HENRY
          Asshole!

The Weasel moves toward him. Henry, sweating, fires again. The Shit Weasel's HEAD EXPLODES, its body blown off the bed. Henry looks at the eggs, thinks, then races out of the room.

67    INT. KITCHEN, HOLE IN THE WALL - DAY                    67

BLACKNESS. Then a cabinet door opens. We're beneath the sink. Henry reaches in and grabs a can of barbecue lighter fluid. From the counter, he snatches a box of matches, then heads back.

68    INT. BEDROOM, HOLE IN THE WALL - DAY                    68

Henry comes to the foot of the bed and extends his arm to squirt the lighter fluid. Suddenly, he stops, peers at something. He squints, not sure what he's seeing, then moves up along the bed.

HENRY'S POV: MOVING IN on some thing, or things, in the shadow of the pillow. We recognize it at the same moment Henry does -- twenty of the weasel eggs, but these are <u>cracked open and empty</u>!

Henry reacts and, simultaneously, HEARS horrible MEWLING CRIES. He looks down at his feet. A dozen worm-like NEWBORN WEASELS are crawling out from under the bed. Two are already climbing up his pant leg and a third is trying to work its way into his boot.

Henry jumps back, kicking out with his foot. The Weasel on his boot flies off. He swats the two on his pants to the floor and STOMPS them. He squirts the lighter fluid on the floor where the others are sliding toward him, then onto the bed. The worms react to the fluid, MEWLING unbearably. <u>And then they keep coming</u> --

Henry backs across the room, sliding open the box of matches. His hands are shaking badly. He gets a couple of the matches out, but juggles the box and loses it. It falls onto the floor.

Henry STOMPS the Weasels in the lead, and tries to light the match in his hand with his thumbnail -- once... STOMP... twice... STOMP, STOMP. His hands won't stay still.

ANGLE DOWN on Henry's shaking hand, flicking desperately at the match head. Beyond his hand, the Weasel worms are sliding toward him. And then, finally --

-- FIRE. Henry drops the match into the puddle of fluid and the floor erupts in flame. And then the bed. As the fire spreads, there are POPPING SOUNDS as the eggs burst, and high-pitched MEWLING as the Weasel worms curl into black crisps. Henry backs out of the bedroom, squirting more fluid as he goes.

69      INT. LIVING ROOM, HOLE IN THE WALL - DAY                    69

Henry passes under The Dreamcatcher as he empties the can of lighter fluid and throws it into the fire. He opens the front door and turns to look once more at the cabin. Anguished --

                    HENRY
          So long, Beav. Love you, man.

He goes out, leaving the door open behind him.

70      EXT./INT. HOLE IN THE WALL - DAY                            70

Henry comes out of the shed wearing ancient cross-country skis and poles, rifle across his back. He glances at the fire through a window, then moves on. The window BLOWS OUT, spraying glass.

He skis awkwardly past the front door, trying to find his rhythm. He goes OUT OF FRAME, but we STAY...

... and PUSH IN toward the front door. Arms of fire pop in and out, beckoning us, and WE GO IN, lingering for a moment on <u>the 20 notches</u> that decorate the doorjamb...

... and ACROSS THE ROOM where the mold is turning black. The Navajo rug appears from beneath, then bursts into flame...

... and RISING UP, to The Dreamcatcher. It's on fire now, too, and a couple of the smaller circles have dropped away. But the other two are hanging onto the center. We continue MOVING IN, until all we can see is the large center circle of The Dreamcatcher. It fills the frame.

                                        FADE OUT.

FADE UP:

71      INT. CAVELL HOUSE, DERRY, MAINE (FLASHBACK -- 1983) - DAY    71

ROBERTA CAVELL stands at the front door looking out, a faint smile on her face. Duddits is being escorted home by the four friends. He rushes ahead to show his mother the item in his hand.

Duddits bursts inside, the other boys following in a noisy jumble, each politely greeting Roberta as Duddits jabbers, displaying a 6-inch circular dreamcatcher (one circle).

                    DUDDITS
          Amma -- ook! Ook ah iss!
          [Mama -- look! Look at this!]

                    ROBERTA
          Douglas, it's beautiful. What is that?

                    DUDDITS
          Eemcacher! Eever make fo me!
          [Dreamcatcher! Beaver make for me!]

                    ROBERTA
               (to Beaver)
          Why, Joe, it's beautiful. You have a real
          talent in those hands.

Beaver is embarrassed, pleased.

                    PETE
               (low)
          It's BS is what it is.

                    JONESY
          No it isn't.
               (indicates Roberta)
          And watch your mouth!

                    PETE
          What? 'BS' is not swearing.

                    JONESY
          Yes it is.

                    PETE
          Bullshit.

                BEAVER
     It's not BS. You hang it over your bed and
     it keeps away bad dreams. It's a
     dreamcatcher.

Jonesy pulls his dreamcatcher from inside a textbook. It's not
quite as good. Duddits snatches it excitedly from his grasp.

                JONESY
     We all made 'em in art.

                BEAVER
     I finished first so I made one for Duddits
     -- um, Douglas.
        (pulls another from his jacket)
     This is mine.

As Roberta admires it, Duddits grabs that one too. Henry pulls
his sad-looking version from his notebook.

                HENRY
     Mine is deformed. I couldn't figure out
     the string...

Duddits snatches it and turns expectantly to Pete, hand out.

                DUDDITS
     Eemcacher, eemcacher, Eet!

                PETE
     Sorry, buddy, I threw mine out.
        (the other boys are suspicious)
     I ain't afraid of any dreams...

                HENRY
     C'mon, Pete...

                JONESY
     Don't make us do the thing in front of
     Mrs. Cavell.

                PETE
     What? I don't got it!

Henry, Jonesy and Beaver start to move toward Pete (a familiar
gang-up move among the friends). Pete backs away, then caves--

                PETE
     All right, all right! Maybe I got it
     somewhere...

He reaches deep into his jeans and extracts his dreamcatcher.
It's been folded in half, but when he flattens it in his hands,
we SEE it's actually the most beautiful of all. Duddits grabs it.

> JONESY
> Hey, man, you're an artiste!

> PETE
> Shut up!

> DUDDITS (O.S.)
> Eemcacher... eemcacher... EEMCACHER!!

Duddits has found a place on the rug and is working intensely at
something they can't see yet. Now, he turns and flashes one of
those dynamite smiles. The boys, one by one, go down around
Duddits, forming a circle on the rug. Roberta moves over to look.

OVERHEAD SHOT: Duddits has placed his larger dreamcatcher in the
center of a design, the four corners of which are formed by each
of the boys' smaller circles. We recognize the overall design as
exactly like the one hanging in Hole in the Wall.

Duddits points to each of the smaller dreamcatchers, naming --

> DUDDITS
> Eever... Henny... Ownzy... Eet!

> HENRY
> That's right, my man...

Duddits' finger moves to the larger circle. Gleeful --

> DUDDITS
> I Duddits.

> BEAVER
> Yeah... I Duddits!

> DUDDITS
> (delighted, louder, raising his
> arms)
> I Duddits!

> ALL THE FRIENDS
> (raising their arms)
> I DUDDITS!

72    EXT. DEEP CUT ROAD, MAINE WOODS (PRESENT DAY) - DAY    72

We HEAR heavy, steady BREATHING and FIND the source -- Henry, who
skis doggedly toward the Loggers' Shelter. The snow has eased up.
His BREATHING is all we hear until --

-- the multiple WHUP-WHUP-WHUP of an approaching HELICOPTER
ARMADA. Henry looks up. Just above tree height come FOUR APACHE
HELICOPTER GUNSHIPS. CURTIS' HELICOPTER flies shotgun. Turbulence
from the rotors makes a snowy WHIRLWIND around Henry.

73     EXT. HELICOPTER ARMADA, ABOVE MAINE WOODS - DAY     73

VARIOUS SHOTS as the copters skim the treetops, armed with .50
MACHINE GUNS and SCORPION AIR-TO-SURFACE MISSILES. Their lethal
appearance and the ROAR of the engines set the heart thumping.

74     INT. OWEN'S COPTER (BLUE BOY LEADER) - DAY     74

Owen is in the lead -- adrenaline coursing. Alongside him is his
pilot, EDWARDS. This is what they live to do. Owen looks out at --

The other Apaches, in a perfect line. Then at the endless woods
below, appearing and disappearing in vapors of white.

                      CURTIS (RADIO)
        Blue Boy Leader... how we doin', bucko?

Owen looks off to his left, at Curtis' chopper.

                      OWEN
               (into radio)
        Right here, Boss... fast and hard.

                      CURTIS (RADIO)
        Wouldn't have it any other way, Blue Boy.

                      EDWARDS
        Sir...

                      OWEN
        I see it...

WHAT OWEN SEES: Down below, the thick forest has been torn apart
in a giant, intermittent PATH OF DESTRUCTION. Something very
large has skipped across the landscape in an extended crash
landing. The devastation gives ominous signs of its massive size.

                      OWEN
        Blue Boy Group, this is Blue Boy Leader...
        Target is imminent. Move to Level 4
        Readiness... Gentlemen, lock and load!

75     INT. ARMADA COPTERS - DAY     75

VARIOUS SHOTS: The COMBAT FLIGHT CREWS hunker down, switch on
guidance systems and rack the big guns to full-auto.

76      EXT. HELICOPTER ARMADA - DAY                          76

The formation is passing directly over one last crater of forest
devastation. Up ahead, the CREST OF A RIDGE. Beyond it... well,
guess.

77      INT. OWEN'S COPTER - DAY                               77

Owen takes out a SNAPSHOT: Owen as a child is sitting on the
shoulders of HIS FATHER, an Air Force Sergeant with a chest full
of combat ribbons. They both look very happy. Owen touches the
snapshot gently with a fingertip for luck, tucks it away.

                    CURTIS (RADIO)
          Conklin, let's have the anthem -- <u>loud</u> --

78      INT. ANOTHER HELICOPTER - DAY                         78

Conklin, sliding in a CD.

                    CONKLIN
                  (into radio)
          Yes, boss, the anthem, blasting off.

Bob Dylan's *"Maggie's Farm"* pierces the air.

                    BOB DYLAN
          'I ain't gonna work on Maggie's farm no
          more./ No, I ain't gonna work on Maggie's
          farm no more.'

79      EXT. HELICOPTER ARMADA - DAY                          79

The formation SWOOPS UP over the ridge. Their target is in full
view now, down the slope, but we SEE it from --

80      INT. OWEN'S COPTER - DAY                              80

OWEN'S POV: Far in the distance, the huge rear edge of the ALIEN
SHIP towers into the air. The front edge, buried in the earth,
has created a new hill of earth and rock where it augered in.

<u>Standing near the wreckage</u>: probably a HUNDRED GRAYBOYS, tiny
figures from back here. But with a familiar shape, the same as
Mr. Gray presented to Jonesy on first look. Naked and unarmed. A
dozen GRAYBOY CORPSES lie scattered around the wreckage -- all in
various stages of red-gold to gray-tinged decay.

The living GRAYBOYS, huge dark eyes staring, raise their arms to
the approaching helicopters. We HEAR various KINDLY HUMAN VOICES
reciting these repeated messages: **"there is no infection here --
please don't hurt us -- we are helpless -- we are dying..."**

Edwards looks over at Owen. The other CREWMEN exchange looks.

81    INT. ARMADA HELICOPTERS - DAY                              81

VARIOUS SHOTS as the Flight Crews on the other ships react.

                    CURTIS (RADIO)
          Owen, whose radio is that?

                    OWEN (RADIO)
          It's not the radio, Boss. They're putting
          it directly into our heads.

Begin to INTERCUT with:

82    INT. CURTIS' COPTER - DAY                                  82

Curtis reacts, talks into the radio, louder than Dylan:

                    CURTIS
          There it is, gentlemen -- directly into
          our heads! That gives you some idea what
          we're up against. And if anybody's
          thinkin' -- 'why those poor helpless
          little folks, all naked and unarmed,
          alongside their crashed intergalactic
          Winnebago -- what kind of a dog, what kind
          of a monster could hear that heartbreak
          and go in just the same?'
              (bigger)
          Well I am that dog, I am that monster... I
          been fighting these mothers for decades
          and they are as harmless as a fox in a
          henhouse --
              (leans into it)
          -- they are cancer. Cancer, yes, and
          praise Jesus, we are one big hot shot of
          chemotherapy -- are you with me?

The Flight Crews affirm it, LOUDLY.

                    CURTIS
          Sing it out, Owen.

83    INT. OWEN'S COPTER - DAY                                   83

Owen looks out at the formation, then down at his electronics.
The bloodlust has gotten to him, too. He's a killing machine.

                    OWEN
              (into radio)
          Blue Boy Group, this is Blue Boy Leader --

OWEN (cont'd)
let's clean up the forest and get rid of
this trash!

84    EXT. HELICOPTER ARMADA, BATTLEGROUND SLOPE - DAY    84

The formation heads down the hillside toward the aliens.

BOB DYLAN
'Well, I wake in the morning.
Fold my hands and pray for rain.
I got a head full of ideas
That are driving me insane.'

INTERCUTTING OWEN, CURTIS, OTHER CREWS, and, finally, the
GRAYBOYS at ground zero. All the while, the accumulated cacophony
of Dylan, the Grayboy pleas, the WHUP-WHUP-WHUPPING rotors,
and... the ARMAMENTS.

OWEN (RADIO)
Blue Boy Group, fire at will!

The Gunships open up with their .50's and FIRE their Scorpions.

AT THE ALIEN SHIP: The Grayboys are torn apart. As each is hit,
it explodes in a mass of gray fiber and red-gold slime. Some, cut
in two at the midsection, go to earth with their arms raised in
surrender. For a spit second before disintegration, we SEE their
true appearance -- the horror, the horror.

85    EXT. ALIEN SHIP - DAY    85

FOUR SPECIAL GRAYBOYS move as a unit, retreating into the shadows
beneath the hull of the massive ship. At an odd-looking section
of the underhull, they position themselves carefully, bodies
actually extending upwards toward the ship.

86    INT. CURTIS' COPTER - DAY    86

Curtis, hovering on the fringe, sees this action and immediately
PULLS HIS COPTER up and away.

87    EXT. ALIEN SHIP - DAY    87

The four Special Grayboys have become part of the underbelly now,
melding with the ship. A design becomes apparent in the ship's
surface there -- it is roughly the design of The Dreamcatcher. A
PULSE BEGINS EMANATING from the ship.

88    INT. OWEN'S COPTER - DAY    88

Owen sees the activity under the ship and Curtis' retreat. Owen
signals for his pilot to pull out and SHOUTS into the radio --

                    OWEN
          Blue Boy Group, withdraw at once! I
          repeat, cease firing and back off!

From here, Owen can see that the other gunships are caught in the
fever of the fight -- going lower, chasing down individual ET's.

                    CONKLIN (RADIO)
          We can get these last mothers --

Owen, SCREAMING orders now --

                    OWEN
          -- no -- no -- back off -- Blue Boy Group,
          get out of there!

89   EXT. ALIEN SHIP - DAY                                      89

The SELF-DESTRUCT CIRCUIT linking the Special Grayboys connects.

THE SHIP EXPLODES INTO INFINITY in a giant RED CLOUD. Three of
the gunships are roiled in the SHOCK WAVES or consumed directly
by the cloud. They go down. The cloud rises in a furious spiral,
speeding toward --

-- Owen's copter and Curtis' copter. INTERCUT both copters and
the shooting cloud.

90   INT. CURTIS' COPTER - DAY                                  90

Curtis is pulling like crazy on his stick. His chopper is almost
sideways, so he has a good view down to the cloud that's chasing
him and, between them, Owen's copter.

91   INT. OWEN'S COPTER - DAY                                   91

Owen, helping Edwards pull the gunship skyward, is in agony about
the three lost crews, but hides it. He watches --

THE RED CLOUD, coming closer to them, the spiral widening.

92   EXT. SKY ABOVE BATTLEGROUND - DAY                          92

The helicopters, rising higher, ever higher, racing the red
cloud, finally getting away, rising above it all...

93   EXT. LOGGERS' SHELTER, DEEP CUT ROAD - MAGIC              93

Henry skis up, exhausted. He picks up some snow and eats it as he
peers around: Becky looks like a prone snow sculpture. The
crisped Weasel is recognizable in the now-frosted fire.

                          HENRY
                        (to Weasel)
               I hope your stay has been pleasant so far.

Henry peers at the tracks of the snowmobile into the woods.

                          HENRY
               What's out <u>there</u>? The highway?... It
               doesn't want to go to Gosselin's... too
               many soldiers.
                        (V.O.)
               *Where is it taking you, Jonesy? Have you
               got Pete with you?*

Henry turns back to the road and heads off. As he does --

                          HENRY
               Speak up, Jonesy... I can't hear you.

94     EXT. SCOUT WRECK, DEEP CUT ROAD - MAGIC                94

The overturned truck is covered in snow. Some shakes off the
windshield as Henry climbs out with a packet of butcher's paper.
He sits against the car, opens the packet of nearly-frozen hot
dogs, starts scarfing them down. As he eats, he begins to cry.

95     EXT. DEEP WOODS - MAGIC                                95

No road. <u>The snow is beginning to fall harder again</u>. It takes a
moment to see the Arctic Cat coming up a gully in the distance.

ON THE SNOWMOBILE, MOVING: Pete sits on the back, his arms
wrapped around Jonesy/Mr. Gray. Pete is in bad shape, covered
with fungus, woozy. He almost falls off as they bump along.

                          PETE
               Jonesy, help me. I can't hold on anymore.

                          JONESY
               We're gonna get you fixed up, Pete. Just
               hang in there.

                          MR. GRAY (V.O.)
               *Ask him if we're still going the right
               way.*

                          JONESY
               Pete... are we getting close to I-95?

                          PETE
               What...?

                         JONESY
              Are we close to 95?

                         PETE
              Yeah, man... it's right over this hill.

STILL MOVING, we're BEHIND THEM now.

                         PETE
              Jonesy, I think I'm dying here. And I've
              been thinking...
                    (drifting)
              ...about our friend...our little Scooby-
              Doo buddy. For a long time, I've been
              thinking maybe he was sent to us, to warn
              us about something. But I could never
              figure what it was...

                         JONESY
              -- Don't talk about him, Pete! Not now --

                         PETE
              ...not till today. It was this, buddy, it
              was this right now. He wanted to warn us --

                         JONESY
                    (overlapping)
              -- not when you're feeling this way...

                         MR. GRAY
              Go ahead, Pete, tell me about your friend.

                         PETE
                    (reacts to the English accent)
              ... No... Jonesy's right.

                         MR. GRAY
              Come on, Pete, let's talk --

Something happens to Pete, some last jolt of energy. He speaks to
the back of Jonesy's parka hood and his tone is defiant.

                         PETE
              Bite my bag, motherfucker.

                         MR. GRAY
              All right, Pete, I'll bite...

The snowmobile skids to a stop.

                         MR. GRAY
              ... your bag and everything else.

                    JONESY (V.O.)
          *No!*

Mr. Gray turns to face Pete. <u>Except that the body in the parka is</u>
<u>not Jonesy's. Right now, it is the horrible True Mr. Gray.</u>

We get a better look this time. He's like a giant, articulated
Shit Weasel. And now the toothy, slimy MAW that runs vertically
where a head should be -- GAPES OPEN. Impossibly fast, Mr. Gray
bends toward Pete... and <u>Pete's head disappears beneath the hood.</u>

ANOTHER ANGLE: PULLING BACK (we don't see the last gory moments
of Pete's life), we're <u>with Jonesy again</u>, at the window in --

96     INT. JONESY'S OFFICE, MEMORY WAREHOUSE                    96

   --  his office in the Memory Warehouse. He looks on in anguish,
helpless, as another of his friends is murdered.

                    JONESY
          No, no... no. You bastard, you...

In despair, he averts his gaze. When he looks back outside,
there's no sign of Pete, just --

97     EXT. WOODS/INTERSTATE 95 - NIGHT                          97

Mr. Gray steering the snowmobile out of the woods and down to the
shoulder of I-95. There's almost no traffic. Mr. Gray dismounts
and walks out to the center of the snowy road. In the distance,
two headlights appear and get closer. Mr. Gray holds his ground
and begins waving his arms.

The vehicle, an ARMY TRUCK, slides to a stop a few feet from Mr.
Gray, who walks around to the driver's side. We're OVER THE
SHOULDER of Mr. Gray when the driver's door opens.

The driver, SGT. ANDY JANAS, a heavyset soldier, has his 9mm
automatic resting on his thigh, pointed at Mr. Gray. On the seat
beside him, IKE, his K-9 comrade, a handsome GERMAN SHEPHERD.

                    JANAS
          What's up, fella?

                    MR. GRAY
               (English accent)
          Thank god you came by, general. I'm broke
          down here and fearing for my life.
               (Ike growls softly)
          That's a good-looking dog you got there.

                    JANAS
          Where you headed?

                         MR. GRAY
               Gosselin's. Any chance you're going near
               there?

Janas regards him warily, nods.

                         JANAS
               That's where I'm going.

Mr. Gray looks toward the back of the truck.

                         MR. GRAY
               I believe your tailgate has come open.

Janas leans out to see, can't, puts the truck in park and climbs
down, automatic in his hand. He nods for Mr. Gray to go ahead.

                         JANAS
               Let's take a look.

Mr. Gray goes first, his hood obscuring his head. Janas follows.
They come around the back, which is closed up fine.

                         MR. GRAY
               I see you've got some cargo you're taking
               to Blue Base.

Janas reacts to the sight, and to Mr. Gray's words, at the same
instant. He starts to lift the automatic --

98   INT. JONESY'S OFFICE, MEMORY WAREHOUSE                    98

Jonesy turns away, not wanting to see what happens next. We HEAR
a GUNSHOT. Jonesy jumps, but doesn't look. Then, suddenly, Jonesy
gets an idea. He looks at the door to the Memory Warehouse.

99   INT. STACKS, MEMORY WAREHOUSE                             99

Jonesy comes out of his office into the vast facility. He looks
up at the shelves two levels up, grabs one of the big dollies and
starts limping toward the ramp as fast as he can.

100  EXT. JANAS'S ARMY TRUCK - NIGHT                           100

Janas's body lands in a snow-filled ditch.

AT THE BACK OF THE TRUCK, Mr. Gray pulls a tarpaulin aside with a
big WHOOSH, REVEALING a couple DEAD DEER crawling with Ripley and
a decaying GRAYBOY, all wrapped in clear plastic. Mr. Gray urges
Ike up into the truck and begins tearing at the plastic.

                         MR. GRAY
               Got a treat for you, Ike. All you can eat.

101     INT. THIRD LEVEL, MEMORY WAREHOUSE                    101

Jonesy hoists the numerous file boxes marked **"DUDDITS"** onto the
dolly. He's gasping by the time he's got them all, but there's no
time to rest -- he shoves the heavy dolly toward the ramp.

102     INT. MEMORY WAREHOUSE                                 102

Jonesy is on the down ramp, but the dolly's so heavy, he can
barely control it; his hip aches, his feet slide. Another level
to descend. The door to his office below seems a long way off.

103     INT. BACK OF JANAS'S ARMY TRUCK - NIGHT               103

IN THE BACK OF THE TRUCK, Mr. Gray steps back and watches calmly
as Ike makes a meal of the grayish sludge that was once an ET.

                    MR. GRAY
          Take your time, good doggy. Eat all you --

Mr. Gray stops, suddenly aware of Jonesy's movement. Impressed --

                    MR. GRAY
          Jonesy...what are you up to?

104     INT. MEMORY WAREHOUSE                                 104

ON THE OFFICE LEVEL OF THE MEMORY WAREHOUSE, Jonesy is sweating
profusely as he pushes his burden toward the office. He HEARS a
DOOR SLAM. His head whips around to look across the warehouse.

WHAT JONESY SEES: the main entrance door is still RATTLING to a
stop. FLASH PAN through the stacks -- a GLIMPSE of the horrible
True Mr. Gray as he flashes by an opening, coming this way!

Jonesy pushes the dolly with everything he's got. He's close now.

MR. GRAY'S POV: he SEES Jonesy about to reach the office. (Mr.
Gray is moving fast. We HEAR the WET SLOSHING SOUNDS his lower
extremities make on the floor.) Jonesy, at the open door, uses
all his strength to turn the dolly, and disappears behind the
open door. Mr. Gray is almost there -- when the door SLAMS SHUT.
BANG! Then the SOUND of Jonesy frantically WORKING THE LOCK.

FROM BEHIND THE TRUE MR. GRAY (not a pretty sight, his back, from
this close): his tail pincers shoot out, grab the doorknob and
twist it -- it turns!

                    MR. GRAY
          Too late, my gimpy friend --

Mr. Gray throws open the office door -- and finds a SECOND DOOR
inside. Mr. Gray tries it, but it's locked. The alien POUNDS on

it in rage, then notices that something is scrawled across the inner door in white paint: **SSDD**

Mr. Gray: a SOUND OF FRUSTRATION <u>like we've never heard before</u>.

105     EXT. DEEP CUT ROAD - NIGHT                                    105

Henry trudges up a hill on his skis. He crests the hill and suddenly he's moving <u>too fast</u> -- because the far side of the hill is ice. Out of control, losing traction... <u>he falls down</u>. He lies in the snow a moment, blinking. Then, HUGE FLOODLIGHTS.

                    PLATOON LEADER
               (amplified)
          HALT! HALT OR WE'LL FIRE!

                    HENRY
               (weak, to himself)
          I think I've just about halted here.

A truck, loaded with floodlights, blocks the road. A PLATOON LEADER stands on the truck, <u>bullhorn in hand</u>. Six more SOLDIERS with M-16's stand in front. Two move forward to prod Henry.

                    PLATOON LEADER
          ON YOUR FEET NOW!

Henry struggles to his feet, then sees that he's dropped a package from his coat. He bends down to pick it up.

                    PLATOON LEADER
          DON'T TOUCH THAT!

                    HENRY
          Blow me.
               (holds out package)
          I come in peace for all mankind. Anybody
          want a dog?

                                             FADE OUT.

FADE UP ON:

A DISTORTED VIEW, THROUGH A PLASTIC FACE MASK. We're in --

OWEN'S POV: looking at Curtis as he zips up a BIOHAZARD SUIT and adjusts the plastic mask. We HEAR Owen's raspy BREATHING.

Curtis' VOICE is DISTORTED through some sort of device. An ESCORT of four SOLDIERS, in similar protection, waits to accompany them. Curtis leans in to speak confidentially to Owen (and TO CAMERA).

                    CURTIS (DISTORTED)
          Come with me, Owen. I'll show you things
          you'll wish you'd never seen.

Curtis cackles and signals for the escort to open the doors to --

106   INT. BARN, GOSSELIN'S MARKET - NIGHT                    106

It's an eerie sight (made more so by the distortion of the face
mask). The barn now holds close to 200 DETAINEES. BEGIN TO MOVE
behind Curtis and escort down the center, SEEING IT as Owen does.

High-wattage bulbs cast a brilliant glare. Heaters give the place
a feverish warmth. The onetime dairy barn now resembles a refugee
camp. But the men, women and children packed in here are wearing
L.L. Bean, Eddie Bauer and Carhartt.

They cover the main floor, the lucky ones sleeping on Army-issue
cots. A few have <u>hugely distended stomachs</u>, but those are being
located and taken out by Soldiers.

BAD SOUNDS: BELCHES, FARTS, SNORES and GROANS, people dreaming
badly. Children who can't stop CRYING. Over it all, MUZAK: just
now Fred Waring's Orchestra is doing "*Some Enchanted Evening.*"

Detainees, including Old Man Gosselin, recognize Curtis and Owen
as "people-in-charge" and gravitate toward them, shouting their
grievances and entreaties:

                    VARIOUS DETAINEES
          I demand to see my lawyer!... When are we
          getting out of this hellhole?... Listen,
          you fascist, you can't do this to people
          in America!... Sir, oh sir, could I have a
          word with you?... We need more doctors in
          here! My wife's hurtin' awful bad...

<u>And on and on</u>. Only the presence of the escort (and the GUARDS
stationed in here) keeps the crowd from mobbing Curtis and Owen.

Curtis seems not to hear any grousing. He moves through the
throng like a demented politician, responding to every complaint
with a smile and a reassuring, running patter:

                    CURTIS (DISTORTED)
          Yes, yes, everyone will be taken care
          of... It should only be a matter of hours
          till you're on your way home... Sorry for
          any inconvenience, but we have only your
          safety in mind... Your government wants to
          do everything it can to make this easy...

<u>Curtis repeatedly looks back at Owen</u>, indicating certain details:

-- <u>half the people are infected with Ripley</u>. The stuff's growing on their faces and hands, in their ears. Up above, it's thriving in the lofts, on beams, even on the electrical cord. A hellish scene. We're as relieved as Owen when the escort heads to the door at the other end, which lets us out into --

107    EXT. CORRAL, GOSSELIN'S - NIGHT                         107

The snow is falling heavily, but the area where the biohazard suits will be removed is under a roof. Owen gazes at the contrasting peace of the snowfall.

<u>Still in OWEN'S POV</u>: an Army truck has backed up to the corral. A NEW LOAD OF DETAINEES is being herded in. One of those NEWCOMERS <u>looks sharply over at Owen's face</u>. IT IS HENRY, who stops short. Owen's hands pull away his hood and we CUT TO:

Curtis and his escort discarding their suits, and Owen, who stands looking through the fence at Henry, a man he does not know.

                    OWEN
          Can I help you, sir?

Henry shakes his head; abruptly his gaze switches off Owen, to Curtis, who has stepped up, ready to go. To Owen --

                    CURTIS
          Let's go, laddie, I'll buy you a cuppa.

Henry regards Curtis with alarm. <u>Owen sees it</u>. Henry backs away, staring at Curtis, who now shows some interest.

                    CURTIS
          You sir, where you from?

                    HENRY
          Boston.

                    CURTIS
          Beantown. Great city. We'll have you back
          there in no time -- maybe by morning.

CU Henry, as he listens to Curtis. He's HEARING SOMETHING ELSE, something we can't hear. He nods and starts to turn away --

                    CURTIS
               (to Owen, leaving)
          C'mon, bucko.

                    OWEN
               (to Henry)
          Excuse me, sir. What's your name?

                              HENRY
                    Henry... Dr. Henry Devlin.

                              OWEN
                    A doctor? Good, we need doctors in there.

108    EXT. OUTSIDE THE FENCE, CORRAL, GOSSELIN'S - NIGHT          108

Owen catches up to Curtis as he walks along the fence toward his
Winnebago in the distance. Curtis idly throws a snowball into the
electrified fence, which ZAPS it with a HISS.

                              CURTIS
                    You see that crud on the faces of the
                    children and you know why I relish a spin
                    in the country like we had today.
                         (Owen nods)
                    You were excellent out there today, O. It
                    made me feel mighty proud to --

Suddenly, Curtis stops, JOLTED, blinking. As though he'd just had
a shock. He shakes his head once, to clear it.

                              OWEN
                    Abe, you okay?

                              CURTIS
                         (it's over, moving on)
                    Yeah. Damn, I must be gettin' too old for
                    this shit... I don't know what that was.

They move off toward the Winnebago, but we SMASH CUT TO:

109    EXT. CORRAL - NIGHT                                         109

-- Henry, who stands staring at Curtis and Owen as they walk
away. He knows exactly what that was -- it was him, probing.

110    INT. CURTIS' WINNEBAGO - NIGHT                              110

Curtis has just poured a good portion of Scotch into Owen's
glass. But Owen is in shock from what he's just heard. Curtis
looks him over, taking a long swallow.

                              CURTIS
                    It's the only way, Owen. We've got to
                    cauterize the site. They've all got to
                    die. It's the only way.

                              OWEN
                    But we don't know that. The studies point
                    to the strong possibility of recovery for
                    many of the exposed subjects --

                    CURTIS
-- The studies show <u>squat</u>, that's what
they show. If Three-Star General Matheson
had been in my spot for the last quarter
century, you'd have never made it to your
first jerk-off. Those gray bastards and
their weasels woulda had you for lunch
back in Armpit, Kentucky.

                    OWEN
Abe, some of them get better. Half of 'em,
at least, will be over it in a few days --

                    CURTIS
<u>Which ones</u>, Mother Teresa? Can you
guarantee me they won't take it home with
them like a present for the family?

                    OWEN
You're saying better safe than sorry.

                    CURTIS
That's it. That's it in a nutshell.
     (comes toward Owen)
<u>I'll tell you what you should be worried</u>
<u>about</u> -- here's what should be on your
mind. Not these few --
     (gestures toward barn)
-- <u>unfortunates</u>. You should be worrying
about a Hitchhiker.

                    OWEN
What?

                    CURTIS
<u>A Hitchhiker</u>. That's been our greatest
fear. That a Grayboy would catch a ride
with someone who could carry it out of
here... without being consumed. Someone
who passes for one of us.

                    OWEN
Are you sure there isn't such a person?

                    CURTIS
No -- but I'm sure that if there is, <u>he's</u>
<u>not getting out</u>. Not with the net my boys
have thrown up around the Blue Zone...
<u>and</u>...

Curtis is looming over Owen now. He leans in further.

                    CURTIS
        ... <u>if we do a thorough job on the ones
        we've got</u>. If we don't go all gooey about
        the little picture when our job is taking
        care of the big one. *Capishe*?

He goes to the window and raises the shade to look at the corral.

                    CURTIS
        Owen, if you think this is easy for me,
        you're crazier than my mother was.

CURTIS' POV: a SINGLE FIGURE -- Henry -- standing in the corral,
staring up in his direction.

                    CURTIS
        Those poor schmucks down there... Those
        folks drive Chevies, shop at Walmart, and
        never miss an episode of *Friends*.  These
        are Americans.  The idea of slaughtering
        Americans...that turns my stomach.

Curtis lets the shade drop and turns back to Owen. Quietly --

                    CURTIS
        But I'll do it.  I'll do it because it
        needs to be done. If we start at two, we
        can be done at two-thirty. Then it's
        behind us.

                    OWEN
        Except for the dreams.

                    CURTIS
        Yes. Except for them.

111  EXT. OUTSIDE THE FENCE, CORRAL, GOSSELIN'S - NIGHT        111

Owen walks through the slanting snow. Henry, inside the fence,
falls in step with him. Owen glances at him, no more.

                    HENRY
        What are you going to tell Rita about what
        you did here, Owen?
            (Owen's pace slows)
        What'll you tell Katrina when she's old
        enough to ask?

Owen stops dead. He turns to look at Henry through the fence.

                    OWEN
        You know me, don't you? I don't remember
        when we met, but you know me.

                    HENRY
          We don't have time to screw around, Owen,
          so I'm going give it to you straight.
          You've got two problems -- one you know
          about and one you don't.

                    OWEN
          Go ahead.

                    HENRY
          First, what you know -- your longtime
          mentor Col. Curtis has gone insane from
          hunting aliens for 25 years... and he
          wants you to help him kill hundreds of
          innocent people.

                    OWEN
              (shaken, but hides it)
          Who are you?

                    HENRY
          Me? We can talk about that later, once
          we're out of here.

Owen can't believe this guy, but he can't walk away either. Henry
leans close to the electric fence. Owen warns him with his eyes.

                    HENRY
          ... You're predictable, Owen. You won't
          let me burn on this fence any more than
          you'll let Curtis slaughter all those
          people. So what you're thinking about is
          whether that digital satscan transmitter
          you've got in your duffle will let you get
          through to someone...
              (Henry searches Owen's mind for it)
          ... someone named... Gen. Matheson!

Owen can't help throwing a paranoid look back at Curtis' trailer.

                    OWEN
          Shut up, whoever you are.

                    HENRY
          Don't worry, Owen, your secret is safe
          with me. And if it makes you feel better,
          I'll tell you this -- you're doing the
          right thing, working for Matheson. No
          matter how disloyal you think you're being
          to Curtis, no matter how guilty you feel --
          you're doing the right thing.
              (nods toward Winnebago)
          Your hero's gone round the bend.

                    OWEN
          Who do you work for?

                    HENRY
          I never thought about it that way, but I
          guess the answer would have to be... a guy
          named Douglas Cavell. Duddits to his
          friends.
               (Owen is blank)
          The shit I know, I know for reasons you'll
          never understand.

                    OWEN
          Try me.

                    HENRY
          'Sometimes we have to kill, but our real
          job is to save lives.'

Owen is <u>rocked, stunned</u>.

                    OWEN
          Those were his last words.

                    HENRY
          Your father was a great soldier. You carry
          his picture always, you take it with you
          when you go into combat.

                    OWEN
               (quiet, shaken)
          Tell me everything.

                    HENRY
          You will save these people. When we're
          done talking, you get on that transmitter,
          you contact Matheson... the cavalry rides
          in. We hope. That takes care of one
          problem.
               (beat)
          Now comes the hard part. You think the
          infection is contained. You think there
          hasn't been a Hitchhiker, but you're
          wrong. He's riding with my best friend on
          earth, a guy named Gary Jones... and <u>he's
          out there</u>.

                    OWEN
          Where? Where is he?

                    HENRY
               (hesitates)
          I'm not sure where he is right now.

                    HENRY (cont'd)
Somewhere south. This... <u>thing</u>, whatever
it is, is using Jonesy to get where it
wants to go... <u>to do what it wants to do.</u>

                    OWEN
What is that?

                    HENRY
          (doesn't know)
I can tell you this -- if you and I don't
get after him right away, he'll be out of
my range and some kind of shit's gonna hit
the planetary fan.

112   INT. EQUIPMENT SHED, GOSSELIN'S - NIGHT          112

CAMERA MOVING among the shadowy tangle of rusting equipment. The
door opens, closes fast (a glimpse of the floodlit camp). Henry,
who's made a furtive dash here, quickly hides in the jumble.

113   EXT. CURTIS' WINNEBAGO - NIGHT                    113

Owen, having knocked, stands outside with a Sentry in the snow.
<u>He checks his watch.</u> Curtis opens the door and motions him in.

114   INT. CURTIS' WINNEBAGO - NIGHT                    114

Curtis hands coffee to Owen, whose unzipped parka reveals he's
wearing Curtis' gift, the shiny .45 Colt. Curtis indicates gun --

                    CURTIS
Suits you, son. Just as I thought.

                    OWEN
Thanks, Abe. It means a lot to me.
          (gets intense)
I'm afraid we may have the Hitchhiker you
were worried about. You remember the
doctor we saw being brought in?

                    CURTIS
Mr. Beantown.

                    OWEN
He says his friend's been shanghaied by a
Grayboy and he's gotten outside our net.
The doctor says <u>he's</u> the only one who can
track this guy... and he wants us to help.

Curtis considers, very suspicious.

                    CURTIS
Our nightmare Hitchhiker. And all Dr.
Mystery wants is for us to give him a free

                    CURTIS (cont'd)
          pass... to catch his friend. Very
          convenient.

                    OWEN
          I'm not saying I believe him. I'm saying
          you ought to hear his story.

                    CURTIS
          Okay... Where is he?

                    OWEN
          I had him taken down to the tractor shed.
          You don't want him tellin' his story
          around the other prisoners.

                    CURTIS
          That's good. I'll check him out and we can
          compare notes.

                    OWEN
          Whatever you say, Boss. If you need me,
          give a holler.

Owen goes out.

115    INT. EQUIPMENT SHED, GOSSELIN'S - NIGHT                115

Henry checks his watch nervously.

                    HENRY
          C'mon, c'mon... time's a-wastin'...

116    EXT. CENTER OF COMPOUND, GOSSELIN'S - NIGHT            116

TRACKING SHOT with Curtis as he makes his way toward the corner
of the compound, carrying a LETHAL-LOOKING RIFLE WITH SCOPE. He's
on alert, checking his surround, giving his suspicions full play.

117    EXT. GUARD TOWER, OUTER PERIMETER, GOSSELIN'S - NIGHT  117

Up on the newly-constructed tower, two TOWER SENTRIES watch the
compound and try to keep from freezing. Gosselin's sits at a
crossroads and now, behind the Sentries, on one of the roads --
LIGHTS. Some large convoy is about to appear over the rise.

118    EXT. TRACTOR SHED, GOSSELIN'S - NIGHT                  118

Curtis prepares to enter the shed. He puts on a plastic mask,
checks his rifle and, standing aside, throws open the door.

119    INT. TRACTOR SHED, GOSSELIN'S - NIGHT                  119

A yellow bulb illuminates the shed. No one in sight. Curtis
enters cautiously, calls out --

                    CURTIS
          Dr. Boston... are you here?

                    VOICE
          I'm here... where I been put...

From behind a tractor steps Old Man Gosselin.

                    OLD MAN GOSSELIN
          ... a prisoner on my own damn property.

CU CURTIS as he digests this.

120    INT. EQUIPMENT SHED, GOSSELIN'S - NIGHT                    120

Henry is ready to jump out of his skin from impatience. Suddenly
the back wall of the equipment shed IMPLODES and a LAND ROVER
smashes into view, Owen at the wheel. He comes within a foot of
hitting Henry, who's stunned.

                    OWEN
          Get in! Time to go.

Henry is still climbing aboard when Owen slams into reverse and
backs out of the shed, spinning the steering wheel.

                    HENRY
          You almost ran me down!

                    OWEN
          I figured you'd read my mind and get outta
          the way.

121    EXT. ELECTRIFIED FENCE, COMPOUND, GOSSELIN'S - NIGHT       121

FAST TRACKING SHOT: the Land Rover tears along the outside of the
fence -- headed for the road. SIRENS begin BLARING.

122    EXT. GUARD TOWER, OUTER PERIMETER, GOSSELIN'S - NIGHT      122

The two Tower Sentries look out in amazement at the roads.

WHAT THEY'RE SEEING: a MAJOR FORCE of REGULAR ARMY is rolling up
to the gates along both roads. And above them, FLOODLIGHTS
BEAMING like UFO'S, a half dozen TROOP-CARRIER HELICOPTERS.

123    EXT. TRACTOR SHED, GOSSELIN'S - NIGHT                      123

Curtis steps out of the shed (we SEE Old Man Gosselin trailing
behind him) and right UP INTO CAMERA.

CURTIS' POV: the massive arrival outside the compound, the
helicopters above.

Curtis understands that he has been betrayed by Owen. And at that moment, he sees --

WHAT CURTIS SEES: the Land Rover, Owen on this side, driving along  the last stretch of fence to the road, almost clear.

Curtis raises the rifle to his eye and we SEE through the NIGHT VISION SCOPE: Owen is visible in the crosshairs. It would take a great shot, but, hey, this is Curtis. He settles on Owen and --

-- his shot is obstructed by a line of Regular Army Vehicles taking up their position along the fence. Curtis lowers his rifle.

                    CURTIS
          Okay, Owen, okay!  You just drove over the
          Curtis Line!

124   INT. LAND ROVER, ROAD OUTSIDE GOSSELIN'S - NIGHT          124

Owen tears along past the arriving convoy, going the other way. His arm is out the window and his fist is raised in an odd finger/thumb SIGNAL that the Regular Army Guys return. To Henry --

                    OWEN
          Where we going?

                    HENRY
          South. That's all I know right now.

                    OWEN
          I just blew a 23-year military career out
          my ass, and all you know is 'south'?

                    HENRY
          You get me in range of Jonesy and we'll
          know everything we need.

125   INT. JANAS'S ARMY TRUCK, I-95 (TRAVELING) - NIGHT          125

Ike, the German Shepherd, is lying on the passenger side of the seat, having a twitchy dream. Something is moving in his belly. Jonesy/Mr. Gray looks over at him, then returns his attention to the difficult driving.

                    JONESY (V.O.)
          Why pick on an innocent dog? Why not just
          plant that booger in me?

                    MR. GRAY (V.O.)
          You're immune. I don't know why, but I'm
          sure you do.

>                    JONESY (V.O.)
>               *No, I don't...*
>
>                    MR. GRAY
>               (surprised, out loud)
>          Really? That would explain why I couldn't
>          find it in your memory. As opposed to the
>          information <u>I know you're hiding</u> -- about
>          your little friend. Information I've
>          repeatedly requested, in the politest way
>          possible --

                                             SMASH CUT TO:

126   INT. JONESY'S OFFICE, MEMORY WAREHOUSE                126

Jonesy watches the door anxiously as it QUAKES from the POUNDING
Mr. Gray is giving it. Again, that HORRIBLE SOUND. CUT BACK TO:

127   INT. JANAS'S ARMY TRUCK (TRAVELING) - NIGHT           127

The part of the driver that is Jonesy -- smiles.

>                    JONESY
>          Why are you so interested in my friend?
>
>                    MR. GRAY
>          Oh, there's a slim possibility that he's
>          someone I've been told about.
>
>                    JONESY (V.O.)
>          *Told about?... Or <u>warned</u> about?*
>
>                    MR. GRAY
>          <u>Uh-uh-uh</u>... You expect me to tell all, but
>          you've given me nothing in return.
>
>                    JONESY
>          Unless you count the free use of my body.

Suddenly, there's a MUFFLED BANG and the truck begins to FISHTAIL
crazily on a blown tire. Ike wakes, BARKING. Jonesy/Mr. Gray
wrestles the steering wheel.

128   EXT. JANAS'S ARMY TRUCK, I-95 - NIGHT                 128

The truck leaves the highway and comes to rest in a deep ditch.

129   INT. LAND ROVER, I-95 (TRAVELING) - NIGHT             129

Owen drives. Now, locating the source of some discomfort, he
reaches down and unhooks his holster, then pulls it off and puts
it on the seat. Henry regards the shiny Colt with interest.

                    HENRY
          That's some gun. Can I take a look?

Owen picks up the automatic, ejects the shell in the chamber and
drops the clip into his lap. Then he hands it to Henry.

                    HENRY
          Kinda flashy for a guy like you, isn't it?

                    OWEN
          It was a gift.

                    HENRY
          I know.

Henry points the gun out the window ahead, then gets thoughtful,
looking at the snowy highway.

                    HENRY
          <u>Where are you</u>, Jonesy? Just pick up the
          phone and call 1-800-HENRY.

130   EXT. JANAS'S ARMY TRUCK, DITCH, I-95 - NIGHT              130

Jonesy/Mr. Gray stands in the highway waiting for a car to come
by, because the truck isn't going anywhere tonight.

131   INT. JONESY'S OFFICE, MEMORY WAREHOUSE                    131

Jonesy stands at the window observing the above scene. He glances
once at the door to the Warehouse -- quiet now. A thought -- he
hurries over, picks up the phone on the desk and <u>dials like mad</u>.

132   INT. LAND ROVER, I-95 - NIGHT                             132

Henry is still holding the gun. Now he hears RINGING (Owen does
not). Henry gives the Colt an odd look and puts it to his ear.

                    HENRY
               (into gun)
          Hello... Jonesy! Jesus Christ, I <u>knew</u> it
          was you!

Owen looks at him like he's crazy. But it's a crazy night.

                    HENRY
               (into gun)
          Where is he taking you?... Massachusetts?
          What's there? ... No idea?... He is?...
          <u>Duddits</u>!... Okay, I will, Jonesy, just
          hang in there -- Jonesy... <u>Jonesy</u>!

Henry, grim, lowers the gun from his ear. To Owen --

                    HENRY
He hung up.

                    OWEN
Gimme back my gun.

                    HENRY
     (intensely, looking out)
We have to go to Derry.

                    OWEN
Is that where they're going?

                    HENRY
No, they're headed toward Massachusetts.
But he says we need Duddits. He says
Duddits will know what to do. Jonesy says
Mr. Gray is <u>afraid</u> of Duddits.

                    OWEN
Why?

                    HENRY
     (no idea, looks ahead)
The exit for Derry is about ten miles
ahead.

                    OWEN
He's alive, your buddy. He's still alive
after all this time with Mr. Gray.

                    HENRY
He's immune. I think it's because he died.
     (on Owen's look)
He got hit by a car and his heart
stopped... twice. I don't think he even
knows it. He came back from dead and that
must have changed him. It means this Mr.
Gray can use him without consuming him, at
least so far.

                    OWEN
... hitch a ride...

                    HENRY
     (something clicks)
... It's almost like Duddits saw this
whole thing coming -- Is that it?
     (figuring, to himself)
Jonesy told me it was Duddits who drew him
into the accident... Duddits...

Owen doesn't try to follow this. He's done his own calculation --

                    OWEN
          If we catch him, we're going to have to
          kill him. You know we have to do it, don't
          you? Killing him's the only way to stop
          Mr. Gray. Assuming we <u>can</u> catch him.

                    HENRY
          I know the math says we have to. Six
          billion people on Spaceship Earth, versus
          one Jonesy.

                    OWEN
          Those are the numbers.

                    HENRY
          Numbers can lie.

A133    EXT. I-95 - NIGHT                                      A133

Near Janas' truck, a State Trooper's dead body lies in a
snowbank. His cruiser is pulling away, headed south.

133     EXT. DERRY EXIT RAMP, I-95 - NIGHT                    133

The exit sign is almost obscured by the heavy snowfall. The Land
Rover has to take the off-ramp slowly.

134     INT. LAND ROVER - NIGHT                               134

Owen peers into the snow. Henry is drifting, thoughts elsewhere.

                    OWEN
          Guide me.

                    HENRY
          Oh... take a right at the top of the ramp.

                    OWEN
          What's the matter?

                    HENRY
          Huh?... I don't know, I just got scared.
          The closer we get, the more scared I feel.

                    OWEN
          Of Duddits?

                    HENRY
          <u>For</u> Duddits. I feel like there's something
          wrong with him. I don't know if we should
          be asking him to help.

                        OWEN
           When did you last see him?

A sore subject. Henry feels guilty.

                        HENRY
           A long time ago. Years.

                        OWEN
           What makes you so sure he can help?

                        HENRY
           Duddits can do anything. I didn't
           understand that back then, but I think
           it's always been true. He's the one who
           made us like this.

                        OWEN
           Like what?

                        HENRY
           You know... weird. I can tell you the day
           it happened. It was in June, after school
           was out the year we met Duds...

135   EXT. STRAWFORD PARK, DERRY (FLASHBACK -- 1983) - DAY        135

A GLASSED-IN NOTICE BOARD: **DERRY DOIN'S.**

Standing in front of it: Henry, Jonesy, Beaver and Pete, staring
at the board. And their new friend, Duddits (wearing wraparound
sunglasses and clutching his lunch box), who's not looking. He's
distracted by a spiderweb, reminiscent of The Dreamcatcher.

Crammed in among the announcements is <u>a photo of a lost girl</u>: a
smiling girl with puzzled eyes. Above her picture, these words:
**"MISSING. JOSIE RINKENHAUER. LAST SEEN JUNE 7, STRAWFORD PARK."**

                        JONESY
           That's yesterday. Right here.

                        BEAVER
           She's the one from the Retard Academy who
           always waves.

                        HENRY
                (sharp, indicates Duddits)
           Don't call it that.

                        JONESY
                (to Duddits)
           We've got to save this girl.

                    DUDDITS
                 (confused)
          -- ave iss urld?
          [-- save this world?]


                    HENRY
          Not the world, Duds, a <u>girl</u>. We'll save
          the world some other time.

                    DUDDITS
          Ister gay?

                    HENRY
          Yeah, Duds, it's a mystery.

                    JONESY
          And we need you to help us solve it.

Duddits looks confused. Jonesy takes his hand. Henry takes his
other hand and gives Pete and Beaver a look, motioning them into
the circle.

                    HENRY
          Come on, guys. Dreamcatcher. Duds'll read
          our minds.

                    PETE
          Not this again.

                    HENRY
          Shut up.

                    JONESY
          We all gotta think of Josie.

Pete and Beaver crowd in, hands on Duddits' shoulders.

They all close their eyes, concentrating. No good. Nothing
happens. Duddits looks expectantly from one to the other, trying
to figure out the game. Then, suddenly, he smiles.

OVERHEAD SHOT: the four friends have surrounded Duddits in the
same relationship as The Dreamcatcher.

<u>Something odd</u>. The five boys begin to give off a VIBRATION,
making an unearthly SOUND. <u>Their images become smeared,
indistinct</u>. Seen from above, their separate figures MELD INTO an
ABSTRACT DESIGN. It builds and builds.

And suddenly it's over. CUT TO:

SERIES OF CLOSE-UPS: Each of the friends. Their lives have been
changed forever and they don't understand it yet. But they know

something large has happened. Henry and Pete have tears rolling down their cheeks. Jonesy is flushed; he GASPS for air. Beaver falls down in a faint, breaking the contact in the circle.

> DUDDITS
> Osie?

Beaver wakes up as he hits the ground, pretends he didn't faint.

> HENRY
> That's right --- can you find Josie?

> DUDDITS
> (clutching his lunch box)
> We ot-sum urk oo-do-now.
> (to Pete)
> Eet, do-oo see Uh Ine?

> PETE
> (confused)
> Do I see what?

> DUDDITS
> Uh Ine, Eet, do-oo see Uh Ine?

> PETE
> Duds, I don't know what --

He stops suddenly, looking across the field. For the first time in his life, he raises his hand in that particular way and waggles his index finger back and forth. He sees The Line. The others watch Pete.

> JONESY (V.O.)
> (his thoughts)
> *This is completely crazy!*

> HENRY
> (out loud)
> You can say that again.

Jonesy's head snaps around to Henry.

> JONESY
> I didn't say anything.

> BEAVER (V.O.)
> *Yes, you did, I heard you. You said, 'This is completely crazy.'*

> JONESY
> I didn't <u>say</u> that, I thought it --

He stops, realizing, now truly scared. Beaver scowls --

> BEAVER
> Kiss my bender... Duds can hear people's
> thoughts, <u>we can't</u>!

> HENRY (V.O.)
> *Are you sure of that, Beav?*

They all comprehend what's happened at the same moment. The three exchange stunned looks, then turn and see that <u>Duddits is beaming at them</u>.

And that Pete has started off across the field, finger waggling. They go after him.

WIDE SHOT OF THE PARK: Pete in the lead, the others following. Duddits almost skipping.

136     EXT. FENCE, RAILROAD PROPERTY (1983) - DAY                 136

Jonesy, Henry, Beaver and Duddits squeeze through a rickety old fence bordering the railroad property. Once through, they scan to find Pete, who's running far ahead of them, across the tracks.

137     EXT. SLOPE, RAILROAD PROPERTY (1983) - DAY                 137

WITH PETE as he slides down a dirt slope, coming right UP TO CAMERA. He picks up a white plastic purse and pulls out Dancing Dawn and Ron dolls, then smiles in triumph. He spins to wave the dolls at the others, who have now reached the top of the slope.

> PETE
> Guys! She's around here for sure!

He puts the dolls back in the purse, sets it down and takes off PAST CAMERA.

138     EXT. DRAINPIPE, RAILROAD PROPERTY (1983) - DAY             138

A drainpipe sticks out of the ground, covered with foliage. Pete arrives, pushes away the brush and sticks his head in.

PETE'S POV: Spooky. It slopes sharply downward into blackness.

REVERSE looking up at Pete, and then Jonesy, Henry and Beaver, all trying to squeeze in and look down the pipe.

> PETE
> Josie!... You down there, Josie?

Silence.

                    BEAVER
                (certain)
        Fuck me Freddy, she's down there. I know
        it. I can see her in my head.

                    HENRY
                (does too; quietly)
        Yeah.

                    JONESY
        Me too.

Then, from far down, a TERRIFIED VOICE.

                    JOSIE (O.S.)
        ...<u>help</u>...<u>pleeeese</u>...

They look at each other. This is it. Beaver is the first to move,
climbing headfirst into the mouth of the pipe.

                    BEAVER
        Grab my feet. We'll make a chain. <u>Hold on,</u>
        <u>Josie, we're coming</u>!
                (singing, it echoes)
        'Here we come, to save the day...'

WAY DOWN THE DRAINPIPE, Josie sits in creepy, wet darkness. When
she HEARS Beaver's singing, her tear-streaked face brightens.

Pete has got hold of Beaver's ankle. Now he crawls in headfirst.

                    PETE
        Don't sing, Beav, she's scared enough!

Henry and Jonesy laugh and prepare to become part of the chain.
They're giddy with triumph. <u>And an otherworldly gift</u>. CUT TO:

Duddits, sitting in the dirt a few feet away, introducing Dancing
Dawn and Ron to his Scooby-Doo toys.

                    DUDDITS
        DonRon... Ooby-Doo.
        [Dawn and Ron ... Scooby-Doo.]

He looks up at Henry's feet hooked over the lip of the pipe, the
last piece of the chain.

                    HENRY
                (echoing, from pipe)
        Duds, <u>we got her</u>!

Duddits is smiling that great smile.

                    DUDDITS
                  (quietly)
          Ere's Osie. *[Here's Josie.]*

                    HENRY (V.O.)
              (pre-lap, present day)
          Here's the street. Turn there.

139    EXT. LAND ROVER, DUDDITS' STREET, DERRY(PRESENT DAY)-NIGHT 139

The Land Rover punches through a pile of snow into the side
street.

140    INT./EXT. LAND ROVER, CAVELL HOUSE, DERRY - NIGHT        140

FROM INSIDE THE LAND ROVER as it rolls down the street. Henry
points to a house, but lowers his hand when he sees a woman is
standing in the doorway, silhouetted by the warm interior light --
Roberta Cavell, Duddits' mother. Owen pulls the Land Rover into
the driveway.

141    INT. FRONT HALL, CAVELL HOUSE - NIGHT                     141

MOMENTS LATER. Roberta and Henry break from a warm embrace. Owen
stands to the side, already introduced.

                    ROBERTA
          He's been waiting for you.

                    HENRY
                  (not surprised)
          Blizzard slowed us up.

Now an EXCITED VOICE, coming nearer --

                    DUDDITS (O.S.)
          -- Henny -- Henny -- HENNY --

-- and here he comes down the stairs, the now-grown Dudster
himself. He throws himself into Henry's arms, kissing him. Henry
shuts his eyes at the touch, but mostly he's shocked by the
emaciated body. Duddits is dying.

He's bald under his Red Sox cap. Crusts of blood around his
nostrils. Deep dark circles under his eyes. Light as milkweed
fluff, he seems ancient. Henry is rocked.

142    INT. UPSTAIRS HALL, CAVELL HOUSE - NIGHT                  142

Henry follows Roberta down the hall. (Duddits stays with Owen.)

                    HENRY
          My god, Roberta, what is it?

> ROBERTA
> Lymphocytic leukemia.

> HENRY
> I'm so sorry, Roberta. We should have been
> here... we let him down.

Roberta stops at a bedroom door, looks at Henry. Just love here.

> ROBERTA
> What you boys did was give Douglas the
> happiest times of his life.

143    INT. DUDDITS' BEDROOM, CAVELL HOUSE - NIGHT                143

Not what you want for your child. A hospital crank-up bed, an IV
pole alongside. Rows of pills. Roberta collects Duddits' things.

> ROBERTA
> I'm going to let you take him, but I have
> to tell you why. Just now, when he was
> getting ready -- Henry, he was <u>so excited</u>.
> Like he hasn't been in such a long time.

She looks at Henry. It's hard for her to say, but --

> ROBERTA
> I think if he's with you, he might die
> happy, instead of in this awful room.

She takes a huge **BOSTON RED SOX** parka from the closet. Roberta
opens a small fridge, takes out the yellow Scooby-Doo lunch box.

> ROBERTA
> Be sure the parka stays on tight. The cold
> devastates him. Medication and
> instructions are in here.

144    EXT. FRONT PORCH, CAVELL HOUSE - NIGHT                     144

Henry and Owen wait outside as Roberta stands with Duddits at the
door. She fusses with his parka, though it's fine.

> ROBERTA
> You mind Henry now.

> DUDDITS
> I-ill, Amma. *[I will, Mama.]*

Excited, he turns away and steps toward Henry.

> ROBERTA
> Haven't we forgotten something?

Duddits runs back to her, gives her a big kiss. She holds him
tightly, but only for a moment. Owen leads Duddits to the Land
Rover. Roberta and Henry exchange a look, then Henry turns away.
Roberta watches as Owen helps Duddits climb aboard.

                    ROBERTA
          Goodbye, Duddie -- be a good boy.
               (beat)
          Now go save the world.

She raises her arms in Duddits' gesture.

145    INT. LAND ROVER, DRIVEWAY, CAVELL HOUSE - NIGHT          145

Owen has settled Duddits in back with Henry and now gets in. He
pulls the .45 Colt from his parka, re-inserts the clip and
chambers a round. He puts the gun snugly in its holster on the
seat. As he backs the Land Rover out WE PUSH IN on the shiny
Colt, VERY CLOSE and CUT TO:

A RADAR SCREEN. A green dot is pulsing on and off, accompanied by
a BEEP-BEEP... BEEP-BEEP. PULL BACK to REVEAL we are --

146    INT. CURTIS' WINNEBAGO, GOSSELIN'S - NIGHT              146

The radar screen is part of a small ELECTRONICS CENTER shut off
from the bedroom by a sliding door. A TECHNICIAN, outfitted in
the overalls of Curtis' unit, graphs a location on a map. The
door slides open, the Technician startles. It's Curtis.

                    CURTIS
          It's all right, laddie. They haven't
          worked up the nerve to take over my
          trailer. Not yet. What've you got?

                    TECHNICIAN
               (points)
          They're on the move again, sir.

                    CURTIS
          Where?

                    TECHNICIAN
          Leaving Derry, Maine. Headed south again,
          on 95, toward Massachusetts.

                    CURTIS
          Massachusetts... hmm. Keep at it, bucko.

There is a loud KNOCKING from out front. Curtis goes out.

FRONT ROOM. Curtis comes in from the bedroom, closing that door
behind him. He opens the outside door. Big smile, friendly --

                    CURTIS
          General Matheson, please come in!

GENERAL HERMAN MATHESON steps in. He's as tough as Curtis, but
without the insanity. He looks around the Winnebago.

                    MATHESON
          This is very nice, Abe.

                    CURTIS
          It's been home through some tough times.
          Is there something we haven't covered?

Matheson knows exactly what Curtis thinks of him.

                    MATHESON
          Two things really. I don't think I got to
          say before how much I respect the work
          you've done. It was with sincere regret --

Curtis raises a hand to stop him.

                    CURTIS
          Herman -- may I call you Herman? -- we may
          not agree about every strategic
          initiative, but we do agree about this --
               (dramatic Curtis pause)
          -- I am past it... burned out. I just
          needed a push. I probably should have quit
          after that mess in Montana.
               (he laughs)
          Even I don't trust my judgement any more.

                    MATHESON
          You're very gracious.

                    CURTIS
          And the other thing?

                    MATHESON
          Oh. My techies tell me we've still got
          some electronics reading hot from in here.

                    CURTIS
          That's right. I've been talking to the
          wife on my sat-phone -- I don't know if
          you ever met Barbara. She's been after me
          for years to retire. She's plenty happy,
          I'll tell you that.
               (Matheson understands)
          I'll have everything shut down in an hour
          or so...

                    CURTIS (cont'd)
                  (the injured warrior)
             ... if that's soon enough.

                    MATHESON
             That'll be fine.

147    EXT. STATE POLICE CRUISER, I-95 - NIGHT          147

       START ON the revolving BUBBLE LIGHTS on the roof, which flare the
       falling snow red and blue. DOWN TO Jonesy/Mr. Gray driving slow.

148    INT. STATE POLICE CRUISER - NIGHT               148

       The flashing lights are bugging Mr. Gray, but he has to keep his
       eyes on the road and can't find the switch.

                    MR. GRAY
             How do you turn off these goddamn lights?

                    JONESY
                  (loathing)
             Maybe you shouldn't have been so fast to
             kill that trooper.
                  (V.O.)
             *'Goddamn lights'? You're making yourself
             at home here, aren't you?*

                    MR. GRAY (V.O.)
             *You have no idea, Jonesy. Tell me how you
             like this --*

       Mr. Gray says the next OUT LOUD, but this time he sounds like an
       Englishman doing <u>a very good imitation of Jonesy</u>:

                    MR. GRAY
             'Maybe you shouldn't have been so fast to
             kill that trooper.'

       Jonesy reacts, grim. Mr. Gray appears in the next second,
       gleeful. Back to English accent --

                    MR. GRAY
             Not bad, huh?... Oh, you don't like that,
             Gary, do you?
                  (glances into the back seat)
             How about you, Ike, did you like it?

       In the back seat, Ike WHIMPERS. His stomach is now massively
       bloated and contracting spasmodically.

                    MR. GRAY
             Won't be long now, boy... won't be long.
                  (doing Jonesy again)
             Ah, <u>there's that sucker.</u>

Mr. Gray reaches across the dash and switches off the flashers.

149    INT. LAND ROVER, I-95 - NIGHT                              149

The Land Rover is making better time than the cruiser. Owen
glances in the rearview mirror at Henry, sitting close to
Duddits, who stares out the window as if watching a movie.

                    DUDDITS
          No more pitty ites. Ownzy in plees-ar
          now... no more ites.
          [No more pretty lights. Jonesy in police
          car now... no more lights.]

                    HENRY
               (half to Owen)
          He's in a police car now. Can you see
          where he is, Duds?

Duddits nods, with as much energy as he's got right now.

                    DUDDITS
          Ownzy in Ister Gay.

                    HENRY
          Ister -- Mr. Gray!
               (Duddits confirms)
          That's right, Duds. He's in Mr. Gray.
               (jolted, a sudden connection)
          Ister Gay is Mr. Gray --

                                        SMASH CUT TO:

150    EXT. STRAWFORD PARK, DERRY (FLASHBACK -- 1983) - DAY    150

THE SCENE WE SAW in front of the bulletin board: the whole group,
about to go find Josie, about to become telepathic.

                    JONESY
               (to Duddits)
          We've got to save this girl.

                    DUDDITS
               (confused)
          -- ave iss urld?
          [-- save this world?]

                    HENRY
          Not the world, Duds, a girl. We'll save
          the world some other time.

                    DUDDITS
          Ister Gay?

                    HENRY
          Yeah, Duds, it's a mystery.

151   INT. LAND ROVER, I-95 - NIGHT                    151

Henry stares in awe at Duddits.

                    DUDDITS (V.O.)
               (echoing from previous)
          *Ister Gay*?

                    HENRY
          You already knew...

                    OWEN
          Can he tell where they are? Ask him again.

Henry takes a moment to come back from his revelation.

                    HENRY
          Where is the police car, Duddits? Are we
          going in the right direction?

Still looking out at the snow, Duddits nods, then points out the
front windshield. His eyes flicker; he's getting weaker.

                    HENRY
          I think we're good.
               (to Duddits)
          Where is he going, Duds? Where is Mr. Gray
          taking Jonesy?

Duddits is drifting, doesn't seem to hear. Henry reaches down --

CLOSE UP of Henry taking Duddits' hand in his. Duddits' fingers
immediately entwine Henry's. TILT UP to Duddits, as he comes back
to alertness, looking directly at Henry.

                    DUDDITS
          Ister Gay want war.

                    OWEN
          War?

                    HENRY
          Not war... water. Mr. Gray wants water...
               (an abrupt realization)
          I know where he's going.  He's going to
          Quabbin Reservoir.

                    OWEN
          Why? What's Quabbin?

                    HENRY
               (distracted, mind racing)
          Quabbin Reservoir supplies the drinking
          water for all of Boston.

Duddits squeezes Henry's hand, drawing his attention back.

                    DUDDITS
          Un urm ill urld.
          [*One worm kill world.*]

                    HENRY
          One worm kills the world...
          Omigod.  One worm?
               (to Owen)
          Back at our cabin, I saw the worms that
          come out of those weasels.  Mr. Gray must
          want to get one into the Boston water
          supply.
               (looks at Duddits)
          Just one worm could infect the whole
          world?

Duddits nods.

                    OWEN
          Are we going right?

                    HENRY
               (peering out)
          Yes, take 495 to the Mass. Pike. It's not
          far...

Henry turns his attention back to Duddits, lifting their hands up
between them. Duddits' eyes shine.

                    HENRY
          You're doing great, buddy. Now, I'm going
          to ask you something hard. Are you ready
          to try something hard?

                    DUDDITS
          Ess, Henny.

                    HENRY
          Good... Can you talk to Jonesy? Can you
          make him hear you?

Duddits stares blankly at Henry for a moment, as though he hasn't
understood. But what he says, is --

                    DUDDITS
          Ownzy and Ister Gay.

152     INT. STATE POLICE CRUISER, INTERSTATE 495 - NIGHT          152

CLOSE UP on the face of Jonesy/Mr. Gray. There's no way to tell
which one, but it doesn't matter much, because at this instant
both of them are VIOLENTLY JOLTED by the incoming message from --

                    JONESY/MR. GRAY
          Duddits!

Jonesy/Mr. Gray loses control of the cruiser. It starts to slide
and he hits the brakes hard. The skid gets worse.

                                        SMASH CUT TO:

153     INT. JONESY'S OFFICE, MEMORY WAREHOUSE                      153

OVER JONESY'S SHOULDER toward the door to the Warehouse. It is
just about to come off its hinges, so violent is the POUNDING
from Mr. Gray outside.

CLOSE ON Jonesy, expecting to face the True Mr. Gray in the next
second. He shoots a look over at --

-- the Duddits file boxes stacked in the corner. Then FLASH PAN
to the door again. All of a sudden, the POUNDING STOPS. SILENCE.

Jonesy is mystified. Then, the SOUND of the DEADBOLT SLIDING
BACK. The inside BOLT slides away. The doorknob turns. The door
swings open. There is no one there. Jonesy reacts, quickly turns
to the Duddits files -- but they're gone. CUT BACK TO:

154     EXT. STATE POLICE CRUISER - NIGHT                          154

The state police cruiser SKIDS directly AT CAMERA and slams to a
stop in the snowbank on the shoulder. Ike, thrown forward, HOWLS.

155     INT. STATE POLICE CRUISER - NIGHT                          155

Jonesy/Mr. Gray has banged his head on the steering wheel, where
it rests now. He lifts his head and, for the first time, there is
fear in him.

                    MR. GRAY
          I knew it, I knew it. He's been here all
          along... waiting.

Now a slow realization comes to Mr. Gray.

                    MR. GRAY
          Jonesy, it appears we didn't meet by
          accident.  We owe it to our friend
          Duddits.

                    JONESY
          I don't know what you mean.

                    MR. GRAY
          No?... Maybe not. Maybe your clever friend
          didn't want you to know what he was up
          to...
               (following the thread)
          ... That's why you had nothing in the
          warehouse about... me. Duddits didn't
          bother to tell you what job he had in mind
          for you.

Mr. Gray tries to collect himself, preparing to go on.

                    MR. GRAY
          It doesn't matter. His little scheme
          didn't work out. We're almost there.
               (works the gear shift)
          What was it your poetry file had to say?
          '...I have promises to keep, and miles to
          go before I sleep, and miles to go...'

He begins to rock the cruiser, extracting it from the snowbank.

                    MR. GRAY
          Slowly, slowly... easy does it.

Mr. Gray is worried. But he's also got a new skill to show off --
he speaks OUT LOUD, in a voice that's exactly like Jonesy's:

                    MR. GRAY
          Thank you, Jonesy. Your files on winter
          driving are very helpful... Slow and easy.

156     INT. LAND ROVER, I-495 (TRAVELING) - NIGHT                156

The Land Rover is kicking ass, closing in. But Duddits seems
weaker again, even with his hand in Henry's.

                    DUDDITS
          Slo an ezy, Ister Gay.

Henry and Owen exchange a look. DAWN begins to light the sky.

157     EXT. HELICOPTER AREA, GOSSELIN'S - SUNRISE                157

Curtis glances at the brightening sky as he walks along the line
of choppers to his Kiowa. The snow is finally stopping. He pulls
his copter's door open and swings in.

158   INT./EXT. CURTIS' COPTER - SUNRISE                      158

Curtis fits a super-GPS unit into its dock on the control panel
and flips it to life: the GREEN DOT we saw earlier begins
BLINKING and BEEPING on a military grid-map of Massachusetts.

A HELICOPTER SENTRY comes running down the line of helicopters as
Curtis TURNS THE ENGINE OVER with a ROAR.

                    HELICOPTER SENTRY
          Colonel Curtis... Colonel Curtis, sir!
          We're not authorized to let any of these
          birds --

                    CURTIS
                 (friendly)
          It's all right, laddie. I've got my
          authorization right here.

Curtis shoots the Sentry dead with his standard-issue automatic.
He pulls the door shut, hits another switch, then checks the
controls: the machine gun mounted in the nose of the Kiowa
SWIVELS side to side, up and down. He starts the rotors.

                    CURTIS
          I'm comin', Owen. Need to take you to
          school. Teach you what happens to buckos
          who cross the Curtis Line.

159   EXT. COMPOUND, GOSSELIN'S - SUNRISE                      159

SOLDIERS run PAST CAMERA, which PANS AROUND AND UP to SEE Curtis'
chopper lift away toward the lightening southern sky.

160   EXT. STATE POLICE CRUISER, RT 9 OUTSIDE WARE, MASS. - DAY  160

A sign: **QUABBIN RESERVOIR -- NEXT RIGHT.** The cruiser comes by and
makes the right turn, carefully.

161   INT. STATE POLICE CRUISER - DAY                           161

Ike lies WHINING on the floor in back, rear legs twitching. Mr.
Gray's hand passes over Ike's head; the dog goes deeply to sleep.

                    MR. GRAY
          Sleep, doggy... Not yet, little one...

The cruiser loses traction and Mr. Gray has to return his
attention to driving. He SLOWS the car to a crawl.

                    JONESY (V.O.)
                (taunting)
          C'mon, Mac, I got a hot date. Why doncha
          step on it?

                    MR. GRAY
                (practicing, mimics Jonesy)
          C'mon, Mac, I got a hot date...

162   EXT. LAND ROVER, ROUTE 9 - DAY                        162

A sign: **QUABBIN RESERVOIR - 3 MILES**. The Land Rover speeds by.

163   EXT. AERIAL SHOT, WESTERN MASSACHUSETTS - DAY         163

Beautiful. Red sky at morning... Flying low over the countryside.
Curtis' chopper ENTERS UNDER CAMERA, at exhilarating speed.

A164  INT. CURTIS' HELICOPTER - DAY                         A164

Curtis' visage is set, scary, invigorated by the hunt.

164   INT./EXT. POLICE CAR, ACCESS ROAD, QUABBIN - DAY      164

The cruiser labors up the unplowed access road now. In the
distance WE SEE an old, square stone building, the SHAFT HOUSE.

INSIDE NOW, Mr. Gray struggles as the car drifts in deep snow.

                    JONESY (V.O.)
          Give it gas... put the pedal to the metal!

Reflexively, Mr. Gray steps on the gas. It works. The cruiser
takes hold and picks up speed. Surprised by the help --

                    MR. GRAY (V.O.)
          Thank you, Gary Jones.

Mr. Gray gives it _more_ gas: the cruiser CRASHES NOSE FIRST into a
GULLY hidden by the snow -- <u>end of the line</u>! Jonesy LAUGHS.

165   INT./EXT. LAND ROVER, HEAD OF ACCESS ROAD, QUABBIN - DAY   165

The Land Rover skids to a stop. Owen looks back at Henry, who
cradles Duddits in his arms. Duddits manages to point a finger.

                    HENRY
          Go up around the Reservoir. The aqueduct
          to Boston starts in Shaft 12.

Owen turns in, fast; drives in tracks just cut by the cruiser.

166     INT./EXT. STATE POLICE CRUISER, ACCESS ROAD, QUABBIN - DAY 166

Jonesy/Mr. Gray staggers out of the cruiser -- trousers ripped,
knees bleeding, hip screaming, shivering in the frigid air. His
damaged body has been used hard. Now the tough part:

He reaches in the back and pulls the dog out. GRUNTING, he swings
Ike up around his neck, almost falling. In agony, he walks toward
Shaft 12 House. The dog's hind quarters are <u>contorting violently</u>.

167     EXT. SHAFT 12 HOUSE, QUABBIN - DAY                          167

Jonesy/Mr. Gray barely makes it to the door, puts Ike down and
tries the door. Locked. Damn! He looks at the adjacent window.

168     INT. SHAFT 12 HOUSE, QUABBIN - DAY                          168

The window is SMASHED by a rock. Jonesy/Mr. Gray knocks out the
remaining glass, then, with difficulty, climbs inside. He catches
his breath, unlocks the door and brings Ike inside.

He looks around: a rectangular room, thirty feet long. Across the
room, A ROUND IRON SHAFT COVER -- 150 pounds, maybe more.

169     INT./EXT. LAND ROVER, ACCESS ROAD - DAY                     169

Owen drives, his face set. He takes the photo of his father from
his pocket, touches it with his fingertip for luck, puts it back.

170     INT. SHAFT 12 HOUSE - DAY                                   170

Jonesy/Mr. Gray is struggling to lift the iron cover to Shaft 12.
He pushes with all his might -- it doesn't even budge. He looks
around the room -- in a corner are some tools, including a
crowbar. He glances at Ike, awake now, ready to give birth.

171     EXT. STATE POLICE CRUISER, ACCESS ROAD - DAY                171

The cruiser is blocking the road. Owen stops the Land Rover fifty
feet behind it, checks the scene: cruiser and Shaft House beyond.

172     INT./EXT. LAND ROVER, ACCESS ROAD - DAY                     172

Owen pulls out the .45, checks it and reholsters. To Henry --

                    OWEN
          Stay here and take care of your friend, no
          matter what you hear.
               (he opens the door, pauses)
          So long, Doctor.

Cautious, staying low, Owen moves to the rear of the Land Rover
and pops open the back gate. He takes out an MP5 auto-fire rifle

and three banana-clips of ammunition. Henry turns to watch as Owen <u>snaps in a clip and slides back the action</u>.

Henry embraces the fading Duddits as Owen heads off toward the Shaft House, almost certainly to kill their friend Jonesy.

173     INT. SHAFT 12 HOUSE - DAY                                    173

Jonesy/Mr. Gray struggles to lift the cover with the crowbar.

174     EXT. APPROACHING SHAFT 12 HOUSE, QUABBIN - DAY               174

Owen raises the MP5 as he comes up to the cruiser. He checks the vehicle and moves on, hugging the treeline. Now he HEARS something he hadn't expected: WHUP-WHUP-WHUP. Owen looks up.

<u>Here comes Curtis in his Kiowa</u>, swinging in low over the trees and heading down the access road toward Owen. The machine gun in the nose ERUPTS IN BLAZING BURSTS.

The ground EXPLODES in a deadly trail of hits. Owen dives for cover and returns fire as the Kiowa sweeps by. Curtis unloads on the cruiser and the Land Rover, <u>riddling them with bullets</u>.

175     EXT. LAND ROVER, ACCESS ROAD - DAY                          175

Henry pulls Duddits, lunch box clutched to his chest, out of the vehicle and carries him into the snowy woods.

176     INT. SHAFT 12 HOUSE, QUABBIN - DAY                          176

Jonesy/Mr. Gray, sweating now, looks up anxiously at the sound of GUNFIRE, then returns to the cover, which is starting to lift.

177     INT. CURTIS' COPTER - DAY                                   177

Curtis is smiling as he pulls the Kiowa into a looping turn over the reservoir. Here's the shocking thing: <u>we've never seen him so happy before</u>. He's defending the honor of the Curtis Line... trying to kill Owen. He heads back in, triggering a new BLAST.

178     EXT. ACCESS ROAD - DAY                                      178

Bullets tear up the ice of the frozen lake, then pock the snow as they tear into the road. Owen takes a hit in the leg. He grunts, goes down hard -- there's blood, lots of it.

179     INT. CURTIS' COPTER - DAY                                   179

Curtis smiles and swings the copter into a turn over the woods. He heads around for the end of the road, ready to make another pass. In the distance, he sees Owen struggle to his feet and limp <u>out into the open road</u>. Curtis can't believe his good luck -- an

open target. He BLASTS away. BEGIN TO INTERCUT THE HELICOPTER
WITH:

180     EXT. ACCESS ROAD - DAY                          180

Owen stands his ground as the shells hit around him. He FIRES an
entire clip from the MP5 at the bottom of the copter. Some of the
bullets hit, but the damage isn't critical.

Curtis swings the Kiowa sideways, staying over the trees so Owen
can't get under him.

Owen drops the depleted MP5 and pulls out Curtis' gift -- the
hidden bug that has let Curtis track him -- the shiny .45 Colt
automatic.

BLAM-BLAM-BLAM! Owen's bullets find the rear rotor of the Kiowa.
The copter jolts and starts to spin.

Curtis knows what's coming -- there's no safe landing possible.
He aims the copter toward Owen, struggling to stay aloft. Curtis
shucks his seat belt, grabs a machine pistol from the seat beside
him... and throws open the door of the Kiowa.

Duddits clings to Henry in a snowbank as they watch the lurching
copter and Owen standing in the road, emptying his gun.

Curtis is still two hundred feet up, but he won't be cheated of
his final dance. So he does an amazing thing: Curtis jumps out,
firing the machine pistol as he goes.

Owen is stunned. Curtis is falling to certain death... and even
that doesn't stop his attack; the warrior keeps BLASTING away.

Curtis, falling, falling. He doesn't stop firing until... he is
impaled on a treetop. The narrow spear bends and breaks. Curtis'
body SMASHES down through the limbs, jolted and jerked like a
ragdoll. And lands at the trunk, dead.

Off in the woods, the Kiowa EXPLODES in flame and smoke.

Henry and Duddits are stunned. They come toward Owen, moving as
fast as they can manage. When they reach him, we SEE --

-- Owen lies dead in the road, blood staining the fresh snow.

181     INT. SHAFT 12 HOUSE, QUABBIN - DAY              181

Jonesy/Mr. Gray has gotten the shaft cover open a few inches. If
he can just get it on the edge of the hole, he'll be able to
slide it away.

182     EXT. ACCESS ROAD - DAY                                    182

Henry, kneeling in the snow by Owen, reaches down and closes
Owen's eyes. Duddits, mimicking, reaches out and puts his hand
over Owen's face; it seems strangely appropriate.

Then Henry does what Owen didn't have time to do: he takes a
fresh banana-clip from Owen's coat and, hands shaking like the
amateur he is, snaps it into the MP5 and pulls back the action.
To Duddits, pointing at the vehicles --

                              HENRY
                    Go back to the car, Duddie. You'll be
                    safer there --

Henry stands, faces the building, takes a breath. He heads off.

183     INT. SHAFT 12 HOUSE, QUABBIN - DAY                        183

Jonesy/Mr. Gray is straining to lift the cover away. We HEAR an
awful sound -- Ike's HOWLING DEATH THROES. And then, CHITTERING.
Jonesy/Mr. Gray looks in that direction.

A newborn SHIT WEASEL writhes into view over the dead body of the
German Shepherd, its body shiny with bloody slime. Its eyes shed
a milky film and their bottomless blackness takes on intelligent
life. It looks at Jonesy/Mr. Gray and starts toward the shaft.

With a smile, Jonesy/Mr. Gray watches the Weasel move toward him.

                         HENRY (O.S.)
                    Look out, Jonesy... or whoever you are.

Jonesy/Mr. Gray looks sharply to the door. As does the Weasel.

Henry's got the MP5 pointed at the Shit Weasel, but when he pulls
the trigger, the gun, <u>set for auto-fire</u>, goes off in a HUGE
BURST, something Henry is not prepared for.

Bullets smash down around the Weasel, but don't hit it. The
Weasel rears up, CHITTERING, and bares its needle-like teeth.

So shocked is Henry by the lightning in his hands, he almost
drops the gun. Finally, he manages to stop firing. In an instant,
the Shit Weasel is attacking, SNAKING in a blur toward Henry.

Henry tries to regain control of his weapon, but his hands are
shaking, his finger can't find the trigger -- and the Weasel is
SHRIEKING and coming on like a rocket.

The Weasel is about ten feet from Henry when it draws its body up
and <u>launches itself into the air</u>.

Henry looks up from his fumbling to see the Weasel flying toward him. Reflexively, he's brought the gun up too. And then it happens, a frozen instant in time:

The Shit Weasel arrives, jaws wide to bite out Henry's throat. What it gets instead is a mouthful of the MP5 muzzle. For one instant, total confusion: the Weasel WRIGGLES to disengage; Henry stares at what he's caught on his line. Henry's finger finds the trigger and a tiny smile flicks across his lips as he FIRES --

The Shit Weasel takes a gullet full of lead and is blown across the room, where it hits the wall with a SPLAT and slides to the floor. A moment later, one last egg comes out its end and rolls a few inches away. Henry and Jonesy are oblivious to this.

Henry stops firing. He looks down at the MP5, uncertain how much ammunition he's got left, then up at Jonesy/Mr. Gray.

Jonesy/Mr. Gray appears to be in convulsion, his body wracked by some violent exorcism. The last wrenching paroxysm heaves him to the floor in a helpless puddle -- hip ruined, bloody, spent -- not so different from his condition after the accident.

Jonesy/Mr. Gray raises his head -- blinking back tears -- and speaks in the perfect voice of Gary Jones.

> JONESY/MR. GRAY
> I knew you'd come, Henry. I knew you
> wouldn't let me die.

Henry isn't sure what to do. Legs shaking, he stumbles back to the support of the wall, holding the gun up as best he can.

> HENRY
> Who the fuck are you?

> JONESY/MR. GRAY
> Don't you know me, H.?

> HENRY
> (honestly)
> I don't know. I think I'm gonna have to
> shoot you, just to be sure.

Jonesy/Mr. Gray's face drops, but into melancholy resignation, not resistance.

> JONESY/MR. GRAY
> Maybe you're right, my friend. I don't
> know myself if Mr. Gray is gone... He
> could be hiding in here somewhere, waiting
> for his chance.

Henry, in agony, sinks to the floor, back against the wall. Now they're looking across the floor at the same level. He doesn't want to kill his friend. He doesn't know what to do. Finally --

                    HENRY
          Tell me something Mr. Gray couldn't
          possibly know. Tell me something only we
          could know...

CLOSE ON Jonesy/Mr. Gray as he lifts his head, hope returning.

                    JONESY/MR. GRAY
          SSDD.

Henry looks at him a long moment.

                    HENRY
          Not good enough.

                    JONESY/MR. GRAY
          You decide. Ask me anything.

                    HENRY
               (long beat)
          At Tracker Brothers... the day we met
          Duddits... what was painted on the wall by
          the window?

Jonesy/Mr. Gray closes his eyes, thinks back, shuffling through thousands of memory files.

Henry raises the barrel of the MP5 directly at the other guy.

                    JONESY/MR. GRAY
               (retrieving it slowly)
          No... bounce... no...

A SHADOW crosses the floor and hits Jonesy/Mr. Gray.

                    DUDDITS (O.S.)
          ...no pway.

Startled, Henry looks up to find Duddits leaning against the doorjamb, his Scooby-Doo lunch box in tow.

                    DUDDITS
          Ello, Ister Gay.

Henry HEARS an EERIE SOUND -- like some interstellar vacuum breaking -- and turns to look across the room.

WHAT HE SEES: Jonesy lies exhausted on the floor, just as before. And that's all he can do, lie there.

But rising above him, a full seven feet tall, is the True Mr. Gray, in all his horror. Except at this moment, it is Mr. Gray who is afraid. The point of his tail, pincer-sharp, moves up between his legs to point at Duddits. He speaks only one word, but it's with an English accent.

                    MR. GRAY
          You.

                    DUDDITS
          Ooby-Ooby-Doo... we ot-sum urk oo-do-now.

Duddits is so weak he can barely remain standing, but he lifts his right hand and points his finger at Mr. Gray.

                    DUDDITS
          Ister Gay... go away.

Mr. Gray steps quickly over Jonesy and heads toward Duddits, baring his teeth and making a ghastly sound.

Jonesy's head snaps around to watch.

Henry is horrified. He lifts the gun in his hands, but when he pulls the trigger, nothing -- empty. WE SEE WHAT HE SEES:

Duddits staggers forward to meet the rush of Mr. Gray -- in our view, he is dwarfed by the giant alien. Duddits' infirm, emaciated shape is completely contained within the outline of the advancing creature.

CLOSE ON DUDDITS' FACE: looking up. No fear, only resolve and concentration. His image is WIPED by the gray mass of Mr. Gray's body, looking and sounding like a freight train.

QUICK CUT: the solitary egg that came out of the Shit Weasel cracks open. A newborn Weasel-worm pokes out.

FROM BEHIND DUDDITS as he is lifted off the floor by what must be Mr. Gray's tail (we can only guess -- it's BELOW FRAME). PUSH PAST HIM into the ghastly maw of the alien, which opens wide with an ear-splitting victory ROAR.

ANGLE DOWN on the black crescent where the manhole cover has been shifted away from the shaft. We HEAR the RUSH OF WATER. TILT UP along the floor behind Jonesy. The Weasel-worm is coming toward us from the distance, headed toward the water.

FLOOR LEVEL: Duddits is slammed down on the hard tiles. He looks about finished. Mr. Gray's legs COME INTO VIEW, straddling Duddits, who looks up --

DUDDITS' POV: a horrifying look up the front of Mr. Gray, whose lethal tail swings into view and rises above us, pincers gathered into a deadly point, poised for the *coup de grace*, as with a medieval broadsword.

Henry reacts, helpless to stop this.

QUICK CUT: the Weasel-worm slides along the floor behind Jonesy's green parka. TILT UP as Jonesy, oblivious, struggles painfully to his feet.

Jonesy's face rises into frame, horrified as he watches the battle.

HIGH SHOT: looking down past Mr. Gray at Duddits. The pincer sword slams down, thrusting into Duddits' chest.

Henry SCREAMS in anguish.

Mr. Gray looks at Henry, as if to say, "You're next." He begins to withdraw his pincers from Duddits, but... something's wrong, they won't come out. Mr. Gray reacts, struggling.

DOWN ON DUDDITS: Something strange is happening to his body where the pincers are imbedded in his chest.  He's changing. His human face is triumphant as he speaks, addressing them all --

                    DUDDITS
          I Duddits!

Duddits reveals his true self, at last. Quickly radiating out from his chest, his whole body changes, becoming a creature much like Mr. Gray... but different.  And whatever force is holding Mr. Gray's pincers now seems to fully meld the two aliens.

TIGHT SHOTS: Mr. Gray writhes in agony, unable to free himself, as the strange energy fills Duddits' alien body and shoots right up Mr. Gray's tail, invading his whole frame.

Mr. Gray is sucked down into Duddits, as if drowning in quicksand. When Duddits has consumed Mr. Gray, their melded bodies implode.

Henry shields his face with his arm.

Jonesy, standing now, must turn away to protect his sight.

The mass that was the two aliens SWIRLS INTO RED BYRUS. Henry's astounded look goes to the spot where Duddits died.  He sees the last of the byrus take the form of the dreamcatcher...then disappear. He SHIFTS HIS GAZE across the room to his friend Jonesy.

HENRY'S POV: Jonesy too has seen this last message from Duddits.

                    JONESY
          H.

                    HENRY
          Jonesy.

EDGE OF THE SHAFT OPENING: the Weasel-worm has reached the
precipice and is about to disappear down the shaft, into the
water below. Its body curls in preparation... hesitates at the
apex and --

SPLATTT! Jonesy's boot smashes the Weasel-worm into pudding.
FLASH TILT UP TO JONESY'S FACE -- satisfaction!

CUT TO BLACK. END MUSIC -- BIG.


                    THE END

# BOOK TO SCRIPT TO FILM
# METAMORPHOSIS

WHEN I READ FICTION, IMAGES OF the characters—how they look and what they say and do as they journey through the landscape of their world—fill my mind. As I watch the events unfold like a movie playing in my head, these images are tangible and supplant my time and reality with their own. The experience is real. This is the magic good fiction inspires. In the novel *Dreamcatcher* Stephen King makes real not only people and places, but also horrific monsters, which come to life with shocking clarity.

Although the images flow easily while reading, the process of turning these words and mental pictures into filmic ones is both challenging and daunting. In adapting a novel to a screenplay, the screenwriter makes the difficult choices that will hopefully transform the story from page to screen, from one art form to another. If the adaptation is successful, the story and the message of the original text will remain vital and true in spirit. It will work despite the loss of characters and events—what at times feels like radical amputations. These sacrifices are necessary to effectively tell the same story in a new way, one that is both concise and compelling.

The collaborative nature of filmmaking often feels like a battleship hurtling through a dark sea at night. With the director at the helm and his crew on board to help manifest his vision, they navigate through this sea of decisions as storyboards are drawn, locations are chosen, and sets are designed and built. Together they move through myriad intricacies necessary to the process. And in this case, there are special complexities as aliens are designed and manufactured both physically and digitally. The actors inhabit the characters, giving them breath, while the camera rolls. Then after months of filming, the metamorphosis is completed with the final editing, scoring, laying in sound effects, finessing and fine-tuning.

In the best of all worlds the magic of the written word is thus transmuted into the wizardry of cinema.

What follows are five scenes from *Dreamcatcher* that show in a nutshell how this particular story progressed from the imagination of Stephen King, through the adaptation by William Goldman and Lawrence Kasdan, and then finally into its realization on film by Lawrence Kasdan and his crew.

—**Elizabeth Dollarhide**, Associate Producer

131

# SCENE: ANIMAL EXODUS

## Q and A with **Stefen Fangmeier**, Visual Effects Supervisor

**Stefen Fangmeier,** won BAFTA Awards for *The Perfect Storm* (2000), *Saving Private Ryan* (1998), and *Twister* (1997). Fangmeier is a member of the extraordinary team at Industrial Light and Magic.

Text from the Stephen King novel (hardcover, page 105) and the corresponding scenes from the screenplay by William Goldman and Lawrence Kasdan *(opposite).*

failed to make Jonesy feel happy, might peg four or six or ten or two fucking dozen. The rule when you played the Duddits Game was that you never complained, never said *Duddits, that's too many* or *Duddits, that's not enough.* And man, they'd laugh. Mr. and Mrs. Cavell, they'd laugh, too, if they happened to be in the room, and Jonesy remembered once, they must have been fifteen, sixteen, and Duddits of course was whatever he was, Duddits Cavell's age was never going to change, that was what was so beautiful and scary about him, and this one time Alfie Cavell had started crying, saying *Boys, if you only knew what this means, to me and to the missus, if you only knew what it means to Douglas—*

"Jonesy." Beaver's voice, oddly flat. Cold air came in through the open kitchen door, raising a rash of gooseflesh on Jonesy's arms.

"Close the door, Beav, was you born in a barn?"

"Come over here. You need to look at this."

Jonesy got up and went to the door. He opened his mouth to say something, then closed it again. The backyard was filled with enough animals to stock a petting zoo. Deer, mostly, a couple of dozen assorted does and bucks. But moving with them were raccoons, waddling woodchucks, and a contingent of squirrels that seemed to move effortlessly along the top of the snow. From around the side of the shed where the Arctic Cat and assorted tools and engine parts were stored, came three large canines Jonesy at first mistook for wolves. Then he saw the old discolored length of clothesline hanging around the neck of one of them and realized they were dogs, probably gone feral. They were all moving east, up the slope from The Gulch. Jonesy saw a pair of good-sized wildcats moving between two little groups of deer and actually rubbed his eyes, as if to clear them of a mirage. The cats were still there. So were the deer, the woodchucks, the coons and squirrels. They moved steadily, barely giving the men in the doorway a glance, but without the panic of creatures running before a fire. Nor was there any smell of fire. The animals were simply moving east, vacating the area.

"Holy Christ, Beav," Jonesy said in a low, awed voice.

Beaver had been looking up. Now he gave the animals a quick, cursory glance and lifted his gaze to the sky again. "Yeah. Now look up there."

---

*When you first read the script, how did you think this scene could be accomplished?*

It was clear to me that this scene could be very difficult and expensive to execute if it couldn't be laid out in a way that would allow us to use real animals. Computer-generated animals could have been an option. However, they would have been costly to create and animate, especially since there would have to be a fair number of different animals, as the script described this scene as "the biggest animal parade since the Ark."

                    BEAVER
          Radiation would explain those nu-cular
          farts he's got...

                    JONESY
               (stands up)
          Beaver...

Beaver looks up at him, then turns to look. Whispering --

                    BEAVER
          Criminettlies...

40    **EXT. PICTURE WINDOW, HOLE IN THE WALL - DAY**        40

      **We're LOOKING IN at the two friends as they come to stand at the
      window. But WHAT WE NOTICE is the <u>reflection in the window</u> of the
      ANIMAL EXODUS that's happening outside in the snowstorm.**

41    **INT. PICTURE WINDOW, HOLE IN THE WALL - DAY**        41

      **FROM INSIDE, over the friends, we SEE the biggest animal parade
      since the Ark. Deer, raccoons, woodchucks, squirrels... and,
      right along with them, bears and wildcats. Animals that usually
      attack each other. None of the animals pays any attention to the
      others. They just keep moving quickly in the same direction. A
      lot have <u>red-gold moss on their fur</u> -- like on McCarthy's cheek.**

42    EXT. SCOUT WRECK, DEEP CUT ROAD - DAY                  42

      Henry and Pete are finally up to making a move. Henry helps Pete
      up and they hobble toward the woman in the road.

                    PETE
          I ought to warn you -- when we get up
          there, I'm gonna strangle this broad.

                    HENRY
          If I had to guess, I'd say she's dead.

                    PETE
          I don't care... I'll strangle her anyway.
          She almost got us both killed.

---

*What other options were discussed?*

Visual effects co-supervisor Tim Alexander and I discussed a few options for shooting the various animals in separate passes that could be composited into the outdoor scene shoot on location. We quickly
determined that using a motion-control camera rig would be too costly and time-consuming. So we
decided to work with director of photography John Seale during the shoot in order to photograph all
elements for the shots in a manner that would make them relatively easy to combine.

SNOW FALLING

EXT./INT. CABIN: WE SEE BEAVER & JONESY THRU ⑥
REFLECTION OF ANIMALS IN WINDOW: PUSH
IN AS THEY APPROACH

NOTE: CAMERA ANGLE SHOULD
BE MORE OBLIQUE RELATIVE
TO WINDOW; ALSO, MORE
INTERIOR CABIN DETAILS
SHOULD BE VISIBLE

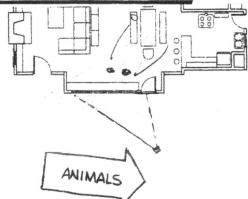

ANIMALS

Storyboard of the Animal Exodus scene showing Beaver and Jonesy looking out the window.

---

***How was the scene shot? Describe the process both exterior and blue-screen.***

The scene was shot in various passes. First up was all of the exterior photography on location in Prince George. This would provide the landscape seen from inside the cabin through its picture window. The cabin location also provided all the reverse angles that showed Jonesy and Beaver coming out of the cabin with animals passing between them and the camera. Tim Alexander worked with the animal trainer and the second unit crew at this location to capture several passes of animals running through the snowy landscape from the various camera angles. When principal photography moved to the stages in

134

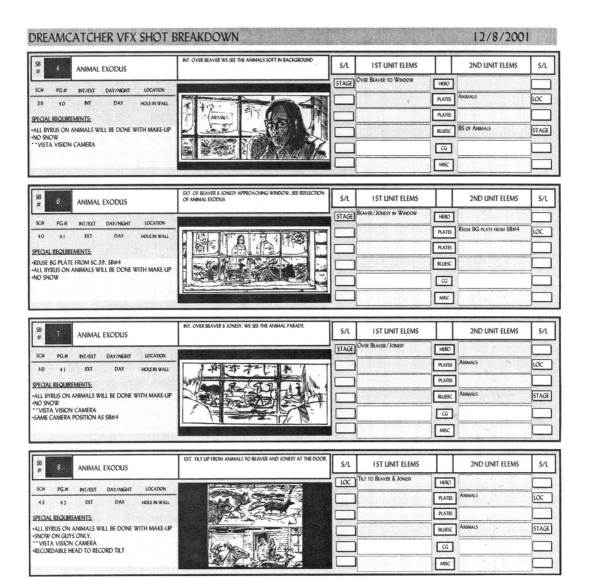

Breakdown sheet of individual special effects shots.

Vancouver, Tim spent another two days on a blue-screen stage again working with second unit and the animal trainer to shoot even more passes of a greater number of animals.

The last group of elements were the shots with Jonesy and Beaver inside the cabin set on stage that were shot with a blue screen outside the window. The camera angles were initially defined during the exterior shoot in Prince George and carefully reproduced during the subsequent shoots in Vancouver. In order to make the tracking of these numerous elements for each shot feasible, the camera setups were limited to lock-offs and pan-tilt movements.

**Damian Lewis** and **Jason Lee**, in the cabin interior on a stage in Vancouver, looked out at a blue screen, which ILM replaced with a composite of the woods outside the cabin exterior 500 miles away, plus multiple passes of animals and snow and haze elements. (The mountain lion would be unusual but not impossible in the Maine woods, and its beauty couldn't be resisted.)

*How did you complete the scene? Describe the process.*

Once Larry and his editorial team selected the plates of the actors and those POVs of the exterior snowy landscape outside the cabin for the cut of the sequence, they were scanned in at ILM along with all the other elements that would be composited into these shots.

Tim then supervised the selection and compositing of these secondary elements, layering more and more animals until Larry liked the population for each angle. Many of the shots turned into very com-

**Jason Lee** and **Damian Lewis** outside the exterior shell of the cabin in Prince George. Here the trees are part of the original scene, but the animals were filmed later in painstaking multiple passes: deer close, middle distance, far; rabbits on similar tracks; and so on for each species.

plex composites with a great number of layers and difficult blue-screen extractions. Computer-generated snow elements were added as well as hazing that increased with distance away from the camera to achieve the proper feel of a snowstorm as one might experience it in the woods of Maine. Once the levels of all these elements were adjusted properly across the scene, the shots created a magical, slightly surreal feeling of a very unusual event that was yet entirely based in nature.

# SCENE: MEMORY WAREHOUSE

## Q and A with **Jon Hutman**, Production Designer

Production designer
**Jon Hutman**
*(French Kiss)* won an
Emmy for *The West
Wing.*

Selected text from
the novel (hardcov-
er, pages 331–33)
and the correspon-
ding scenes from the
screenplay *(opposite)*.

Outside the dingy office was a room so vast Jonesy couldn't see the end of it. Overhead were endless acres of fluorescent bars. Beneath them, stacked in enormous columns, were millions of cardboard boxes.

*No,* Jonesy thought. *Not millions. Trillions.*

Yes, probably trillions was closer. Thousands of narrow aisles ran between them. He was standing at one edge of eternity's own warehouse, and the idea of finding anything in it was ludicrous. If he ventured away from the door into his office hideout, he would become lost in no time. Mr. Gray wouldn't need to bother with him; Jonesy would wander until he died, lost in a mind-boggling wasteland of stored boxes.

*That's not true. I could no more get lost in there than I could in my own bedroom. Nor will I have to hunt for what I want. This is my place. Welcome to your own head, big boy.*

• • •

When he had first looked out at this enormous storeroom, all the boxes had been plain and unmarked. Now he saw that those at the head of the row closest to him were labeled in black grease-pencil: DUDDITS. Was that surprising? Fortuitous? Not at all. They were *his* memories, after all, stored flat and neatly folded in each of the trillions of boxes, and when it came to memory, the healthy mind was able to access them pretty much at will.

*Need something to move them with,* Jonesy thought, and when he looked around he was not exactly amazed to see a bright red hand-dolly. This was a magic place, a make-it-up-as-you-go-along place, and the most marvelous thing about it, Jonesy supposed, was that everybody had one.

Moving quickly, he stacked some of the boxes marked DUDDITS on the dolly and ran them into the Tracker Brothers office at a trot. He dumped them by tipping the dolly forward, spilling them across the floor. Untidy, but he could worry about the Good Housekeeping Seal of Approval later.

---

*How did the description in the book and in the screenplay of the Memory Warehouse translate into the initial designs?*

The key conceptual challenge of the Memory Warehouse was to come up with a physical representation of the interior of Jonesy's mind. Jonesy's body becomes the unwilling host to the alien villain, Mr. Gray. The Memory Warehouse becomes the setting within which Jonesy struggles to resist Mr. Gray's attempt to take control of his mind as well.

Stephen King describes the Memory Warehouse as a sort of infinite storehouse contained within the familiar confines of the Tracker Brothers' warehouse—the abandoned factory where the four friends first met Duddits. King's notion of infinity is linear:

This vast storage facility has a funky, burnished quality, like
some aging, Victorian library. The overall design is circular --
level upon level of overloaded stacks spiraling up into the
gloom. It's so impossibly big and crowded and baroque, it could
only exist in a dream, or in someone's imagination.

TIGHT SHOT, somewhere in the stacks, of several aging file boxes
labeled *"ROCK 'N ROLL LYRICS -- Real and Mis-remembered."*

Jonesy, as he is today, minus the limp, is barely glimpsed as he
loads the files on a dolly. In their place, he stacks a new box
labeled *"APPLE G3 Laptop -- how the damn thing works."*

                         •   •   •

99      INT. STACKS, MEMORY WAREHOUSE                          99

Jonesy comes out of his office into the vast facility. He looks
up <u>at the shelves two levels up</u>, grabs one of the big dollies and
starts limping toward the ramp as fast as he can.

                         •   •   •

101     INT. THIRD LEVEL, MEMORY WAREHOUSE                    101

Jonesy hoists the numerous file boxes marked **"DUDDITS"** onto the
dolly. He's gasping by the time he's got them all, but there's no
time to rest -- he shoves the heavy dolly toward the ramp.

102     INT. MEMORY WAREHOUSE                                 102

Jonesy is on the down ramp, but the dolly's so heavy, he can
barely control it; his hip aches, his feet slide. Another level
to descend. The door to his office below seems a long way off.

                         •   •   •

104     INT. MEMORY WAREHOUSE                                 104

ON THE OFFICE LEVEL OF THE MEMORY WAREHOUSE, Jonesy is sweating
profusely as he pushes his burden toward the office. He HEARS a
DOOR SLAM. His head whips around to look across the warehouse.

WHAT JONESY SEES: the main entrance door is still RATTLING to a
stop. FLASH PAN through the stacks -- a GLIMPSE of <u>the horrible
True Mr. Gray</u> as he flashes by an opening, <u>coming this way</u>!

Jonesy pushes the dolly with everything he's got. He's close now.

---

"Outside the dingy office was a room so vast Jonesy couldn't see the end of it. Overhead were endless acres of fluorescent bars. Beneath them, stacked in enormous columns, were millions of cardboard boxes....Thousands of narrow aisles ran between them. He was standing at one edge of eternity's own warehouse."

Larry and I came up with a circular notion of infinity—radial, spiraling, like a nautilus shell. The final design (as translated and executed by art director Steve Graham and assistant art director Marion Kolsby) ended up as a synthesis between the stacks of a library (Jonesy is an academic) and an industrial warehouse (Tracker Brothers).

4

From the first, the storyboards indicated an alternation of close-ups of Jonesy with wide shots of the set, but drawings like number six were adjusted after the design of the warehouse was decided.

5

(*Opposite*) From plan to set, here seen with the actual lights used in filming the core, as opposed to the elegant skylight ILM laid in later.

Finally, production designer **Jon Hutman** checks the set dressing, as first assistant director Steve Dunn looks on.

OFFICE

6

TRK. JONSEY POV

2ND UNIT

### What action in the screenplay determined aspects of the design?

The key action sequence that takes place in the Memory Warehouse is Mr. Gray's pursuit of Jonesy, who is racing to secure his Duddits memory files behind the locked door of the warehouse office. Larry and I conceived the Memory Warehouse as an infinite stack of endless rows of bookshelves, built around a circular central core. A spiral ramp wraps around the perimeter of this core, connecting the various levels.

The design of the set evolved in response to the choreography of the chase scene: Where is Jonesy when he hears Mr. Gray? Where is Jonesy when he sees Mr. Gray? What obstacles can we put in the way of Mr. Gray?

The symmetry of the set allowed us to cheat a few extra laps around the spiral ramp, concealing the fact that the entire set was only thirty feet tall! (Special thanks due here to John Seale and his wide-angle lenses, as well as a couple of discreet set extensions by our friends at ILM.)

***Once the design was decided, what was involved in making the set? How was it constructed?***
The set was constructed (by Doug Hardwick and his team of metal magicians) like a giant erector set. The entire three-story spiral ramp was prefabricated as a free-standing structure and assembled in pieces on the soundstage.

The shelves which surround the ramp were similarly prefabricated and assembled in place with the decorative railings, rivets, and architectural details applied in place.

Director of photography **John Seale**, production designer **Jon Hutman**, director **Lawrence Kasdan**, and first assistant director **Steve Dunn** plan a shot in the completed set.

**Damian Lewis** (Jonesy) discarding old memories *(opposite)* and racing to hide sensitive ones from Mr. Gray *(right)*.

*What was the inspiration for the set dressing and how challenging did you find it to do?*

The set dressing (courtesy of Rose Marie McSherry and her crew of paper bundlers) was all crafted by hand. Our desire was to create a storehouse of memories, mementoes, and experiences—both vast and varied. Rather than the endless rows of file boxes that King describes in the novel, we strove for the quality of the world's biggest attic—crammed full of things that have fallen into disuse, but too precious to throw away.

I hate to admit that our inspiration and model for the dressing came from another movie—the first *Harry Potter*. I thought that the wand shop at Diagon Alley was a perfect model for our Memory Warehouse. There was a tremendous variety of specific individual boxes, and yet as a mass, they blended into a dense, even texture. While the contents of the shelves appeared to be rather crammed and chaotic, there seemed to be an underlying sense of logic and order—the kind that could only be navigated and decoded by the singular hand that created it.

This seemed an apt metaphor for the storehouse of Jonesy's memories—a rich, dense texture of specific details, unified by an indecipherable pattern of disorder.

# SCENE: LOGGERS' SHELTER

## Q and A with **Lawrence Kasdan**

Director **Lawrence Kasdan** has directed ten films, including *Body Heat, The Big Chill, Grand Canyon,* and *Mumford*, and has written or co-written four of the most successful pictures in motion-picture history (*Raiders of the Lost Ark, The Empire Strikes Back, Return of the Jedi,* and *The Bodyguard*).

Text from the novel (hardcover, page 195) and the corresponding scene from the screenplay *(opposite).*

Pete looked into the woods. Nothing. The flood of animals had dried up. He was alone.

*Except I'm not.*

No, he wasn't. Something was out there, something that didn't do well in the cold, something that preferred warm, wet places. Except—

*Except it got too big. And it ran out of food.*

"Are you out there?"

Pete thought that calling out like that would make him feel foolish, but it didn't. What it made him feel was more frightened than ever.

His eye fastened on a sketchy track of that mildewy stuff. It stretched away from Becky—yeah, she was a Becky, all right, as Becky as Becky could be—and around the corner of the lean-to. A moment later Pete heard a scaly scraping sound as something slithered on the tin roof. He craned up, following the sound with his eyes.

"Go away," he whispered. "Go away and leave me alone. I . . . I'm fucked up."

There was another brief slither as the thing moved farther up the tin. Yes, he was fucked up. Unfortunately, he was also food. The thing up there slithered again. Pete didn't think it would wait long, maybe *couldn't* wait long, not up there; it would be like a gecko in a refrigerator. What it was going to do was drop on him. And now he realized a terrible thing: he had gotten so fixated on the beer that he had forgotten the fucking guns.

His first impulse was to crawl deeper into the lean-to, but that might be a mistake, like running into a blind alley. He grabbed the jutting end of one of the fresh branches he'd just put on the fire instead. He didn't take it out, not yet, just made a loose fist around it. The other end was burning briskly. "Come on," he said to the tin roof. "You like it hot? I've got something hot for you. Come on and get it. Yum-fuckin-yum."

Nothing. Not from the roof, anyway. There was a soft *flump* of snow falling from one of the pines behind him as the lower branches shed their burden. Pete's hand tightened on his makeshift torch, half-lifting it from the fire. Then he let it settle back in a little swirl of sparks. "Come on, motherfucker. I'm hot, I'm tasty, and I'm waiting."

Nothing. But it was up there. It couldn't wait long, he was sure of it. Soon it would come.

---

*In the book, the shit weasel is on the roof of the loggers' shelter. Why did you decide to place it in the snow berm? In the film, the scene is very creepy because the audience knows what Pete does not—that the shit weasel is coming to get him. What was involved in creating the effect?*

It was obvious that the movie should use the great scene in the book when Pete, left alone at an abandoned loggers' shelter, battles a shit weasel. At this point in the film, another shit weasel would already have had a big introduction in the bathroom, and its terrible capabilities would have been demonstrated in the attack on Beaver. That gave me the freedom to pursue a really delicious idea: We could see the weasel's path toward Pete only as an ominous, moving bulge in the snow. Naturally, that meant bringing the weasel down off the roof of the shelter and onto the ground.

WIDE SHOT, snow falling on the lovely woods. In the distance, Pete sits by the fire, apparently in conversation with someone.

AT THE FIRE. Pete is pretty sloshed. Lots of empties around. He throws some more wood on the fire.

PETE'S POV: the leaping flames, and through them, Becky, apparently in blissful sleep.

> PETE
> ... well, it's very nice of you to say so. I find you very attractive, also. I have the feeling you're one of those rare women who could handle the full-size Ford Expedition, 'the truck that handles like a luxury car'... a <u>really big</u> luxury car...
>      (laughs, losing it)
> ... but seriously, folks, there is one issue I'd like to bring up, just in case I should, you know, kick the bucket out here... turn into a goddamn Petesicle... not that I think that's inevitable...

IN THE SNOWBANK behind Pete, we SEE that <u>something is moving under the snow</u>, creating a raised, moving map of its progress toward Pete's back. Pete takes a final swig and flips the empty over his shoulder into the snowbank -- <u>the moving bulge stops</u>.

> PETE
> ... I'm sure Henry or Jonesy or Beaver will be coming to get us soon. They're my friends, see, we're all best friends, and friends don't let each other down...

The bulge in the snow starts moving toward Pete again.

> PETE
> ... which relates to what I wanted to mention here... Now, ma'am, don't get freaked out or think I'm some kind of weirdo who you shouldn't meet for the best fried clams in Maine -- just some <u>innocent</u>

---

The advantages of this idea kept revealing themselves. If Pete didn't know that Becky was dead and went on with his monologue to her, but the audience knew a shit weasel had come out of her into the snow and was creeping up behind Pete—well, the potential for suspense was terrific. And so was the chance to do a little comedy in the midst of the terror, by having Pete's discarded beer bottle momentarily stop and divert the unseen shit weasel. But after such an elaborate build-up, the reveal of the weasel to Pete would have to be good, and the attack different from Beaver's scene. That train of thought produced the image of Pete peeing in the snow and uncovering the weasel, which would then strike him in the exposed area.

So much for dreaming up the ideal scene. Getting it on film was hard work for everybody. We had decided that the loggers' shelter was going to be a set on a stage in Vancouver; nobody wanted to try all

Pete looks around at his surroundings...

Pete takes a final swig from his beer... THE WEASEL, BURIED UNDER THE SNOW, MOVES DOWN THE SNOW BANK...

The first step from words to pictures: the storyboards.

that complicated effects work in the snowy woods outside Prince George as the brief winter daylight ran out. Jon Hutman, our production designer, and his crew built an amazingly convincing set of the shelter and the surrounding woods, and cinematographer John Seale devised a lighting scheme that produced an uncanny likeness of the gray overcast in a snowstorm. The practical special effects team, led by Bill Orr, covered everything in artificial snow, which looked great but produced so much fine dust that we all worked for more than a week in painters' masks.

The working part of the set was the snowbank or berm facing the shelter, against which Pete would sit and over which the weasel would approach. Shaped like a boomerang and built in movable ("wild") sections, it had an opening near one end through which the puppeteers could launch the shit weasel. (In

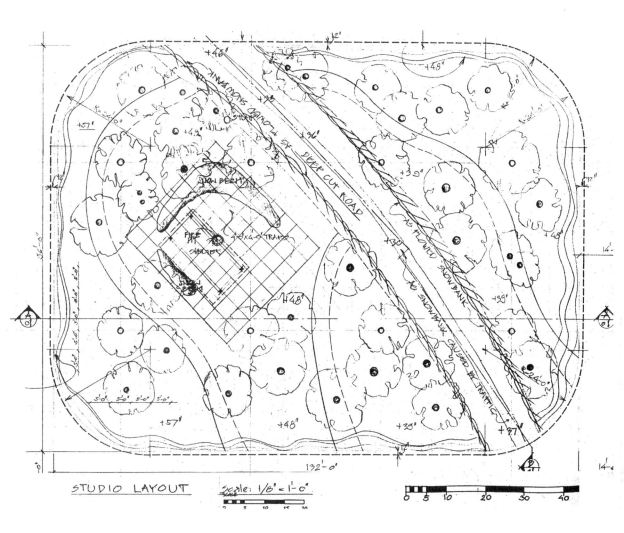

STUDIO LAYOUT     Scale: 1/8" = 1'-0"

The plan of the Loggers' Shelter set, which was built on a stage in Vancouver but had to cut seamlessly into scenes shot in the woods outside Prince George. The critical berm is the boomerang-shaped piece at the top of the gridded area.

the finished scene, the weasel is sometimes a puppet, with the rods and wires optically removed later, and sometimes an identical computer-generated image.)

A good deal of experimentation went into finding the right materials to cover the berm. The bulge of the advancing weasel had to show up distinctly and yet not crack or shift unnaturally. In the end, a precise thickness of a second kind of artificial snow was laid over a white sheet or "snow blanket."

The greatest challenge was simulating the weasel's distinctive zigzag movement while advancing it along exactly the right path toward Pete's back. Orr and company built a curving groove in the top of the berm and pulled a wooden model of the weasel's body through it, geared to zig and zag as it rolled. The whole thing looked like a toddler's pull-toy, but after much adjustment, it did the trick.

**Timothy Olyphant** worked day after day at the loggers' shelter, doing first Pete's bemused, tipsy monologue, then his life-or-death battle with a shit weasel. The weasel was sometimes a cumbersome puppet attached to the actor, and sometimes wasn't there at all (it would be added digitally later), but the desperate mood had to be maintained throughout.

Then there was getting a beer bottle that Timothy Olyphant, playing Pete, tossed over his shoulder to land just in front of the buried weasel. The special effects people built an ingenious, ski-jump-like chute on the roof of the shelter and sailed bottle after bottle through the air and onto the berm. But the ballistics defeated us. What finally worked was having one man catch in a long-handled net the bottle Timothy tossed, while another man, above the frame, dropped an identical bottle straight down into the "snow."

The crew swarms over the loggers' shelter set, some in painters' masks against dust from the artificial snow. Note the grid of lights that simulated the even illumination of winter overcast.

I could go on about simulating Pete's peeing Duddits' name in the snow, and about getting all the other shots for his battle with the weasel, but you get the idea. And beyond that, there was still the work of post-production: editing the picture, adding the sound effects, laying in James Newton Howard's score. But it will all be worth it if the audience, caught between screaming and laughing, has a good time.

# SCENE: JONESY'S ACCIDENT

## Q and A with **Charles Okun**, Producer

Producer **Charles Okun** has worked with director Lawrence Kasdan on nine films. He produced *Mumford, Grand Canyon*, and *The Accidental Tourist*, and was executive producer on *Silverado, I Love You to Death, Wyatt Earp*, and *French Kiss*.

Text from the novel (hardcover, pages 46 and 272) and the corresponding scene from the screenplay *(opposite)*.

In mid-March of 2001, Jonesy had been struck by a car while crossing a street in Cambridge, not far from John Jay College, where he taught. He had fractured his skull, broken two ribs, and suffered a shattered hip, which had been replaced with some exotic combination of Teflon and metal. The man who'd struck him was a retired BU history professor who was—according to his lawyer, anyway—in the early stages of Alzheimer's, more to be pitied than punished. So often, Jonesy thought, there was no one to blame when the dust cleared. And even if there was, what good did it do? You still had to live with what was left, and console yourself with the fact that, as people told him every day (until they forgot the whole thing, that was), it could have been worse.

And it could have been. His head was hard, and the crack in it healed. He had no memory of the hour or so leading up to his accident near Harvard Square, but the rest of his mental equipment was fine. His ribs healed in a month. The hip was the worst, but he was off the crutches by October, and now his limp only became appreciable toward the end of the day.

• • •

"What?" he says, and the man who has stopped beside him, the first one to bend over him in a past which now may be blessedly cancelled, looks at him suspiciously and says *"I didn't say anything,"* as though there might be a third with them. Jonesy barely hears him because there *is* a third, there is a voice inside him, one which sounds suspiciously like his own, and it's screaming at him to stay on the curb, to stay out of the street—

• • •

Sunlight twinkles on a windshield; he sees this in the corner of his left eye. A car coming, and too fast. The man who was beside him on the curb, old Mr. *I*-Didn't-Say-Anything, cries out: "Watch it, guy, watch it!" but Jonesy barely hears him.

---

*How did the description in the book and in the screenplay of Jonesy's Accident translate into the initial designs?*
The location was chosen to reflect the run-down urban setting of the college in Boston where Jonesy teaches. The street needed to be wide enough to have two lanes of traffic in each direction, with a crosswalk in the middle of the block.

Jonesy, hurrying along a busy Boston sidewalk. He comes to a major street and stops at the crosswalk. Lots of traffic. Jonesy flinches, then turns to the STRANGER next to him.

                    JONESY
          What'd you say?

                    STRANGER
          I didn't say anything.

                    JONESY
          Right. Sorry.

PUSH IN as he tries to shake a weird feeling. Then, stunned, he stares at something across the street <u>which we don't see</u> --

-- and suddenly he plunges into the street.

This big old clunker of a car, an ANCIENT MAN at the wheel, driving way too fast, SMASHES INTO JONESY. He spins crazily in the air, then crashes down onto the pavement. As his SCREAMING gets louder and louder --

JONESY'S POV: A CROWD OF PEOPLE around him, but he's having trouble looking up, so <u>what he's seeing mainly is their shoes</u>.

Someone is saying, "Get a cell phone, call an ambulance!", and an OLD WOMAN replies, "It won't do any good." And now the ANCIENT MAN who hit him pushes his way through the crowd. Jonesy can see his antique brown wingtips --

                    ANCIENT MAN (O.S.)
               (early Alzheimer's)
          I looked away for one second and then I
          heard a thump... What happened?

Jonesy sees something he recognizes: a pair of tattered, black and white Converse sneakers have worked their way forward.

                    DEFUNIAK (O.S.)
               (distraught)
          Omigod, that's Prof. Jones! He can't die.

---

*What action in the screenplay determined aspects of the design?*

The area of Vancouver where this scene was shot was actually a little too run-down for the area of Boston where we wanted to set our college. We changed the name of the pawn shop across the street from San Francisco to something New-Englandy (Liberty), and we spruced up the theater marquee where Jonesy waits at the crosswalk to make it look like a nightclub. We installed those wonderful chaser lights that you see behind him. We also made our own "Walk/Don't Walk" signs at the crosswalk so that we could control them on cue.

3C

continuous, as Jonesy walks across frame

3D

continuous DOLLY AROUND stranger as he reacts...

DOLLY

Perhaps the most extensively used storyboards of the film. From these drawings of the director's conception of the accident flowed choice of location, camera move, stunt rigging, green screen placement, and sequencing of vehicles.

---

### Once the design was decided, what was involved in making the set? How was it constructed?

The accident was shot in two pieces which were composited together. First a car drives into frame and screeches to a halt (with no one in front of it). Then a stuntman walks into the street, and is yanked out of frame by a cable (in front of a green screen). When these two pieces of film are put together, you see the car screeching to a stop and (apparently) hitting the body which flies into the air at the moment of "impact."

Larry conceived this sequence as a single shot, so the whole thing had to be very carefully choreographed. There is a moment when Damian (the actor playing Jonesy) steps out of frame, and is replaced by the stuntman.

3E

continuous, DOLLY BEHIND STRANGER and
Jonesy as he walks across PUSH DOLLY PUSH toward
street...

3F

continuous, as CAR SMASHES INTO JONESY...

3G

continuous...

**Damian Lewis** (Jonesy) lies in a real street wearing fake blood and an elaborate appliance simulating a smashed hip. *(Inset)* The stuntman doubling Damian Lewis warms up before being yanked violently out of frame by a cable and landing on a pile of gymnastics pads.

*What was the inspiration for the set dressing and how challenging did you find it to do?*
Our access to this location was extremely limited. Because Hastings Street is a major thoroughfare, we could not control the street until 7:00 p.m. Because it is a night scene, we had to finish before the sun came up. Of course the individual technical elements had been rigged and rehearsed well in advance, but the careful timing and integration of all of the separate elements could only be truly synchronized on the spot.

First assistant director **Steve Dunn** and producer **Charles Okun** *(inset)* had overall responsibility for the location on Vancouver's Hastings Street, which included an elaborate crane-dolly camera mount *(top)* and a large green screen *(bottom)*.

# SCENE: SCOUT CRASH

## Q and A with **E. J. Foerster**, 2nd Unit Director

**E. J. Foerster,** the second unit director, directed the stunts in *Dreamcatcher.*

Text from the novel (hardcover, pages 85-86) and the corresponding scene from the screenplay *(opposite).*

*"Look out!"* Pete shouted, and Henry snapped his gaze back to the windshield.

The Scout had just topped the steep rise of a tree-covered ridge. The snow here was thicker than ever, but Henry was running with the high beams on and clearly saw the person sitting in the road about a hundred feet ahead—a person wearing a duffel coat, an orange vest that blew backward like Superman's cape in the strengthening wind, and one of those Russian fur hats. Orange ribbons had been attached to the hat, and they also blew back in the wind, reminding Henry of the streamers you sometimes saw strung over used-car lots. The guy was sitting in the middle of the road like an Indian that wants to smoke-um peace pipe, and he did not move when the headlights struck him. For one moment Henry saw the sitting figure's eyes, wide open but still, so still and bright and blank, and he thought: *That's how my eyes would look if I didn't guard them so closely.*

There was no time to stop, not with the snow. Henry twisted the wheel to the right and felt the thump as the Scout came out of the ruts again. He caught another glimpse of the white, still face and had time to think, *Why, goddam! It's a woman.*

Once out of the ruts the Scout began to skid again at once. This time Henry turned against it, deliberately snowplowing the wheels to deepen the skid, knowing without even thinking about it (there was no time to think) that it was the road-sitter's only chance. And he didn't rate it much of one, at that.

Pete screamed, and from the corner of his eye, Henry saw him raise his hands in front of his face, palms out in a warding-off gesture. The Scout tried to go broadside and *now* Henry spun the wheel back, trying to control the skid just enough so that the rear end wouldn't smash the road-sitter's face backward into her skull. The wheel spun with greasy, giddy ease under his gloved hands. For perhaps three seconds the Scout shot down the snow-covered Deep Cut Road at a forty-five-degree angle, a thing belonging partly to Henry Devlin and partly to the storm.

---

*How did you and Larry decide on what the crash should look like?*

When I first met Larry to talk about the Scout Crash sequence, he was absolutely clear on how he wanted this event to feel. "Pete and Henry are driving in the middle of the dense forest on a logging road, during a snowstorm, it's beautiful, almost serene…and then it happens, it's violent!" he explained. I understood he wanted to go for the contrast between the calm of one moment and the adrenaline of another. "I don't want this to feel like a stunt," he said. "It should catch us off guard, and put us in that surreal moment that happens when we are in an accident." Having had my fair share of winter driving accidents, I knew exactly what we were going for.

Henry, driving through the storm, Pete alongside, with beer.

>                    PETE
>           You want a beer?

>                    HENRY
>           Later.

Pete chugs his beer, then points up ahead -- a steep hill.

>                    PETE
>           Better get a run at it.

Henry guns the gas, squints to see. The Scout takes the hill with
no problem. As they fly over the crest, Pete's eyes go wide --

>                    PETE
>           Watch it!

>                    HENRY
>           I see him!

A man is sitting in the center of the road, a hundred feet down
the slope of the hill. Just sitting there, like a serene Buddha.
The headlights flood him. The guy does not move an inch.

Henry twists the wheel to the right. The Scout's tires fight to
get out of the deep ruts. Still no movement from the man in the
road as the car rushes closer and starts to SKID broadside.

Pete braces his hands on the dashboard. Henry fights the car,
turning the wheel the other way now.

FROM BEHIND the man in the road: the Scout skidding toward us,
about to obliterate this guy.

Henry gets a close-up view out his side window and reacts in
surprise -- it's a woman. Her hooded face flashes by Henry's
window as the Scout misses her by inches.

FROM OVERHEAD we SEE the Scout slide by her, practically taking

---

*How difficult was it to do? Describe the process.*

The location for "Deep Cut Road" was exactly that. We had actually cut a road out of a section of forest in Prince George, B.C. Jon Hutman, the designer, and Larry did a great job in engineering the road so it had enough curves, bends, and rises to work with. I set up the initial driving shots with wide angles and aerials to show the loneliness of the Scout driving amidst this vast snow-covered forest. When the Scout crests the hill, I added a small snowdrift for the Scout to crash through to momentarily obliterate Pete and Henry's view of the road. As the windshield wipers reveal their POV, we see the woman sitting in the middle of the road and all hell breaks loose. The near-miss shots were very important to me because I wanted the Scout to miss the woman in the road so close that it would put you back in your

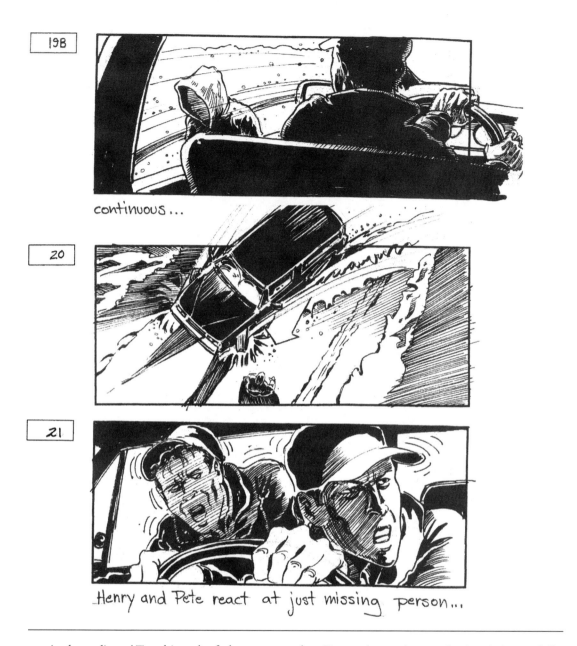

198

continuous...

20

21

Henry and Pete react at just missing person...

seat in the audience! To achieve the feel, we mounted an Eyemo (camera) on a pivoting 4x4 on a dolly. As the stunt driver turned into the skid, we dollied right revealing the woman's back. The Scout hit the marks perfectly and it's right in your face.

**How much is luck an element in stunts like this? How exactly can you predict the results?**
Shooting the actual "Scout Flip" was a little nerve-racking as we only had one Scout to use for the "Flip" itself, which meant I could only count on one take! We found a nice section of road with a larger open space at the end to dress with small trees and sprigs that would break during impact. A

| SB # 6 | SCOUT FLIPS | POV OUT WINDSHIELD OF BECKY IN ROAD (BOARDS 6 & 13) | | S/L | 1ST UNIT ELEMS | | 2ND UNIT ELEMS | S/L |
|---|---|---|---|---|---|---|---|---|
| SC# 38 | PG.# 38 | INT/EXT EXT | DAY/NIGHT DAY | LOCATION DEEP CUT ROAD | | | HERO | SCOUT, BECKY DUMMY (OR ACTOR) | LOC |
| | | | | | | PLATES | | |
| SPECIAL REQUIREMENTS: | | | | | | PLATES | | |
| •SNOW NEEDED FOR ENTIRE SEQUENCE | | | | | | BLUESC | | |
| •PROSTHETIC BECKY DUMMY (OR ACTOR) | | | | | | CG | | |
| | | | | | | MISC | | |

| SB # 17 | SCOUT FLIPS | OVER BECKY TO SCOUT SLIDING INCHES FROM HER | | S/L | 1ST UNIT ELEMS | | 2ND UNIT ELEMS | S/L |
|---|---|---|---|---|---|---|---|---|
| SC# 38 | PG.# 38 | INT/EXT EXT | DAY/NIGHT DAY | LOCATION DEEP CUT ROAD | | | HERO | SCOUT, BECKY DUMMY (OR ACTOR) | LOC |
| | | | | | | PLATES | | |
| SPECIAL REQUIREMENTS: | | | | | | PLATES | | |
| •SNOW NEEDED FOR ENTIRE SEQUENCE | | | | | | BLUESC | | |
| •PROSTHETIC BECKY DUMMY (OR ACTOR) | | | | | | CG | | |
| | | | | | | MISC | | |

| SB # 19 | SCOUT FLIPS | OVER HENRY TO BECKY AS THEY SLIDE BY | | S/L | 1ST UNIT ELEMS | | 2ND UNIT ELEMS | S/L |
|---|---|---|---|---|---|---|---|---|
| SC# 38 | PG.# 38 | INT/EXT EXT | DAY/NIGHT DAY | LOCATION DEEP CUT ROAD | | | HERO | SCOUT, BECKY DUMMY (OR ACTOR) | LOC |
| | | | | | | PLATES | | |
| SPECIAL REQUIREMENTS: | | | | | | PLATES | | |
| •SNOW NEEDED FOR ENTIRE SEQUENCE | | | | | | BLUESC | | |
| •PROSTHETIC BECKY DUMMY (OR ACTOR) | | | | | | CG | | |
| | | | | | | MISC | | |

| SB # 20 | SCOUT FLIPS | FROM OVERHEAD WE SEE THE SCOUT SLIDE BY BECKY | | S/L | 1ST UNIT ELEMS | | 2ND UNIT ELEMS | S/L |
|---|---|---|---|---|---|---|---|---|
| SC# 38 | PG.# 38 | INT/EXT EXT | DAY/NIGHT DAY | LOCATION DEEP CUT ROAD | | | HERO | SCOUT, BECKY DUMMY (OR ACTOR) | LOC |
| | | | | | | PLATES | | |
| SPECIAL REQUIREMENTS: | | | | | | PLATES | | |
| •SNOW NEEDED FOR ENTIRE SEQUENCE | | | | | | BLUESC | | |
| •PROSTHETIC BECKY DUMMY (OR ACTOR) | | | | | | CG | | |
| | | | | | | MISC | | |

The original storyboards were refined, elaborated, and integrated into the shot breakdown. With such detailed planning—and an investment of time the first unit could not afford—the second unit made each shot as effective as possible. And did it safely.

one-wheel car ramp was placed at the end of the run-in to initiate the Scout to flip. For story point and to help the Scout use its momentum to flip, a large tree trunk was placed to the right of the ramp so the front right tire would dig in. I used my psychic handicapping powers to approximate where the first impact would be, and positioned the trusty Eyemo to get the shot. We lensed three other camera angles including one mounted in the back seat for Pete and Henry's "trip in the washing machine." The rest would be up to the skills and bravado of David Jacox and Marshall Virtue, the stuntmen in the Scout. After much discussion about speed, angle of attack, snow traction, and our mandatory safety meeting, we were ready to go. With all the planning and calculations, there is still

The crash was staged, the actors (**Timothy Olyphant** and **Thomas Jane**) faked their limps, and the figure in the road is a dummy modeled on the actress who played Becky. But the snow, the cold, the fast-fading winter light in the woods outside Prince George—those were real.

a component of luck that is associated with stunts to get the shots you want. In this case, as I probably had one shot at it, I needed as much luck as I could get. The Scout hammered down the road, hit the ramp, slammed the tree trunk, and flipped like a Russian gymnast! Perfect! Thumbs up from the camera crew and a quick playback ensured we had shots better than expected. Unfortunately, the Eyemo had to go to the camera hospital as the Scout had landed directly on the crash housing, cracking the case but delivering an epic impact shot. As it turned out the Scout incurred only minor damage as a result of flipping in the snow. We repositioned the cameras, went for take two, which ended the Scout's film career, but not before delivering a wealth of angles to complete the sequence.

**Were you pleased with the outcome?**
The Scout Crash sequence had all the right elements: a good concept, proper planning, sensible stunt coordination, talented performers, professional crew, and most importantly a director who knows what he wants and collaborates within those elements. I think we were able to deliver the visuals that convey the tone and energy that Larry was looking for, and hopefully a little more to jump the audience out of their seats!

**Morgan Freeman** as Col. Abraham Curtis, in the high-tech command center from which he leads the fight against invasion by extraterrestrials.

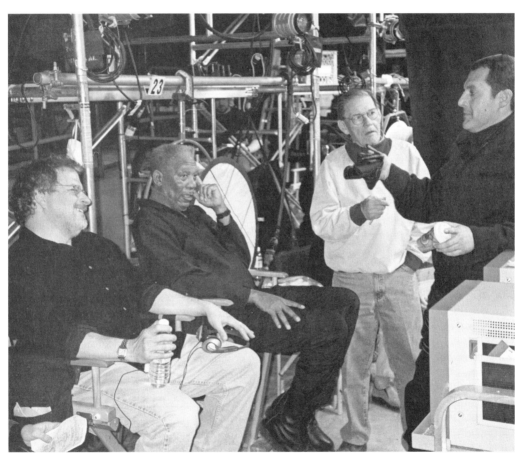

*(L to R)* Outside the command center set, director **Lawrence Kasdan**, actor **Morgan Freeman**, and producer **Charles Okun** listen to a tall tale from actor **Tom Sizemore**.

# THE ACTORS

## MORGAN FREEMAN

Col. Abraham Curtis is the commander of Blue Unit, an elite, top secret military task force whose mission is eradication of alien invaders and containment of the contagion they spread. After twenty-five years of clandestine operations, confronting horrors unimagined by civilians, he is no longer entirely sane.

MORGAN FREEMAN RECENTLY STARRED WITH Ben Affleck in the Tom Clancy thriller *The Sum of All Fears* and with Ashley Judd in *High Crimes.*

Mr. Freeman received an Academy Award® nomination for Best Actor for his work in Frank Darabont's adaptation of Stephen King's *The Shawshank Redemption*, which like *Dreamcatcher* was made by Castle Rock Entertainment. He received a Golden Globe Award and an Academy Award® nomination for his performance in *Driving Miss Daisy.*

Earlier in his career he won the Los Angeles, New York, and National Society of Film Critics Awards and received Academy Award® and Golden Globe nominations for Best Supporting Actor for his work on *Street Smart.*

Mr. Freeman's recent work includes *Bruce Almighty* with Jim Carrey.

# THOMAS JANE

A psychiatrist who can actually read his patients' minds, Dr. Henry Devlin feels that his "gift" has led him to speak too much truth and thus do more harm than good. In despair, he is on the verge of suicide—until events sweep him into a lethal struggle, and he is surprised to find himself clinging to life.

**THOMAS JANE** RECENTLY PLAYED BASEBALL legend, Mickey Mantle, in *61\**, the Emmy-nominated film, directed by Billy Crystal for HBO, about the competition to break Babe Ruth's single season home run record.

Jane is also known for his performances in *Stander, Deep Blue Sea, The Thin Red Line,* and *Boogie Nights.*

# JASON LEE

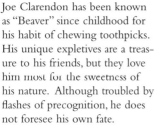

Joe Clarendon has been known as "Beaver" since childhood for his habit of chewing toothpicks. His unique expletives are a treasure to his friends, but they love him most for the sweetness of his nature. Although troubled by flashes of precognition, he does not foresee his own fate.

JASON LEE'S BIG BREAK CAME IN 1995 WHEN HE was cast in the leading role of the slacker "Brodie" in writer/director Kevin Smith's comedy *Mallrats*. *Mallrats* was the first of four movies with Smith. Lee's performance as Ben Affleck's insecure, outspoken roommate "Banky" in *Chasing Amy* won him an Independent Spirit Award for Best Supporting Actor. He also starred in Smith's supernatural comedy *Dogma* as the demonic "Azrael" and in *Jay and Silent Bob Strike Back*.

Lee was the lead singer of the 1970s rock band, *Stillwater*, in writer/director Cameron Crowe's Golden Globe-winning film *Almost Famous*. He recently re-teamed with Crowe for *Vanilla Sky*.

His other films include *Big Trouble*, *Heartbreakers*, *Mumford*, *Enemy of the State*, and *Kissing a Fool*.

166

# DAMIAN LEWIS

Gary Jones—"it's Jonesy to everybody"—is an associate professor of history and a family man. Universally liked, he still feels the deepest bond with his boyhood friends. He doesn't realize that the accident that nearly kills him also prepares him for his role in the conflict that breaks over them all.

**DAMIAN LEWIS** MAKES HIS AMERICAN MOVIE debut in *Dreamcatcher*. In 2002 he received a Golden Globe nomination for Best Actor in a Mini-series or TV Drama for his performance as Major Richard Winters in HBO's *Band of Brothers*. Already well known in his native Britain, Lewis recently starred in the Galsworthy classic *The Forsyte Saga*.

Lewis starred in the BBC mini-series *Hearts* *and Bones* and in *Warriors*, which won a European Film Award and a BAFTA Award. His television credits also include *Robinson Crusoe*, *Life Force*, and two popular, highly rated British series *A Touch of Frost* and Agatha Christie's *Poirot*.

He recently starred as Jeffrey Archer in *Jeffrey Archer—The Truth*, a satirical drama based on the disgraced politician's life.

# TIMOTHY OLYPHANT

The boy Pete Moore wanted to be an astronaut and go to Mars, but the man finds himself selling cars. Even his ability to see "The Line," which guides him to lost people and objects, brings him more grief than joy: it scares people. His friends can only watch as Pete, in his disappointment, turns increasingly to alcohol.

**TIMOTHY OLYPHANT** IS EQUALLY IN DEMAND FOR major studio productions and films by independent filmmakers. He starred with Glenn Close and Dermot Mulroney in *The Safety of Objects* and in *A Man Apart*, opposite Vin Diesel.

On television, Olyphant appeared in the HBO film *When Trumpets Fade* by director John Irvin and in *Sex in the City*. He joined ABC's critically acclaimed drama series *High Incident*, which was created by Steven Spielberg and Eric Bogosian for Dreamworks.

Olyphant's other films include *Go, Rock Star, Broken Hearts Club—A Romantic Comedy, Gone in Sixty Seconds*, and *Scream 2*.

# TOM SIZEMORE

Lt. Col. Owen Underhill is a dedicated soldier and the protégé of Col. Curtis, who is ready to turn Blue Unit over to him. But Owen's loyalties are torn when Curtis embarks on an extreme course of action and a stranger who can read Owen's mind presents him with an incredible story.

**TOM SIZEMORE** HAS WORKED WITH SOME OF THE best directors in the industry—Steven Spielberg, Martin Scorsese, Oliver Stone, Ridley Scott, Tony Scott, and Lawrence Kasdan—playing the kind of tough guy characters he idolized in the movies he saw growing up.

Sizemore recently starred in *Black Hawk Down* and *Pearl Harbor*. The role of Sergeant Horvath in Spielberg's Academy Award®-nominated *Saving Private Ryan* first introduced him to a broader audience. He has played major roles in *Big Trouble*, *Red Planet, Bringing Out the Dead*, and *Play It to the Bone*. His performance in the 1997 suspense thriller *The Relic* brought him a Best Actor Award at the Madrid Film Festival.

His other films include *Born on the Fourth of July, Natural Born Killers, Wyatt Earp, Heat, Devil in a Blue Dress*, and *Strange Days*.

# DONNIE WAHLBERG

"Duddits," as Douglas Cavell calls himself, has obvious deficits and attends a school for exceptional children. But when he becomes the boys' fifth friend, the center of their circle, they discover his assets: a loving heart—and paranormal powers that bond them all. And then one day everything depends on the dying Duddits....

**DONNIE WAHLBERG** PLAYED IN THE *SIXTH SENSE* and recently appeared in the award-winning HBO series *Band of Brothers*. He currently stars in the NBC hit drama *Boomtown*.

Wahlberg made his movie debut in *Bullet* and attributes his big break to director Ron Howard, who cast him in *Ransom*.

Although Wahlberg's love of acting dates from his schooldays, any thoughts of an acting career had to be put on hold when the band he started in his freshman year of high school, *New Kids on the Block*, became a huge success, racking up nine top ten hits and selling over fifty million records.

*(top, L to R)* **Mikey Holekamp** as Henry, **Andrew Robb** as Duddits, **Reece Thompson** as Beaver, **Giacomo Baessato** as Jonesy, and **Joel Palmer** as Pete. Five boys who had to be believable as youthful versions of the adult characters—and extraordinary actors themselves. Here Duddits bestows the gift of seeing "The Line" on Pete.

*(Left)* **Andrew Robb** as Duddits; *(right)* **Reece Thompson** as Beaver.

171

# THE FILMMAKERS

## Behind the Scenes

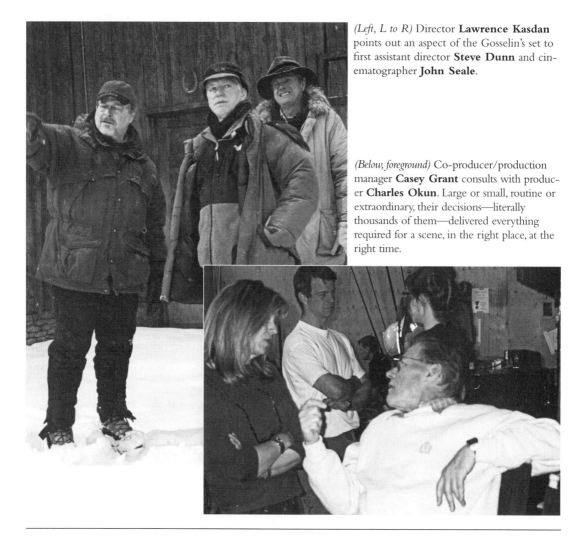

*(Left, L to R)* Director **Lawrence Kasdan** points out an aspect of the Gosselin's set to first assistant director **Steve Dunn** and cinematographer **John Seale**.

*(Below, foreground)* Co-producer/production manager **Casey Grant** consults with producer **Charles Okun**. Large or small, routine or extraordinary, their decisions—literally thousands of them—delivered everything required for a scene, in the right place, at the right time.

"I think science fiction, fantasy, and horror are at their most powerful if you believe in and care about the people involved," says *Dreamcatcher* writer/director/producer Lawrence Kasdan.

Since co-writing *Raiders of the Lost Ark*, *The Empire Strikes Back*, and *Return of the Jedi* early in his career, Kasdan has been looking for a story that would allow him to direct a big effects movie. Known for personal, humanistic films such as *The*

*Big Chill*, *The Accidental Tourist*, *Grand Canyon*, and *Mumford*, Kasdan sought an emotionally engaging story that was rooted in reality.

"In my movies I've always tried to find the most potent metaphor," says Kasdan, "and one of the things Stephen King does really well is find interesting, extravagant metaphors for things that embody our deepest fears. *Dreamcatcher* is about controlling the fear of the chaos that's out there, whether it's somewhere in the universe, outside in the dark, or in your body as it begins to rebel against you. Then there are all the things I've tried to deal with in my other movies, the relationships between characters, friendships, issues of loyalty and redemption; but as with a lot of King's writing, they're married to an exotic, horrifying action story. That's something I've always wanted to try."

By the time Kasdan heard about Stephen King's best-selling novel *Dreamcatcher*, a script was already in development for Castle Rock Entertainment, the company that produced the films *Stand By Me, Misery, The Shawshank Redemption, Dolores Claiborne, The Green Mile*, and *Hearts in Atlantis*, all based on King's books or stories.

"This is the first really successful horror/suspense movie made from one of my books in at least fifteen years," says King. "Not surprisingly, the last one was also a Castle Rock film: *Misery*, with Kathy Bates. Castle Rock is the one company that has never treated me as a horror commodity. They've been able to see that these are actually stories about human beings, and that sometimes the monsters and the elements of horror are good ways of looking at the things that really trouble us in real life."

Two-time Academy Award-winning screenwriter William Goldman (*Butch Cassidy & the Sundance Kid, All the President's Men*), who had previously adapted King's novels *Misery* and *Hearts in Atlantis* for Castle Rock, took on the task of distilling the essence of the six-hundred-page book down to a couple of hours of screen time. Then, as is his custom, Kasdan wrote the final shooting script himself.

*Dreamcatcher* is the story of four friends who perform a heroic act as children and are changed forever by the supernatural powers they gain in return. Over time, Jonesy, Henry, Pete and Beaver grow up to be men who feel isolated from the rest of the world, never quite recapturing the thrill of heroism that they felt in their youth. Unable to understand or master their powers, they are left with the nagging frustration of possessing great potential, but not the ability to realize it.

Associate producer **Mark Kasdan** annotates script changes with brother Lawrence.

When the time came to begin casting, the filmmakers needed actors who could not only embody the characters, but also convincingly portray the strong bond between the friends that sustains them through their loneliness and frustration and forms the core of their story. "This movie is full of wonderful young actors," the director attests. "I feel I've been very lucky in finding terrific actors all through my career, and this is a new crop of great guys." The story offered seven key characters to cast, and *Dreamcatcher* benefited from Kasdan's expertise in bringing together a strong ensemble. The film stars Morgan Freeman (*Seven*) as the mad alien hunter, Colonel Abraham Curtis; Tom Sizemore (*Black Hawk Down*) as Owen Underhill, a military officer under his command; Thomas Jane (*Deep Blue Sea*) as Dr. Henry Devlin; Jason Lee (*Almost Famous*) as Beaver; Damian Lewis (*Band of Brothers*) as Jonesy; and Timothy Olyphant (*Go*) as Pete. Donnie Wahlberg (*Ransom*) plays Duddits, the mysterious figure at the center of their circle.

*Dreamcatcher* is an unusual film in that it encompasses many different genres, and Kasdan used rehearsal time to get his cast on the same page with regard to the tone of the movie. "Larry likes trying to figure out characters more than most writers," says Jason Lee. "Half of the filmmaking process is actually shooting the movie, but the

Associate producer **Elizabeth Dollarhide** gives director **Lawrence Kasdan** an update on the day's critical details.

thing about this movie," says Timothy Olyphant, "is that the moments when you're laughing and you're nervous and you're scared and you're saddened and it's tragic...are all in one scene. The fact that all hell breaks loose is a source of fun, but at the heart of it is a great story about friends who have a chance to be heroes again, to live like they haven't lived since they were kids."

The story's action element enticed Kasdan, as it provided him with an opportunity to work with the latest filmmaking technology. "I've made a lot of movies where people sit around and talk to each other," he says. "This movie has snowmobile chases and car wrecks and spaceships and monsters. It's been wonderful to get out there and discover how you wreck a car, how you simulate a machine gun battle between ground and helicopter, how you depict an animal that's been

other half is the fun and the challenge of figuring out characters, and he does that so well. When we shot *Mumford* we talked and talked and talked as a group for days, and from that comes the development of these characters. And it's amazing that even in an effects-filled action movie like this, he still takes the same approach. I don't care if you're Al Pacino or Robert De Niro, every actor has to have a director. It's like a conductor—the conductor walks offstage, the music just falls apart."

"Larry Kasdan is a storyteller with a fabulous sense of humor and an instinctive ability to make dramatic choices," says Stephen King. "He's not afraid to work on a big canvas with a lot of characters. I think that he may have been attracted to the idea of making *Dreamcatcher* because it's a story that goes back and forth between humor and horror. This is something that we've seen in Larry ever since the opening shot in *The Big Chill*, which appears to be somebody dressing up for a big party to the tune of Marvin Gaye's 'I Heard It Through the Grapevine,' then the camera pulls back and you realize that this is a corpse that's being dressed for burial. And that is maybe the essential Lawrence Kasdan; someone who's able to play both sides of the fence."

His versatility allowed Kasdan to deftly negotiate the film's multilayered landscape. "The great

**Lawrence Kasdan** directs **Morgan Freeman** in the elaborate Winnebago command center set.

infected with an alien body."

Kasdan has learned that the visual effects process is grueling work. "It's incredibly frustrating," he says. "You're doing the mid-step; you're preparing something for an effects shot that's not going to be developed until months later. In addition to the technical challenges, we had to find ways to make it look absolutely realistic, because that's the standard we set for ourselves on this movie."

There are over four hundred visual effects shots in *Dreamcatcher*, created by a post-production

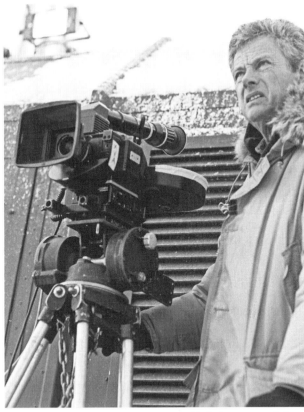

*(Left)* Gosselin's backwoods store is transformed by the arrival of Blue Unit; note the portable light tower and the electrified fence, both custom designed by the art department. *(Right)* Director of photography **John Seale** assesses a shot from the porch of the Winnebago.

group almost as large as the main filming crew. The visual effects team is comprised of some of the most accomplished professionals in the field: Stefen Fangmeier, two-time Oscar nominee and winner of three BAFTA Awards for *The Perfect Storm, Saving Private Ryan,* and *Twister,* headed a huge team at Industrial Light & Magic (ILM); creatures builder Steve Johnson, two-time Emmy winner for Best Makeup in a Miniseries for his work on *The Shining* and *The Stand,* created the puppet versions of the monster known as the 'shitweasel'; and visual effects producer Jacqui Lopez oversaw the realization of it all.

Taking a more down-to-earth, humanistic approach to the story necessitated some changes in the way the team usually works. "Directors who are used to shooting visual effects for science fiction or fantasy tend to work more from a visual discipline," explains Lopez. "They do their storyboards and adhere stringently to the dramatic concepts developed in pre-production. Larry is used to working with actors, so he is much more story and dialogue-driven. The visual effects must be a natural extension of the elicited performances, rather than adhering to the storyboard, so you have to allow for a lot more flexibility. It's more challenging for visual effects, but I think it's a much better way to work."

Some of the effects that appear to be the simplest onscreen were the most creatively challenging for the designers. One example of this is "The Line," the physical manifestation of Pete's inner radar that directs him to things that are lost. "The Line has a very mystical element to it, so when

Director **Lawrence Kasdan** *(center)* works out the intricacies of the dinner table scene, the only one where the four adult friends are seen happy in each other's company, with actors *(L to R)* **Thomas Jane**, **Jason Lee**, and **Timothy Olyphant**.

you try to visualize it, it's very abstract, which is not necessarily easy to translate onto film," explains visual effects supervisor Stefen Fangmeier. "While it's a technical challenge to match the realistic look of an Apache helicopter, we have very good reference photography that's available, so we know exactly what it has to be. With more abstract designs like The Line, we have to invent something completely original."

Bringing the hideous creatures that terrorize the world of *Dreamcatcher* to life was a very laborious process. Based on Crash McCreery's design, the creature team built a clay maquette, which was then digitally scanned into the computer to form the bones of the three-dimensional monster. The computer graphics modeler then "sculpted" it with all the features and details required. Then the model was digitally painted, and the digital armature that the animators use to control the creature's movement was embedded within it. When the creature moves, it bends and might deform in odd ways. So the designers employ a process called "enveloping," which goes over the object and ensures that no matter how the creature moves, the skin will follow the movement naturally, without any kinks. After the animator animates it into a particular shot, the

technical director lights and integrates the creature to blend into the three-dimensional world.

"Finding the right sense of movement for the various creatures requires a lot of creative searching as well," Fangmeier attests. "How do you make something like that move in a very distinctive way? A lot of the personality comes from the movement, from the unique way it approaches and interacts with other characters."

Once those images are rendered by the computer—after all the work done by the modelers, the painters, the animators, and the technical director—the resulting image is then composited together with the filmed footage. Small touches are added that increase the look of authenticity, such as a cast shadow, or a reflection in a puddle of blood on the floor. All these little nuances eventually add up to create an unbelievable creature that the audience can believe in completely.

The makeup team faced similar design challenges. One of the major hurdles for makeup supervisor Bill Corso was designing the disease that is spreading amongst the humans and animals unfortunate enough to be caught in the woods. "We had to come up with an unearthly biological disease that has never been seen before, and create something that is both visually interesting

*(Left)* Actor **Tom Sizemore** focuses on director **Kasdan's** plan for a tense scene in the Winnebago.

*(Below, L to R)* Production designer **Jon Hutman** studies his notes as director **Lawrence Kasdan**, first assistant director **Steve Dunn**, and cinematographer **John Seale** consult in the chill of the British Columbia winter.

and practically effective," Corso explains. "The animals in particular were difficult, because I had to figure out how to replicate the look of the growth that we put on the humans in a way that was safe for the animals. It must be edible and non-toxic because chances are they'll eat it. Will it stay on them? Will the other animals try and eat it off them? But what makes this work fascinating is not just coming up with some creative idea, but figuring out how to implement it in a practical and realistic way."

Usually, the most disturbing scenes in horror films are set in traditionally creepy settings, such as an abandoned house, a pitch-black basement, or a car parked in the woods at night. *Dreamcatcher* brings horror to a somewhat different locale: the audience is first introduced to the film's terrifying monsters…in the bathroom.

"The sequence in the bathroom may be the most fun sequence I've ever done, and also the most gory and grossest and creepiest," says Kasdan. "In some ways I'm prouder of that sequence than anything I've ever done because there were so many people working to make it so textured and varied: the creature designer, the puppeteer, the group at ILM, the actors, the set

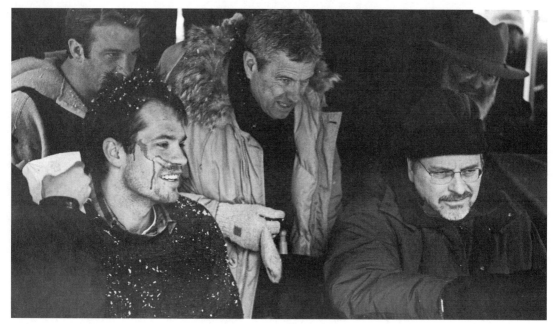

Videotape taps in the film cameras make it possible to check shots immediately. *(L to R)* Actors **Thomas Jane** and **Timothy Olyphant**, cinematographer **John Seale**, and director **Lawrence Kasdan** judge a take from the Scout wreck, the cause of Pete's bloody nose.

textured and varied: the creature designer, the puppeteer, the group at ILM, the actors, the set designer. There's a lot of physical dressing, reflecting the effects of this alien infestation. When you go into the bathroom it's an abattoir, a complete mess. It's out there on the edges of what you can stand to look at – it's funny and exciting and scary all at the same time, and those are the combinations that I wanted. In a movie like this you want to see a horrific effect but only for a glimpse and then have people look at each other and say, *Did I see what I saw?*"

A key figure in establishing the eerie, heart-racing tone of the film was Australian cinematographer John Seale, winner of the Best Cinematography Oscar for his work on *The English Patient*. A man of boundless energy and good humor, Seale is an advocate of working with multiple cameras, often using three cameras in a setup.

"I love being able to work out schemes with a director where two or three cameras might be running during an entire scene," says Seale. "I've heard in the past that a lot of actors like multiple cameras. I remember one actor saying, 'Every time I came around a corner there was a camera in my face, so I could never stop acting. I had to keep the performance going, keep the character alive at all times.' I think that's fantastic, because that surely must make a better film."

"Working with multiple cameras is very stimulating," says Kasdan. "It gives me enormous freedom to move quickly. You automatically have different angles, and it means that you don't need every take to be perfect, because you know you have a lot of options to cut around. It gives you an openness about the process that I haven't always been able to achieve."

When it comes to shooting style, Seale approaches each film as if it's his first. "Larry said, 'I want to get the feeling that we didn't set this up for the camera; that we are there by invitation only. We didn't create it and we're just trying to capture it.' I loved the idea, it's the first time something like that has been asked of me. It makes for a whole new look, the feeling that we're simply about making every shot so beautiful you could frame it. It will be full of grit, misframings, and flat zooms, rather than perfect tracking shots. If it's consistent, it will give the audience the feeling of 'Man, we were there! We saw it happen!'"

Most of the action in *Dreamcatcher* occurs in the midst of a raging blizzard deep in the woods of Maine; unfortunately, filming in Stephen King's home state wasn't an option. Production designer Jon Hutman, winner of an Outstanding Art Direction Emmy for his work on *The West Wing*, scouted the United States and Canada in search of a hilly, forested area with a guaranteed snowfall. As the story often calls for only a single set of tire tracks or footprints in front of the camera, the location also had to make it possible for all the production's support system, crew, camera, lighting and snow-making equipment to remain invisible. It also had to be near a community capable of accommodating two hundred and fifty people.

Hutman settled on Prince George, British Columbia, about 500 miles north of Vancouver. Most of the key exteriors were filmed in the countryside outside Prince George. The shells of a barn, a grocery store, and the cabin known as Hole in the Wall were designed and built in Vancouver, then shipped to Prince George in segments and assembled at the location. They were so beautifully and convincingly aged, some locals wondered if they hadn't been there all along.

Most productions hope for mild, accommodating weather during shooting; *Dreamcatcher*, however, necessitated a harsher climate. Despite a history of severe winter weather, there were a few nervous moments the week before filming began in early January 2002, when the city experienced a period of unseasonably balmy weather. But just as production began, the snow came back to British Columbia.

"The weather was never consistent," says Hutman. "We had real snow that fell, real snow that we trucked in, snow that we made from water and blew in. Then we had paper snow of different sizes, which was mainly what went on the ground, and popcorn snow, made out of cornstarch, for the falling snow. A smorgasbord of snow." But there was always enough of the real stuff in the woods that equipment had to be moved on sleds.

And the cold came as well. The lowest temperatures occurred during a night shoot, when the mercury dropped to –34°F (–37°C). Car fenders dripped with icicles, hotel windows iced up on the inside, water bottles froze solid on set. With few daylight hours, everyone had to work efficiently despite the cold. To save time, the production's caterers carried hot food to the crew along logging paths.

Later the unit moved to Vancouver, first to stages where the interiors were built. These included the cabin and the massive Memory Warehouse, imagined as a spiral library rising to infinity. As spring came on, exteriors for the flashbacks to the boys' childhood were shot in the countryside nearby. The weather was better, and the days gradually grew longer, but the pace was still demanding.

Even after experiencing the seemingly endless challenges and difficulties of creating a film of such enormous scope, his experience working on *Dreamcatcher* has only heightened Kasdan's enthusiasm for filmmaking. "I've been directing movies now for twenty years, and it's only made me hungrier to try different things. I love so many different kinds of movies that I want the opportunity to play in those fields. A lot of what I've done has been about the everyday challenges that people face in the normal world, and I think that the pleasure I found in dealing with this story is that it is so extreme, so beyond the normal world, and takes those basic concerns and amplifies them. To me, this film was the most fun you could possibly have, dealing with extreme situations and doing things I had never done before, combining a lot of disciplines to create a great opportunity."

# ABOUT THE FILMMAKERS

**LAWRENCE KASDAN**, writer/producer/director, has directed ten films: *Body Heat, The Big Chill, Silverado, The Accidental Tourist, I Love You to Death, Grand Canyon, Wyatt Earp, French Kiss, Mumford,* and *Dreamcatcher* (2003 release). He has written or co-written all of these pictures except John Kostmayer's *I Love You to Death* and Adam Brooks' *French Kiss.*

In addition, Kasdan has written or co-written four of the most successful pictures in motion picture history—*Raiders of the Lost Ark, The Empire Strikes Back, Return of the Jedi,* and *The Bodyguard.*

Born in Miami Beach, Florida, and raised in West Virginia, Kasdan attended the University of Michigan, supporting himself with a series of writing awards while he studied English literature.

Kasdan made his critically acclaimed directorial debut with *Body Heat* in 1981. Next, he directed *The Big Chill*, which he co-wrote with Barbara Benedek and which was nominated for three Academy Awards®, including Best Picture. His next effort was the sprawling Western *Silverado*, which he directed, produced, and co-wrote with his brother Mark.

Kasdan next directed *The Accidental Tourist,* based on the novel by Anne Tyler and adapted by Kasdan and Frank Galati. The film was named Best Picture of 1988 by the New York Film Critics, received four Academy Award® nominations, including Best Picture, and earned Geena Davis a Best Supporting Actress award. *I Love You to Death*, written by John Kostmayer, was the first script that Kasdan directed that he did not write.

The script for *Grand Canyon,* co-written with his wife, Meg Kasdan, earned them Academy Award® and Golden Globe nominations for Best Original Screenplay. The film received the Golden Bear Award for Best Picture at the 1992 Berlin Film Festival.

In 1992, Kasdan's seventeen-year-old script for *The Bodyguard* was filmed under the direction of Mick Jackson. Kasdan, Jim Wilson, and Kevin Costner produced the movie, which went on to gross $400 million in theaters worldwide.

In 1994, Kasdan made *Wyatt Earp,* starring Kevin Costner, Dennis Quaid, and Gene Hackman, and in 1995, directed *French Kiss,* a romantic comedy set in Paris and Cannes with Meg Ryan and Kevin Kline.

Kasdan made his theatrical stage debut in the fall of 1995 as director of John Patrick Shanley's *Four Dogs & a Bone*, a dark comedic look at the seamier side of Hollywood, as the inaugural play of the newly renovated Geffen Playhouse.

*Mumford*, a comedy that Kasdan produced with Charles Okun and wrote and directed, was released in 1999.

Kasdan recently directed *Dreamcatcher,* based on the novel by Stephen King, for Castle Rock Entertainment and Warner Bros. The film was adapted for the screen by William Goldman and Lawrence Kasdan and produced by Kasdan with Charles Okun.

**WILLIAM GOLDMAN**, screenwriter, prior to *Dreamcatcher*, adapted the Stephen King books *Hearts in Atlantis* and *Misery* for Castle Rock Entertainment.

Goldman won Academy Awards® for his adaptation of the incisive political exposé *All the President's Men* and for his original script *Butch Cassidy and the Sundance Kid*. Both screenplays also earned him Writers Guild

Awards. Other honors include Lifetime Achievement Awards from the WGA and from the National Board of Review of Motion Pictures, and from the Writers Guild of Great Britain.

Goldman's first screen credit was the 1965 thriller *Masquerade*. The following year his script for the detective drama *Harper* won the Edgar Allen Poe Award for Best Motion Picture Screenplay. His screenwriting credits include *The Princess Bride*, *The Chamber*, *Absolute Power*, *The Ghost and the Darkness*, *Heat*, *Misery*, *Maverick*, *Chaplin*, *Year of the Comet*, *Magic*, *A Bridge Too Far*, *Marathon Man*, *The Great Waldo Pepper*, *The Stepford Wives*, and *The Hot Rock*.

Goldman has been an author for forty-five years. Since his first novel, *The Temple of Gold*, he has written more than two dozen books, both fiction and nonfiction.

Among his novels are *Magic*, *The Princess Bride*, *Marathon Man*, and *Tinsel*.

His nonfiction work includes acclaimed books about the entertainment industry— *Adventures in the Screen Trade*; *Hype and Glory*; *The Season: A Candid Look at Broadway*; and *Which Lie Did I Tell?*

**STEPHEN KING**, novelist, was born in Portland, Maine in 1947, the second son of Donald and Nellie Ruth Pillsbury King. From his sophomore year at the University of Maine at Orono, he wrote a weekly column for the school newspaper, *The Maine Campus*. He graduated from the University in 1970 with a B.S. in English and qualified to teach on the high school level. He and Tabitha Spruce married in January of 1971.

King made his first short story sale to a mass-market men's magazine shortly after his graduation from the University. Throughout the early years of his marriage, he continued to sell stories to men's magazines. Many of these were later gathered into the *Night Shift* collection or appeared in other anthologies. In the fall of 1971, King began teaching high school English classes at Hampden Academy in Maine. Writing in the evenings and on the weekends, he continued to produce short stories and work on novels.

In the spring of 1973, Doubleday & Co. accepted the novel *Carrie* for publication. King wrote his next-published novel, *Salem's Lot*, in 1973, and *Carrie* was published in the spring of 1974. That same fall, the Kings left Maine for Boulder, Colorado. They lived there for a little less than a year, during which King wrote *The Shining*. Returning to Maine in the summer of 1975, King finished writing *The Stand*. *The Dead Zone* was also written in Bridgton.

The Kings have three adult children. King put some of his college dramatic society experience to use when he played bit parts in a George Romero picture, *Knightriders*, and *Creepshow*, a film he scripted. In 1985, King wrote and directed the movie *Maximum Overdrive*, and *Creepshow II* was released in 1987. Many of his works have been adapted for the screen, including *Carrie*, *The Shining*, *Christine*, *Cujo*, *Pet Sematary* (for which King wrote the screenplay and had a bit part as a minister), and *Misery*, as well as *The Green Mile* and *The Shawshank Redemption*. The popular movie *Stand By Me* was adapted from his novella *The Body* from the *Different Seasons* collection. In 1992, the film *Sleepwalkers* was produced from an original screenplay by King. In 2004, King's first TV series, *Kingdom Hospital*, will air on ABC.

**CHARLES OKUN**, producer, has teamed with director Lawrence Kasdan on nine films. They initially met when Okun was preparing Kasdan's first feature film, *Body Heat*, in 1981.

A native of New York, Okun taught school briefly following his graduation from NYU. In the fifties he left teaching to join the film industry, working first as an electrician on documentaries, commercials and industrial training films. In 1961 he became an assistant director, first on commercials and then, in 1968, on feature films.

His film career as an assistant director, unit production manager, and producer has spanned over 30 films. He worked as an assistant director for Frank Perry on *Diary of a Mad Housewife* and *Rancho Deluxe*. This was followed by *Such Good Friends* for Otto Preminger, Michael Winner's *Death Wish*, Jonathan Demme's *Handle With Care*, Sidney Lumet's *Loving Molly*, the first feature from Michael Cimino, *Thunderbolt and Lightfoot*, and Ted Kotcheff's *Fun with Dick and Jane*. Okun worked with Cimino again on *Heaven's Gate* and on *The Deer Hunter*, which won five Academy Awards.

Okun collaborated with Kasdan as executive producer/unit production manager on *Silverado* and as co-producer on *Cross My Heart*, which was produced by Kasdan. He served as producer/unit production manager on *The Accidental Tourist*, nominated for four Academy Awards including Best Picture, and on *Grand Canyon*. Okun was executive producer/unit production manager of *I Love You to Death* and *Wyatt Earp*, executive producer on *French Kiss* and producer on *Mumford*, 1999.

**BRUCE BERMAN,** executive producer, joined the production division of Warner Bros. Pictures and rose through the executive ranks to become President of Worldwide Theatrical Production. Under his aegis, the studio produced and distributed such titles as the Oscar-winning *Driving Miss Daisy*, as well as *GoodFellas, Presumed Innocent, Robin Hood:*

*Prince Of Thieves, Batman Forever, Malcolm X, The Bodyguard, JFK, The Fugitive, Dave, A Time To Kill,* and *Twister*.

In 1996, Berman started Plan B Entertainment, the Warner Bros. Pictures-based independent production company that was later acquired by Village Roadshow Pictures. Village Roadshow Pictures, where Berman now holds the post of Chairman and Chief Executive Officer, currently has 20 projects in various stages of development at Warner Bros. Pictures. Most recently, Berman executive produced the immensely successful *Ocean's Eleven, Showtime, Training Day, Cats & Dogs, Three Kings, The Matrix, Analyze This, Deep Blue Sea, Practical Magic,* and *Space Cowboys* through Village Roadshow's partnership with Warner Bros. Pictures, as well as the hit comedy *Miss Congeniality*, produced jointly with Warner Bros. Pictures and Castle Rock Entertainment. He most recently served as executive producer on the romantic comedy *Two Weeks Notice*. Berman is the executive producer for the next two highly anticipated chapters in the *Matrix* saga, *The Matrix Reloaded* and *The Matrix Revolutions*.

**JON HUTMAN**, co-producer and production designer, won an Emmy® for his work as production designer on "The West Wing."

His recent motion picture credits include *What Women Want* and *Coyote Ugly*.

*Dreamcatcher* is Hutman's fifth collaboration with Lawrence Kasdan. He served as an art director on *I Love You to Death*, and designed *French Kiss* and *Mumford*, for which he also received a co-producer credit.

Hutman has designed three films for Robert Redford—*The Horse Whisperer, Quiz Show,* and *A River Runs Through It*—and two films for former Yale classmate Jodie Foster—*Nell* and *Little Man Tate*. Other credits include

*Lolita*, *Flesh and Bone*, *Trespass*, *Meet the Applegates*, and *Heathers*.

Hutman has a degree in architecture from Yale and studied scenic design, painting, and lighting at the university's School of Drama.

He made his directing debut with episodes of *Gideon's Crossing* and *The West Wing*.

**STEPHEN DUNN**, co-producer and first assistant director, was the first assistant director on Lawrence Kasdan's *Mumford* and *Wyatt Earp*. *Dreamcatcher* is his sixth collaboration with Kasdan, with whom he first worked on *The Big Chill*.

Dunn was recently associate producer, as well as first assistant director, on *The Shipping News*, his fourth film for Lasse Hallstrom. He was first assistant director on *Chocolat*, *Cider House Rules*, and *Something to Talk About*.

His credits also include *What Dreams May Come*, *One Fine Day*, *Kansas City*, *A Little Princess*, *Falling Down*, *Dying Young*, and *Dances With Wolves*.

Dunn started as Tom Laughlin's assistant on *Billy Jack Goes to Washington*. He worked for Paul Schrader on *Blue Collar*, *Hardcore*, *Cat People*, *American Gigolo*, and *Patty Hearst*.

Dunn edited the Robert Altman films *Fool for Love* and *Beyond Therapy*, and recently produced the independent film *Final* for Campbell Scott. He is a graduate of USC's school of cinema.

**ELIZABETH DOLLARHIDE**, associate producer, enjoyed a career in advertising and marketing before she began working in films and commercials in 1990. She worked as assistant to the producer on *Soul Food*, during which she designed and directed the second unit photography of the food montage. At the University of Mississippi she produced a literacy television program, which aired live via satellite to schools across the state.

During *Mumford*, she joined Kasdan Pictures as assistant to Lawrence Kasdan. On *Dreamcatcher*, she was assistant to Charles Okun. She also produced the behind-the-scenes video for the website and managed the marketing and publicity efforts for Kasdan Pictures.

**MARK KASDAN**, associate producer, was born in Miami Beach, Florida, and raised in Wheeling, West Virginia, and grew up loving Hollywood movies of the fifties, particularly the Westerns so numerous at the time. His brother, Lawrence, shared his enthusiasm.

At Harvard, Kasdan began studying linguistics, but spent more time enthralled by the masterpieces of world cinema. He switched majors to focus on movies and later attended film schools in London and Los Angeles.

An internship program sponsored by the Academy of Motion Picture Arts and Sciences led to a job with John Sturges, the veteran director whose credits included several of the Westerns Kasdan had long admired, notably *The Magnificent Seven*.

An even greater thrill came some years later, after a variety of jobs in film and advertising, when Lawrence invited him to co-write and help produce a Western of their own—*Silverado*. The beauty of the New Mexico locations later led Kasdan and his wife, Maxann, to move to Albuquerque.

After writing the thriller *Criminal Law* and co-writing several screenplays with Terry Swann, a friend and collaborator since UCLA Film School days, Kasdan returned to work with his brother and served as an associate producer of *Dreamcatcher*.

**JOHN SEALE**, ACS, ASC, director of photography, is widely respected as one of the world's most accomplished cinematographers. His recent work includes *Harry Potter and the Sorcerer's Stone*, *The Perfect Storm*, and *The Talented Mr. Ripley*.

Seale won an Academy Award®, a BAFTA Award, a European Film Award and the American Society of Cinematographers' Award for *The English Patient*.

He also received Academy Award® nominations for *Rainman* and *Witness* and BAFTA Award nominations for *Witness* and *Gorillas in the Mist*. He is the winner of two Milli Awards, the Australian Cinematographers' Society's highest honor, and an AFI award from the Australian Film Institute for *Careful, He Might Hear You*.

His credits include *City of Angels*, *Ghosts of Mississippi*, *The American President*, *Beyond Rangoon*, *The Paper*, *The Firm*, *Lorenzo's Oil*, *The Doctor*, *Dead Poets' Society*, *Stakeout*, *The Mosquito Coast*, and *Children of a Lesser God*.

After *Dreamcatcher*, Seale re-teamed with Anthony Minghella for *Cold Mountain*.

**CAROL LITTLETON**, editor, edited *The Truth About Charlie* for Jonathan Demme and *The Anniversary Party* for Alan Cummings and Jennifer Jason Leigh.

Littleton, known for her focus on the subtleties of characterization and performance, was chosen by Lawrence Kasdan to edit his first film, *Body Heat*, because she saw the humor, which had escaped the attention of other editors.

Littleton has now worked with Kasdan on seven more movies: *The Big Chill*, *Silverado*, *The Accidental Tourist*, *Grand Canyon*, *Wyatt Earp*, *Mumford*, and *Dreamcatcher*, and continues to appreciate that sense of humor, as well as Kasdan's skill as an observer of human behavior.

Littleton was nominated for an Academy Award® and an ACE Award for her work on *E.T.* Her credits include *Beloved*, *Twilight*, *Benny and Joon*, *China Moon*, *White Palace*, *Swimming to Cambodia*, *Brighton Beach Memoirs*, and *Places in the Heart*.

**RAUL DAVALOS**, editor, edited the first and second seasons of the successful, fast-talking series "Gilmore Girls" before leaving to become one of the editors of *Dreamcatcher*.

Davalos edited *Via Dolorosa*, directed by veteran cinematographer John Bailey, which screened at the Sundance Festival in 2000 and *Cronos*, directed by Guillermo del Toro, which won a prize at the Cannes Film Festival.

*Dreamcatcher* is Davalos' eighth film with Carol Littleton. Their seventeen-year collaboration began in 1985 on Lawrence Kasdan's *Silverado*. Davalos worked with Littleton on *Vibes*, *The Accidental Tourist*, *White Palace*, and *China Moon*, and became associate editor on *Benny and Joon* and *Wyatt Earp*.

His television credits as an editor include HBO's "Blue Ridge Fall," "Judas" (ABC) and several films directed by Douglas Barr, "Conundrum" for Showtime, "Love Lessons" (CBS), "Switched at Birth" (CBS), "Half a Dozen Babies" (ABC), and "Cloned" (NBC).

Davalos was born in Havana and grew up in Key Biscayne, Florida. He first studied pre-med, but changed direction after seeing *The Godfather* and *A Clockwork Orange*. He attended the London Film School and edited commercials in Florida before moving to L.A.

**STEFEN FANGMEIER**, visual effects supervisor and second unit director, won BAFTA Awards for *The Perfect Storm* (2000), *Saving Private Ryan* (1998), and *Twister* (1997), and received Academy Award® nominations for *A Perfect Storm* and *Twister*. His credits include *Galaxy Quest*, on which he was also the second unit director, *Speed 2*, and *Small Soldiers*.

Fangmeier is a member of the extraordinary team at Industrial Light & Magic, where in addition to *Dreamcatcher*, he worked on *Signs*.

He joined the computer graphics department at ILM in 1990. His first major project was *Terminator 2: Judgment Day*. He later worked on *Jurassic Park* and *Hook* as a computer graphics supervisor and on *Casper* as the digital character co-supervisor.

Prior to joining ILM, Fangmeier served as director of production at Mental Images GmbH and Co. in Berlin. He also worked as a scientific visualization program manager at the National Center for Supercomputing Applications at the University of Illinois, as a technical director for Digital Productions in Los Angeles, as a computer operator, and as a systems programmer and image processing analyst at the Aerospace Corporation in California.

Fangmeier received his degree in computer science from California State University of Dominguez Hills in 1983 and has been a member of the DGA since 1999.

**CASEY GRANT**, co-producer, acted as executive producer on *Snow Dogs*, co-producer and production manager on the John Frankenheimer feature *Reindeer Games* and *Excess Baggage*, and as production manager on *Double Jeopardy*, *Along Came a Spider*, and *Cool Runnings*. Grant also served as unit production manager on *Run*, *Leaving Normal*, and *This Boy's Life*, and as associate producer/production manager on the films *The 13th Warrior*, *Carpool*, and *Man of the House*.

**JAMES NEWTON HOWARD**, composer, recently scored *Treasure Planet*, his third feature film for Walt Disney Features Animation after *Dinosaur* and *Atlantis, The Lost Empire*. Howard has scored more than 65 feature films and earned five Academy Award® nominations. Among his most celebrated contributions to film music are the Oscar-nominated scores for *The Fugitive*, *The Prince of Tides*, and *My Best Friend's Wedding*. He has also written the Oscar-nominated songs "Look What Love Has Done" (from *Junior*) and "For the First Time" (from *One Fine Day*).

In addition, his evocative music has enhanced such films as *Signs, The Sixth Sense* and *Unbreakable* for M. Night Shayamalan, *America's Sweethearts, Big Trouble, Snow Falling on Cedars, Devil's Advocate, Liar, Liar, Space Jam, Primal Fear, Restoration, Falling Down, Wyatt Earp, Dave, Alive, Glengary Glen Ross, The Man in the Moon, Dying Young, Grand Canyon, My Girl, Pretty Woman, Flatliners, Everybody's All-American*, and *The Emperor's Club*, among others.

Howard began his music studies at age four. He continued training at Santa Barbara Music Academy of the West and at USC School of Music as a piano performance major. He completed his formal education with orchestration study under the legendary arranger Marty Paich. He subsequently began his industry career performing as a keyboard artist for Melissa Manchester and Elton John. He toured with the latter superstar in the 1970s and early 80s. Additionally, he worked with such legendary artists as Barbra Streisand, Diana Ross, Rod Stewart, and Bob Seger.

For television, Howard has composed and/or written memorable themes for which he has garnered two Emmy Award® nominations for the series *ER*.

# CAST AND CREW CREDITS

FROM WARNER BROS. PICTURES

CASTLE ROCK ENTERTAINMENT Presents in Association with
VILLAGE ROADSHOW PICTURES and NPV ENTERTAINMENT
a KASDAN PICTURES PRODUCTION

A LAWRENCE KASDAN Film

MORGAN FREEMAN    THOMAS JANE    JASON LEE    DAMIAN LEWIS
TIMOTHY OLYPHANT    TOM SIZEMORE    DONNIE WAHLBERG

# DREAMCATCHER

| Casting by | Music by | Co-Producers |
| --- | --- | --- |
| RONNA KRESS, C.S.A. | JAMES NEWTON HOWARD | STEPHEN DUNN |
| | | CASEY GRANT |
| | | JON HUTMAN |

| Creature Designer | Visual Effects Supervisor | Costume Designer |
| --- | --- | --- |
| CRASH McCREERY | STEFEN FANGMEIER | MOLLY MAGINNIS |

| Edited by | Production Designer | Director of Photography |
| --- | --- | --- |
| CAROL LITTLETON, A.C.E. | JON HUTMAN | JOHN SEALE, A.C.S. A.S.C. |
| RAUL DAVALOS, A.C.E. | | |

| Executive Producer | Produced by |
| --- | --- |
| BRUCE BERMAN | LAWRENCE KASDAN    CHARLES OKUN |

| Based on the book by | Screenplay by |
| --- | --- |
| STEPHEN KING | WILLIAM GOLDMAN and LAWRENCE KASDAN |

Directed by
LAWRENCE KASDAN

Production Manager . . . . . . . . . . . . CASEY GRANT

First Assistant Director. . . . . . . . . STEPHEN P. DUNN

Second Assistant Director. . . . . . . . . . PAUL BARRY

### CAST

| | |
| --- | --- |
| Col. Abraham Curtis . . . . . . . . MORGAN FREEMAN | |
| Henry. . . . . . . . . . . . . . . . . . . THOMAS JANE | |
| Beaver . . . . . . . . . . . . . . . . . . . JASON LEE | |
| Jonesy . . . . . . . . . . . . . . . . DAMIAN LEWIS | |
| Pete . . . . . . . . . . . . . . . TIMOTHY OLYPHANT | |
| Owen . . . . . . . . . . . . . . . . TOM SIZEMORE | |
| Duddits. . . . . . . . . . . . DONNIE WAHLBERG | |
| Young Henry . . . . . . . . . . . . . MIKEY HOLEKAMP | |
| Young Beaver . . . . . . . . . . . REECE THOMPSON | |
| Young Jonesy . . . . . . . . . GIACOMO BAESSATO | |
| Young Pete . . . . . . . . . . . . JOEL PALMER | |
| Young Duddits . . . . . . . . . . . ANDREW ROBB | |

Rick McCarthy . . . . . . . . . . . ERIC KEENLEYSIDE
Roberta Cavell. . . . . . . . . ROSEMARY DUNSMORE
Gen. Matheson. . . . . . . . . . . . . MICHAEL O'NEILL
Maples. . . . . . . . . . . . . . . . DARRIN KLIMEK
Old Man Gosselin . . . . . . . . . . . . CAMPBELL LANE
Barry Neiman . . . . . . . . . . . . C. ERNST HARTH
Trish. . . . . . . . . . . . . . . INGRID KAVELAARS
Rachel . . . . . . . . . . . . . . . CHERA BAILEY
Richie Grenadeau . . . . . . . . . . . ALEX CAMPBELL
Scottie. . . . . . . . . . . . . . . . . . T.J. RILEY
Duncan . . . . . . . . . . . . . . . RYAN DE BOER
Becky . . . . . . . . . . . . . . . SUSAN CHAREST
Army Truck Driver . . . . . . . . . . . TY OLSSON
Conklin. . . . . . . . . . . MICHAEL DAINGERFIELD
Tracking Technician . . . . . . . . . KEVAN OHTSJI
EMT #1. . . . . . . . . . . . . MARCY GOLDBERG
EMT #2 . . . . . . . . . . . . DION JOHNSTONE
Josie Rinkenhauer . . . . . . . . . . . SHAUNA KAIN

| | | | |
|---|---|---|---|
| Edwards . . . . . . . . . . . . . . . . . COLIN LAWRENCE | | Supervising Art Director . . . . . . . W. STEVEN GRAHAM | |
| Platoon Leader . . . . . . . . . . . . . . MALIK McCALL | | Art Directors . . . . . . . . . . . . . KENDELLE ELLIOTT | |
| Helicopter Sentry . . . . . . . . . . . . JORDAN WALKER | | | HELEN JARVIS |
| Defuniak . . . . . . . . . . . . . JONATHAN KASDAN | | Assistant Art Directors . . . . . . . . . MARION KOLSBY | |
| Stranger on Curb . . . . MICHAEL RICHARD DOBSON | | | ROXANNE METHOT |
| Bad Driver . . . . . . . . . . . . . . . . JOHN MOORE | | Set Decorator . . . . . . . . . ROSE MARIE McSHERRY | |
| Woman in Crowd . . . . . . . . . . CAROLYN TWEEDLE | | Camera Operators . . . . . . . . . . . . JOHN CLOTHIER | |
| Apache Crewman #1 . . . . . . . . . CHRISTOPHER ANG | | | TRIG SINGER |
| Apache Crewman #2 . . . . . . . . . . CHRIS DUGGAN | | First Assistant Cameramen . . . . . . . PATRICK STEPIEN | |
| Apache Crewman #3 . . . . . . . . . . DANIEL MERALI | | | BOB FINDLAY |
| Apache Crewman #4 . . . . . . . . . . . MATT RILEY | | | PAUL GUENETTE |
| Detainee #1 . . . . . . . . . . . . . JOHN ARMSTRONG | | Second Assistant Cameramen . . . . STEWART A. WHELAN | |
| Detainee #2 . . . . . . . . . . . . . JACK CROWSTON | | | DAVID D. LOURIE |
| Detainee #3 . . . . . . . . . . . TRENNA FRANDSEN | | | GREG BEATON |
| Detainee #4 . . . . . . . . . . . . . . JOHN GAGNE | | Camera Loader . . . . . . . . . . . . MICHELLE HNLICA | |
| Detainee #5 . . . . . . . . . . . . . . SUE HARTLEY | | Camera Trainees . . . . . . . . . . . THOMAS YARDLEY | |
| Detainee #6 . . . . . . . . . . . . . JOHN HOMBACH | | | ANTHONY BOCQUENTIN |
| Detainee #7 . . . . . . . . . . . KAT KOSIANCIC | | | DEAN MORIN |
| Stunt Coordinator . . . . . . . . . . . . . . JACOB RUPP | | | JOSE WILLIAM MANZANO |
| Mr. Freeman's Stunt Double . . . . . . JOPHREY BROWN | | Stills Photographer . . . . . . . . . . DOANE GREGORY | |
| Mr. Freeman's Helicopter Double . . . STEVEN J. WRIGHT | | Supervising Sound Editors . . . . . . . . ROBERT GRIEVE | |
| | | | YANN DELPUECH |

STUNT PERFORMERS

| | |
|---|---|
| CHARLES ANDRE | DENNIS BREST |
| ANDREW KEILTY | GREG SCHLOSSER |
| YVES CAMERON | RON ROBINSON |
| DAVID JACOX | JIM DUNN |
| MARSHALL VIRTUE | JAMES RALPH |
| JASON GLASS | JOE DOSERRO |
| DEAN CHOE | ERNIE JACKSON |
| REG GLASS | KRISTENE KENWARD |
| BRAD KOZLEY | BRAD LOREE |
| KEN KIRZINGER | JJ MAKARO |
| DEB MACATUMPUG | RICK PEARSE |
| KIT MALLET | FIONA ROESKE |
| GERALD PAETZ | HEATH STEVENSON |
| MIKE ROSSELLI | FRED PERRON |
| BILL EDWARDS | |

PUPPETEERS

| | |
|---|---|
| ENRIQUE B. BILSLAND | MARK KILLINGSWORTH |
| BILL BRYAN | LEON LADERACH |
| JENY CASSADY | LEONARD MACDONALD |
| JASON HAMER | ROBERT NEWTON |
| | GEOFF REDKNAP |

| | |
|---|---|
| Associate Producers . . . . . . ELIZABETH DOLLARHIDE | |
| | MARK KASDAN |

| | |
|---|---|
| ILM Visual Effects Co-Supervisor . . . . TIM ALEXANDER | |
| ILM Animation Supervisor . . . . . . . . . . HAL HICKEL | |
| ILM Visual Effects Producer . . . . . . . . . . JEFF OLSON | |

| | |
|---|---|
| Visual Effects Producer . . . . . . . . JACQUELINE LOPEZ | |

| | |
|---|---|
| Re-recording Sound Mixers . . . . . KEVIN O'CONNELL | |
| | GREG P. RUSSELL |
| Script Supervisor . . . . . . . . . . . . BARBARA E. TUSS | |
| Post Production Supervisor . . . . . STEVEN KAMINSKY | |
| Make Up Supervisor . . . . . . . . . . . . BILL CORSO | |
| Dialect Coach . . . . . . . . . . . . . . . TIM MONICH | |
| Production Accountant . . . . . . . . MARGE ROWLAND | |
| Post Production Accountant . . . . . . . PATTI AMARAL | |
| Assistant Production Accountants . . . . . SARAH TROWSE | |
| | JANE MASON |
| | LEONA MADDEAUX |
| Accounting Clerk . . . . . . . . . . . . . . TANIA ROSA | |
| Payroll Accountant . . . . . MICHELE LEE SHELLENBERG | |
| Construction Accountants . . . . . . . . NANCY VIBERT | |
| | DEBBIE LOVEN |
| Accounting Trainee . . . . . . . . . . DIANE McMILLAN | |
| Set Designers . . . . . . . . . . . . . . MICHAEL TOBY | |
| | JAY MITCHELL |
| | ALEXANDER KAMENICZKY |
| | ANNEKE VAN OORT |
| | ALLAN GALJDA |
| Storyboard Artists . . . . . . . . . RICHARD NEWSOME | |
| | MARC VENA |
| | ADRIEN C. VAN VIERSON |
| Assistant Set Decorator . . . . . . . SHANNON GOTTLIEB | |
| Set Decorating Buyer . . . . . . . . . . . . . ZOE JIRIK | |
| Set Decorating Coordinator . . . CYNTHIA BURTINSHAW | |
| Lead Set Dressers . . . . . . . . . . . . . TERRY LEWIS | |
| | LAURIE MARSH |

| | | | |
|---|---|---|---|
| On-Set Dresser | KEVIN GRIFFIN-PARK | Second Boom | CHRIS HIGGINS |
| Set Dressers | KEN SAWATZKY | Video Playback | KLAUS MELCHOIR |
| | MIKE WEBSDALE | Video Assist Operators | ROB PARISIEN |
| | J. TODD LAWLEY | | BENNY BACH |
| | GORD ENVIK | | MAX TORROBA |
| Assistant to Jon Hutman | ASHLEY BURNHAM | Computer Playback | JASON BROWN |
| Art Department Assistants | SHANNON JOHNSTONE | Projectionist | JACQUES BLACKSTONE |
| | STEPHANIE SCOTT | | |
| | | Key Make-Up Artist | VICTORIA DOWN |
| First Assistant Editor | LUCYNA WOJCIECHOWSKI | Assistant Make-Up Artist | RITA CICCOZZI |
| Visual Effects Editor | BRIGITTE DALOIN | Mr. Freeman's Make-Up Artist | NANCY HANCOCK |
| Assistant Editors | OFE YI | Key Hairstylist | SHERRY LINDER-GYGLI |
| | HUGH ROSS | Hairstylist | SANDY MONESMITH |
| | ANNA SOLORIO-CATALANO | Mr. Freeman's Hairstylist | DEENA ADAIR |
| | CHERYL BUCKMAN | | |
| | SHELLY THEAKER | Assistant Costume Designer | CAROLYN J.R. CAMERON |
| | MICHELLE HENDRICKSEN | Costume Set Supervisor | ELIZABETH NEEDHAM |
| | AUDREY CHANG | Assistant Costumers | DEBBIE HUMPHREYS |
| | ALBERT COLEMAN | | CHARRON HUME |
| | PABLO PRIETTO | Assistant Costume Designer (LA) | JOSEPHINE MONMANEY |
| Apprentice Editor | RYAN MALONE | | |
| Editorial Production Assistant | LORI LORDOG DABSON | Gaffer | DAVID TICKELL |
| Visual Effects Coordinators | AMY BERESFORD | Best Boy Electric | JEFF HARVEY |
| | HEIDE WALDBAUM | Rigging Gaffer | JARROD TIFFIN |
| | | Rigging Best Boy | JOHN PIROZOK |
| Unit Manager | YVONNE MELVILLE | Lamp Operators | J.F. RAYMOND |
| Third Assistant Director | PAUL BURGER | | AVRON SHER |
| Production Coordinator | JASMINE MARY ELSWORTH | | SIERRA HURST |
| Assistant Production Coordinators | BRETT DAVIES | Genny Operator | JAY D. ANDERSON |
| | KATHLEEN NURIT | | |
| Second Assistant Production Coordinator | NICOLE FLORIAN | Key Grip | DILLARD BRINSON |
| Set Production Assistants | LUKE FISHER | Best Boy Grip | TOM GREGG |
| | JASON COLLIER | Dolly Grip | GIL FORRESTER |
| Assistant Director Trainees | JENNIFER ZIMMER | Grips | STEVE RINGWOOD |
| | RILEY WALSH | | BEN RUSI |
| | | | CHRIS MARTIN |
| Key Military Advisor | JAMES DEVER | | RICHARD JAMES ZIMMERMANN |
| Boot Camp Manager | JEFF MOSUK | Rigging Grip Best Boy | ROB SHAMRYK |
| Military Advisor Assistants | BRIAN MAYNARD | Rigging Grips | DEAN COLLINS |
| | MATT MORGAN | | KEVIN MCCLOY |
| | JAY FERGUSON | | |
| Location Manager | CONNIE KENNEDY | Property Master | BRYAN KORENBERG |
| Assistant Location Managers | MARNIE GEE | Assistant Property Master | HAIDA GREENLEAF HARPER |
| | DEBORAH D. BOSE | Props Buyer | ANDY NIEMAN |
| Location Scout | DOUG WHITE | Head Greensman | GLENN FOERSTER |
| Location Production Assistants | CHRIS WAYATT | Greens Lead | KEVIN CLARK |
| | MARIAN KOPRADA | On Set Greens | DAVE HENNEBERY |
| | JEFF MOHS | | |
| | LORI BANKO | Special Effects Coordinator | WILLIAM H. ORR |
| | PHILIP NEE NEE | SPFX Buyer | TERESA WILKINSON |
| | LINDSAY DEWHIRST | SPFX Best Boy | LARS LENANDER |
| | OISIN CARROLL | SPFX Snow Coordinator | CLAYTON SCHEIRER |
| | RYAN SHANKS | SPFX Head Fabricator | W.A. ANDREW SCULTHORP |
| Sound Mixer | ERIC BATUT | | |
| Boom Operator | CHRIS GLYN-JONES | | |

SPFX Assistants. . . . . . . . . . . . . . . . . REG MILNE
JOHN WILKINSON
COLIN NASO
CHRIS DAVIS
JOHN S. BLEZARD
GRANT SMITH
STEVE WOLVELY
ELIE T. MERHEB
BRIAN BULLOCK
DENNIS MISHKO BRIEST

Construction Coordinator . . . . . DOUGLAS HARDWICK
Construction Foremen . . . . . . . . . . . MIKE McLEOD
DALE MENZIES
Construction Buyer. . . . . . . . . . . . . JAN HOLMSTEN
Tool Maintenance . . . . . . . . . . . . . . J. JOSEPH LEJA
Lead Carpenters . . . . . . . . . . . . JACQUES PARADIS
GLEN HERLIHY
MARKE K. WALKER
ROB SMITH
ROSS WALSH
PETER MCGREGOR
Standby Carpenter . . . . . . . . . . . . . JOHN KOBYLKA
Lead Labourer . . . . . . . . . . . . SAYURI KATAYAMA
Construction First Aid/ Safety . . . . . . . DEE A. BURDEN
SHAUN WITT
Paint Supervisor . . . . . . . . . . . . . . STEVE CRAINE
Paint Foremen . . . . . . . . . . . . . . . . . DAVE JONES
STEPHEN VANCE
Lead Scenic. . . . . . . . . . . . . . JOHN BRUCE KEYS
Scenic Artists . . . . . . . . . . . . . LYNN-ANNE WEST
LYNN CHAULK
Standby Painter . . . DEREK REMBRANDT BOBOROFF

Assistant to Lawrence Kasdan . . . . . . . . WILMA DAVIS
Assistant to Charles Okun . . . . . . SUSANNAH JULIEN
Assistant to Casey Grant . . . . . . . . . . . . LINDA REA
Assistant to Mr.Freeman . . . . . . . . QUENTIN PIERRE
Driver to Mr. Freeman . . . . . . . ROBERT GASKILL JR.
Assistant to Barbara Tuss. . . . . . CAROL GREEN-LUNDY
Tutor. . . . . . . . . . . . . TRACEY SHELLEY-LAVERY
Office Production Assistants . . . . . . . LISA CANTRELL
BREANNE LARRETT
CHRIS WIMMER
JEREMY H. MARTIN
RYAN FIELDS
BARRY POAGE

Unit Publicist . . . . . . . . . . . . PATRICIA JOHNSON
Videographer. . . . . . STEPHEN JONATHAN TAYLOR
Casting Assistant (LA) . . . . . . . . . CONNIE CZERNEK
Vancouver Casting By. . . . . . . . . . . STUART AIKINS
Vancouver Casting Assistant . . . . . . . . SEAN COSSEY
Extras Casting By. . . . . . . . . . . . ANDREA BROWN
Extras Casting Assistant . . . . . . . . ANDREA HUGHES

First Aid/Craft Services . . . . . . . . . . . PAUL HUNT
RON GREY

Animals provided by . . . . . . . . . . . . . . . . . . . . .
BOONE'S ANIMALS FOR HOLLYWOOD
Head Animal Trainer. . . . . . . . . URSULA BRAUNER
Asst. Animal Trainer . . . . . . . . . . . . . DOUG LEAF
Creative Animal Trainers . . . . . . . . . . MARK DUMAS
DAWN DUMAS
KATHY GRANT
IAN DOIG
KYLE M. DOIG
STEVE WOODLEY
DREW THOMPSON

Aerial Coordinator . . . . . . . . . . STEVEN J. WRIGHT
Assistant Aerial Coordinator . . . . . LAURENCE PERRY
Helicopter Pilots . . . . . . . . . . DARRIN CULPEPPER
DALE CARTER
ANDRE LAFFERMA
Helicopter Engineer. . . . . . . . . . . CHRIS MUELLER

Re-Recorded at . . . . SONY / CARY GRANT THEATER
Re-Recordists . . . . . . . . . . . . . . . . . DAN SHARP
BRIAN P. WILLIAMS
ADR/Dialogue Supervisor . . . . . . . . DARREN KING
Dialogue Editor . . . . . . . . . . . . . WAYNE GRIFFIN
ADR Editor . . . . . . . . . . . . . . . . GREG BROWN
Sound Effects Editor. . . . . . . . . . . . . AI-LING LEE
Foley Supervisor . . . . . . . . . . . . . . . . DAN YALE
Foley Editor . . . . . . . . . . . . VALERIE DAVIDSON
First Assistant Sound Editor . . . . . BARBARA DELPUECH
Second Assistant Sound Editor . . . . . . . MEG TAYLOR
Assistant Sound Editors. . . . . . . . . . KIRA EDMUNDS
SHAUGHNESSY HARE
DAVID MARCUS
Sound Dogs, Inc. Producer . . . . . DEBORAH K. IRWIN
Sound Design Services . . . . . . . SOUND DOGS, INC.
Foley by . . . . . . . . . . . . . . . ONE STEP UP, INC.
Foley Artists. . . . . . . . . . . . . . . DAN O'CONNELL
JOHN CUCCI
Foley Mixer. . . . . . . . . . . . . . . JAMES ASHWILL
ADR Mixers . . . . . . . . . . . CHARLEEN RICHARDS
THOMAS J. O'CONNELL
ADR Recordists. . . . . . . . . . . . . DAVID LUCARELLI
RICK CANELLI
ADR Engineers . . . . . . . . . . . . . DEREK CASARI
JOHN LAWSON
ADR Voice Casting . . . . . . . . . . . . . SANDY HOLT
Special Alien Voices . . . . . . . . . . . GARY HECKER
Special Bodily Sounds. . . . . . . JACQUES BLACKSTONE

Supervising Music Editor. . . . . . . . . . JIM WEIDMAN
Music Editor . . . . . . . . . . . . . . . DAVID OLSON
Score Recorded and Mixed by . . . . . SHAWN MURPHY

Electronic Score recorded and mixed by. . . . JAMES T. HILL
Additional Engineering by. . . . . . . . . . . KIRA LEWIS
Assistant to Mr. Howard . . . . . . ANNICA ACKERMAN
Conductor . . . . . . . . . . . . . . . . . PETE ANTHONY
Orchestrations by  . . . . . . . . . . . . . JEFF ATMAJIAN
                                           BRAD DECHTER
                                           PETE ANTHONY
                              JAMES NEWTON HOWARD
Music Contractor. . . . . . . . . SANDY DE CRESCENT
Auricle Control Systems. . . . . . . . RICHARD GRANT
Music Preparation. . . . . JOANN KANE MUSIC SERVICE
Score recorded at . . . . . . SONY PICTURES STUDIOS
                       JAMES NEWTON HOWARD STUDIOS
Stage Engineer . . . . . . . . . . . . . . . . PAT WEBER
Stage Recordist. . . . . . . . . . . . . ADAM MICHALAK
Stage Hands . . . . . . . . . . . . . . . . JASON LLOYD
                                           MARK ESHELMAN
Score mixed at . . . . . . . . . . . . . . . . . TODD-AO
Music Clearance . . . . . . . . . . . . . . . JILL MEYERS

Main Titles designed and produced by . . . . . . . . . . . .
               IMAGINARY FORCES / KYLE COOPER

Color Timer . . . . . . . . . . . . . . . . . . DAVID ORR
Negative Cutter . . . . . . . . . . . . . . . . MO HENRY
Opticals and End Titles . . . . . . . . . . . PACIFIC TITLE
Dolby Sound Consultant . . . . . . BRYAN PENNINGTON
Preview Technical Supervisor . . . . . . . . . . BILL DUFVA
Post Production Projectionist . . . . . . RUSSELL TURNER

Transportation Coordinator . . . . . . . . ROB VREUGDE
Transportation Captains . . . . . . . . . . KEN MARSDEN
                                           ANDREW O'BRAY

### PRODUCTION DRIVERS

| | |
|---|---|
| MARK PAWLITSKY | NICK DIOMIS |
| STEPHEN CARR | JACQUES ST. HILAIRE |
| BLAKE R. ZICKEFOOSE | TED WASSENAAR |
| BILL HARMER | TED EWING |
| WILL SICKLES | DENNIS FREISEN |
| ROD STONER | GREG LANSINK |
| ERIK STRANDGAARD | LORRIE WARD |
| BRAD BUSKEY | KEITH LAPP |
| ROB CHARTIER | SCOTT DINGO DEAN |
| LES PETERS | ALOOIS STRANNAN |
| GUS BRADLEY | THOMAS CAVAZZI |
| SHAWN HENTER | CHARLES A. HUGHES |
| BARRY H. HENDRICKS | VALERIE ENDERS |
| RON LEWIS | JOE O'NEILL |

### PRODUCTION SECURITY

| | |
|---|---|
| LARRY M. WOODHOUSE | GRAHAM TAIT |
| ANDREW SOLES | PERRY MARRIOTT |
| MARILYN ISADORE | LES MURRAY |
| JERRY MICHAEL BRIGGS | KEVIN MCGILL |
| RANDY COLVIN | |

### TIVOLI CATERING

| | |
|---|---|
| MICHAEL LEVY | CHRISTINE REYES |
| ANNE TROYER | BRANDON OWEN |
| LEE MCNISH | LISA ROWSON |
| | ANTHONY DELL'ORTO |

### SPECIAL VISUAL EFFECTS and ANIMATION
By
### INDUSTRIAL LIGHT & MAGIC
A Division of Lucas Digital Ltd.
Marin County, California

Computer Graphic Supervisors . . . . JOAKIM ARNESSON
   GREGOR LAKNER                  CURT MIYASHIRO
Digital Compositing Supervisor . . . . . . . TAMI CARTER
CG Sequence Supervisors . . . . . . . DAVID HISANAGA
   DAVID HORSLEY                  HAYDEN LANDIS
   HANS UHLIG                     JOHN WALKER
Lead Digital Compositors . . . . . . . MICHAEL CONTE
                                       PATRICK TUBACH
Lead Animators . . . . . . . . . . . . . . . MARC CHU
   ANDY WONG                      SYLVIA WONG
Creature Supervisor . . . . . . . . . . . TIM MCLAUGHLIN
Digital Model Supervisor . . . . . . . ANDREW CAWRSE
Lead Viewpaint Artist. . . . . . . . . . . RON WOODALL
Visual Effects Editor . . . . . . . . . MICHAEL GLEASON
Color Timing Supervisor . . . . . . . BRUCE VECCHITTO
Lead 3D Camera Matchmove . . . . . TERRY CHOSTNER
Lead Digital Paint & Roto Artist . . . . JACK MONGOVAN
Computer Graphic Artists . . . . . . JEFFREY BENEDICT
   MATTHEW BOUCHARD               ZACHARY COLE
   RYAN COOK                      MARC COOPER
   RAÚL ESSIG                     SIMON EVES
   CHRISTIAN FOUCHER              CARL FREDERICK
   TODD FULFORD                   BRANKO GRUJCIC
   ED KRAMER                      JOSH LEVINE
   JONATHAN LITT                  PATRICK NEARY
   MASAYORI OKA                   HIROMI ONO
   MAYUR PATEL                    MARY PAYNE
   VICTOR SCHUTZ                  NOAH TAYLOR
   ALAN TROMBLA
Digital Compositors . . . . . . . . . . . . LEAH ANTON
   AL BAILEY                      PATRICK BRENNAN
   CATHY BURROW                   COLIN CAMPBELL
   SCOTT DAVID                    DAVID FUHRER
   ANGELA GIANNONI                SHAWN HILLIER
   JEN HOWARD                     STEPHEN KENNEDY
   JESSICA LASZLO                 MARCEL MARTINEZ
   STEVE SANCHEZ                  BRIAN SORBO
   RUSS SUEYOSHI
Animators . . . . . . . . . . . . . . . . . ISMAIL ACAR
   PETER DAULTON                  ANDREW DOUCETTE
   ALISON LEAF                    JONATHAN LYONS
   STEVE NICHOLS                  JAKUB PISTECKY
   MARK POWERS                    TIM STEVENSON
   DAVID WEINSTEIN

| | |
|---|---|
| Technical Animator . . . . . . . . . . . KEIJI YAMAGUCHI | Technical Support . . . . . . . . . . . TRENT BATEMAN |
| Lead Concept Artist . . . . . . . . . . . . . RANDY GAUL | ROB DE HAAN       CHRIS DOYLE |
| Concept Artists . . . . . . . . . . . . . . CARLOS HUANTE | ADAM FUCHS       ROBERT GIANINO |

Technical Animator . . . . . . . . . . . KEIJI YAMAGUCHI
Lead Concept Artist . . . . . . . . . . . . . RANDY GAUL
Concept Artists . . . . . . . . . . . . . . CARLOS HUANTE
   ERICH IPPEN           PHILIP METSCHAN
Digital Modelers . . . . . . . . . BRADFORD DECAUSSIN
   DYLAN GOTTLIEB           SCOTT MAY
   GIOVANNI NAKPIL          OMZ VELASCO
Viewpaint Artist . . . . . . . . . . . . TERRY MOLATORE
Digital Matte Artists . . . . . . . . . . . . . PAUL HUSTON
                               WEI ZHENG
Sabre Artists . . . . . . . . . . . . . . . MARK CASEY
   ORIN GREEN          CATHERINE TATE
   CHAD TAYLOR          DEAN YURKE
Visual Effetcs & Animation Coordinators . . . . . . . . . . .
   ADRIENNE ANDERSON      JULIE CREIGHTON
   STACEY SHEAR
Location Matchmove Technician . . . . . JOHN WHISNANT
3D Camera Matchmove Technician . . . . . . . . . . . . . . .
   WENDY HENDRICKSON-ELLIS      DAVE HANKS
   RANDY JONSSON           JODIE MAIER
   MELISSA MULLIN         JEFF SALTZMAN
   DAVID WASHBURN
Digital Paint & Roto Artists . . MICHAELA CALANCHINI
   SUSAN GOLDSMITH        KATIE MORRIS
   ELSA RODRIGUEZ        LESLIE SAFLEY
   ERIN WEST
Lead Pre-visualization Artist . . . . EVAN PONTORIERO
Pre-visualization Artists . . . . . . . . . . BRICE COX , JR.
   ROBERT KINKEAD        DANIEL SLAVIN
Software Research and Development . . KEVIN BLENKHORN
   CHARLIE KILPATRICK        ALEX SUTER
   EMERITO TREVINO
VFX Director of Photography . . . . . PATRICK SWEENEY
VFX First Assistant Camera Operator . . MIKE BIENSTOCK
Modelmakers . . . . . . . . . . . . . . CHARLIE BAILEY
                           STEVE GAWLEY
Stage Technician . . . . . . . . . . . . MICHAEL OLAGUE
Additional Visual Effects Editing . . . . . . . . TIM EATON
Visual Effects Assistant Editors . . . . . . LORELEI DAVID
                        ANTHONY LUCERO
Visual Effects Production Assistants . . JOHANNA D'AMATO
                        LAURA DENICKE
Video Operations Supervisors . . . . NICK PROVENZANO
                        MIKE MORGAN
Video Engineering . . . . . . . . . . . . CRAIG MIRKIN
   DAVID NAHMAN-RAMOS      JEANNE RICH
Still Photographer . . . . . . . . . . . . . . SEAN CASEY
Negative Lineup . . . . . . . . . . . ANDREA BIKLIAN
Projectionists . . . . . . . . . . . ANASTASIA EMMONS
                        KENN MOYNIHAN
Film Recording Engineers . . . . . GEORGE GAMBETTA
   RICHARD GENTNER        TODD MITCHELL
Digital Plate Restoration Artists . . . . MARIANNE HEATH
                         SAM STEWART

Technical Support . . . . . . . . . . . TRENT BATEMAN
   ROB DE HAAN          CHRIS DOYLE
   ADAM FUCHS          ROBERT GIANINO
Art Department Production Assistants . . . . . . GUS DIZON
                          DAVID YEE
Technical Assistants . . . . . . . . . . . . BRIAN FLYNN
   KENNETH GIMPELSON      VIJAY MYNENI
Visual Effects Executive Producer . . . . . MARK S. MILLER

PROSTHETIC AND ANIMATRONIC EFFECTS BY
STEVE JOHNSON'S EDGE FX, INC.

Lead Weasel Effect Designer . . . . . . LEON LADERACH
Effect Technicians . . . . . . . . . . . . . . . TIM JARVIS
                            BILL BRYAN
                         DAVE SNYDER
Lead Artist . . . . . . . . . . . . LENNIE MacDONALD
Lead Weasel Engineer . . . . . . . . . . . LARRY ODIEN
Lead Weasel Technician . . . . . . . . ENRIQUE BILSLAND
Assistant Coordinator . . . . . . . . . . . . JASON HAMER
Weasel Sculptors . . . . . . . . . . . . . JOHN WELDY
                          GLEN HANZ
Weasel Effect Designer . . . . . . . . . BERNIE EICHOLZ
Lead Fabricator . . . . . TAMARA CARLSON-WOODARD
Effect Painter . . . . . . . . . . MARK KILLINGSWORTH
Mold Shop Supervisor . . . . . . . . . . . BRENT BAKER
Lead Hair Technician . . . . . . . . . NED NEIDHARDT
Lead Fur Technician . . . . . . . . . DEBORAH GALVEZ
Fur Technician . . . . . . . . . . . . . RICK LaLONDE
Foam Runner . . . . . . . . . . . . . . . SAM SAINZ
Production Coordinator . . . . . . . ROBERT NEWTON
Effect Coordinator . . . . . . . . . . . . . MARK BOLEY

VISUAL EFFECTS BY
PACIFIC TITLE AND DESIGN

Visual Effects Supervisor . . . . . . . . . MARK FREUND
Digital Compositors . . . . . . . . . . . . . CHRIS FLYNN
                    JENNIFER LAW-STUMP
                       MAUREEN HEALY
3D Supervisor . . . . . . . . . . . MICHAEL WAHRMAN
3D Animator . . . . . . . . . . . . . BRIEN GOODRICH
Visual Effects Producer . . . . . . . RODNEY MONTAGUE

DIGITAL VISUAL EFFECTS BY
ASYLUM

2nd UNIT CREW

2nd Unit Director . . . . . . . . . . . . . E.J. FOERSTER
2nd Unit VFX Director . . . . . . . STEFEN FANGMEIER
First Assistant Director . . . . . . . . . DAVID FOOTMAN
Second Assistant Director . . . . . . . . DARREN ROBSON
2nd Unit Director of Photography ROGER VERNON, C.S.C.
Camera Operator . . . . . . . . . . . PAUL MITCHNICK
First Assistant Camera . . . . . . . . . DOUG LAVENDER
Second Assistant Camera . . . . . . . CHRIS ROTHFELDER
B Camera First Assistant . . . . . . . . . . . . . JIM CLARE

B Camera Second Assistant . . . . . . RANDY MORTON
Video Assist. . . . . . . . . . . . . CAMERON DRINKLE
Video Assist / Puppeteer. . . . . . . . ANDREW PEDLEY
Camera Trainees . . . . . . . . . . . . ROBERT I. KATZ
                                 COLLIN MULLIN
                                 DEAN MORIN
                                 JOSE LAU
Script Supervisor . . . . . . . . . . . . . JEAN BEREZIUK
Assistant Location Manager . . . . . . . TERRY MACKAY
Third Assistant Director . . . . . . . . MISHA BUKOWSKI
Property Master. . . . . . . . . . . . . . MARK HUGHES
Costume Set Supervisor . . . . . . . . . . . DANISE LEE
                                 CHARRON HUME
 Stunt Coordinator/ Stunt Double . . . . DAVID JACOX JR.
SPFX Technician . . . . . . . . . . . . . . . . JAY DOLAN
Chief Lighting Technician . . . . . . . . PHIL KLAPWYK
Key Grips . . . . . . . . . . . . . . . JOHN KUCHERA
                                 JOHN SKILLMAN
Genny Operator . . . . . . . . . . . . . . . . . ROB LEE
Lamp Operator . . . . . . . . . . . . . . . . . ROD FREW
Dolly Grips . . . . . . . . . . . . MATT GREENHOUGH
                                 MIKE MCCLELLAND
Grip. . . . . . . . . . . . . . . . . . BILLY LACHANCE
Crane Grip . . . . . . . . . . . . . . ZANE ROSSOUW
Head Greensman . . . . . . . . . . . . . KEVIN CLARK
Greensmen. . . . . . . . . . . . . . . . . . . JAY HALL
                                 DARRIN MASSEY
On-Set Paint . . . . . . . . . . . . . . . . . RAY ALLEY
First Aid/Craft Services . . . . . . . . . GLENN MOWATT
Production Assistant. . . . . . . . . . . JEFF MacDONALD
                                 DAVID MACDONALD
                                 JINA VEANNE JOHNSON
                                 JITKA DERMISKOVA
                                 JODY RYAN
Transportation Captains. . . . . . . . . . WAYNE POWER
                                 RED MURPHY
Transportation Co-Captain . . . . . MALCOLM JOHNSON
Production Drivers. . . . . . . . . . . . GRANT McPHEE
                                 LYLE W. EDGE
                                 SCOTT DELAPLACE
                                 KATHY VOLD
                                 VASILIOS BILL FTERGIOTIS
                                 GRANT PROFIT
                                 KEVIN PROFIT
                                 BRUCE MOLISON
Catering. . . . . . . . . . . . . . . . FOCUS ON FOODS
                                 STARLIT CATERING
                                 JOANNE RYAN
                                 RAY BAXTER
                                 PAUL SMALE
                                 MARICAN GARCIA

"ALWAYS IN MY HEART"
Written by Barbara L. Jordan & William Peterkin
Performed by Tony Carbone
Courtesy of Heavy Hitters

"BLUE BAYOU"
Written by Joe Melson and Roy Orbison
Performed by Roy Orbison
Courtesy of Orbison Records, Inc.

"SCOOBY DOO, WHERE ARE YOU"
Written by David Mook and Ben Raleigh

"MIGHTY MOUSE THEME"
Written by Philip Scheib and Marshall Barer

"STOPPING BY WOODS ON A SNOWY EVENING"
by Robert Frost. Used by permission of
Henry Holt and Company, LLC.

The Major League Baseball trademarks depicted in this motion
picture were licensed
by Major League Baseball Properties, Inc.

Digital Editing Systems provided by DIGITAL VORTECHS

Gyro-Stabilized Camera System provided by SPACECAM
SYSTEMS, INC.

Color by TECHNICOLOR

KODAK Motion Picture Products

FUJIFILM Motion Picture Products

The Producers wish to thank:
BRITISH COLUMBIA FILM COMMISSION
PRINCE GEORGE FILM COMMISSION
CITY OF PRINCE GEORGE
DR. JOHN CARTER, MEDICAL ADVISOR
CORBIS

Score Album on VARÉSE SARABANDE LPs

Filmed in Vancouver and Prince George,
British Columbia, Canada

American Humane Association was on set to monitor the animal action. No animal was harmed in the making of this film.